S0-BYT-021

BOOK COLLECTING

A Beginner's Guide

BOOK COLLECTING

A Beginner's Guide

Seumas Stewart

With a Foreword
by John F. Fleming

New York
E. P. Dutton & Co., Inc.
1973

To

WALTER ROBSON HUMPHRIES

Sometime Senior Lecturer in Scottish History

at the University of Aberdeen

First published in U.S.A. 1973
by
E. P. DUTTON & CO., INC.

Printed in England
FIRST EDITION

SBN: 0-525-06968-2

Library of Congress Catalog Card Number:
LC 72-76049

Contents

Illustrations

Foreword

by John F. Fleming

The late Dr. A. S. W. Rosenbach, whom the press dubbed "The Napoleon of Books", once wrote, "The greatest sport, next to love, is book-collecting". His friend Christopher Morley thought it a statement worthy enough to include in his edition of Bartlett's *Familiar Quotations!* It is true that any sport, if you are going to excel at it, requires deep interest and dedication. But in practically every sport the rewards are short-lived. They burn you out. Not so in the pursuit of The Book. It is a leisurely, dedicated chase that leaves you exalted, not exhausted, in body and spirit.

There is no explanation in the Annals of Medicine that explains the efficacious effect that the pursuers of the printed word enjoy, nor do they mention the reasons for the longevity of the book collector. The record is long and convincing.

This is in a way an extra dividend for the fledgling book collector who will want to follow the guidance and advice given in this book. There is a very wide range of subjects to collect here, and serious beginners are well advised how they may be able to value a book and escape the pitfalls of this fascinating game.

A rule one must remember: Examine and collate. Examine and collate again. Make sure your purchase is perfect. Even if you become a seasoned collector, don't take the word of anyone.

Many years ago, to be exact forty-five years ago, an eminent

Rare Book dealer bought from a not so eminent Rare Book dealer a copy of the celebrated first edition of William Blake's *Poetical Sketches* for $3,000.00. It contained the bookplates of R. A. Potts. It is a small octavo of only 70 pages. Within easy reach of the famous book dealer's staff was the superb Blake *Bibliography* by Geoffrey Keynes, published by the Grolier Club a few years before. A very young but curious neophyte, just hired, wanted to find out why it was worth $3,000.00. He fumbled his way through the reference catalogue and found the card listing the Keynes *Bibliography*. He located the impressive tome and soon found the listing of the fourteen known copies. Under Copy "K" he read: "R. A. Potts copy. Sold at Sotheby's Feb. 20, 1913 (lot 71, £8-5s) in calf gilt. pp. 49-70 in fac-simile." The great dealer was informed. No, he had not yet paid for it. A young "white-haired boy" was born.

I am happy to admit this occurs rarely, but if one is vigilant he will escape monetary losses, and what is more important, a sense of despair. To me the game is so rewarding that a few mistakes over the decades are trivial.

The demand for the important printed volumes of the world has become universal, and the constant search by collectors and institutions throughout the world has caused a sharp quickening of prices, especially for certain books. Seumas Stewart has provided a scale of value groupings, which as he says are variable and liable to increase with the years. Experience will inevitably help in keeping track of such price fluctuations. What may never need alteration, however, is the very extensive array of facts and knowledge that Mr. Stewart has assembled for you on the great avocation of book collecting.

J.F.F.

New York City
May 1972

Author's Preface

As it is only the aspiring book collector himself who can determine the objects of his pursuit, this book does not presume to inform him what he ought or ought not to collect. It attempts to advise him on the problems he is likely to meet and seeks to open windows for him on the areas where he may operate with pleasure and, perhaps, profit.

It has been thought best to deal almost exclusively with printed books and pamphlets originating among the English-speaking peoples—and even within this limitation there are certain unavoidable omissions. Sporting books have hardly been touched on and there is no mention of collecting in such areas as heraldry, naval and military matters, and the literature of arms and armour.

Believing that the primary justification for a book's existence is its content, the author has occasionally tried to communicate his delight in certain literary oddities by means of short quotations. He has made no attempt to conceal his own predilections and prejudices, for book collecting has always the better flourished in an atmosphere of controversy. If the names of many important books and their writers do not appear in the pages which follow, no slight is intended. The aim has been to illustrate desirability, demand, supply, price, etc, representatively rather than comprehensively.

The scale of values given is based on a study of prices paid at important book auctions over the past twenty years, as recorded in the yearly *Book Auction Records*, now published by Dawsons of Pall Mall. Help has also been obtained from various catalogues issued by important international book dealers over the same period. There is no fixed price for any antiquarian or out-of-print book, so the indications given here cannot be regarded as Median and Persian.

While every effort has been made to ensure that the information given is correct, it would be surprising if there were no minor inaccuracies in a book of this compass. The publishers and the author would be grateful for any authoritative information which would help to eliminate errors in subsequent editions.

The author would like to thank the many friends and colleagues who gave him their advice and assistance, particularly Mr T. N. Jellis, Macclesfield, England, Mr and Mrs Piers Plowman, Welwyn Garden City, England, and the publishers for their patient co-operation at all times.

Scale of Values

As prices of books are variable and are likely to increase year by year, it has been thought advisable in most cases not to give precise amounts which might soon become outdated, but to suggest values by means of the following scale. Book-collecting being an international activity, roughly approximate equivalents in sterling, American dollars and Australian dollars are given.

(A) up to	£900	$2,340	$A1,980	(a) up to	£90	$234	$A198
(B) ,, ,,	£800	$2,080	$A1,760	(b) ,, ,,	£80	$208	$A176
(C) ,, ,,	£700	$1,820	$A1,540	(c) ,, ,,	£70	$182	$A154
(D) ,, ,,	£600	$1,560	$A1,320	(d) ,, ,,	£60	$156	$A132
(E) ,, ,,	£500	$1,300	$A1,100	(e) ,, ,,	£50	$130	$A110
(F) ,, ,,	£400	$1,040	$A880	(f) ,, ,,	£40	$104	$A88
(G) ,, ,,	£300	$780	$A660	(g) ,, ,,	£30	$78	$A66
(H) ,, ,,	£200	$520	$A440	(h) ,, ,,	£20	$52	$A44
(I) ,, ,,	£100	$260	$A220	(i) ,, ,,	£10	$26	$A22

Where prices are likely to be above the range of (A), or below that of (i), approximate figures will be given in sterling and American dollars, or, if the book is of particular interest to Australian collectors, in sterling and Australian dollars. The table is adjusted to take into account the varying ideas of value in the different countries and is not accurate enough to be used for exchange transactions.

CHAPTER ONE

The Quarry and its Anatomy

Everybody who buys a book once in a while and, having read it, keeps it on his shelves, is a book collector of sorts. By common consent, however, it is only the enthusiastic, systematic buyer and keeper who is accounted a book collector, or more exaltedly, a bibliophile. When his enthusiasm reaches boiling point, the bibliophile becomes a bibliomane and when it boils over so that he loses all sense of proportion, he becomes a bibliomaniac. Book collecting is one of the world's great joys to a literate man; bibliomania is a cursed tyranny —though some have been able to live quite happily under its domination.

Most of us have some kind of bee in our bonnets. It is usually such a bee that stings the collector into activity. He acquires a burning interest in some subject and therefore decides to obtain as many books on the subject as he can. Or the interest is in a particular author and the desire is to possess everything his favourite wrote as well as everything written about him. It is neither enough for the collector to have access to the books in some library, nor to have them in paperback reprints or battered old copies; he must get as close as he can to the fountainhead, so he begins to look for first editions in good condition. Outsiders may scoff, but the collector who is truly hooked knows that his pursuit will bring him delights which will far outweigh the depression of incidental disappointments.

Sometimes the beginning collector is stimulated by no more than a general love of books which urges him to build up a worthwhile library. By comparison with the single-minded specialist he starts at a disadvantage, particularly if he is short of money, for his field is as wide as the world. Let him begin by listing the hundred books he would most like to own, checking his list against what he already has, then setting out to fill the gaps. By the time he has completed the list the chances are that he will have found a special niche as a collector.

He should learn quite a lot in his progress towards his initial target, especially about cutting his coat according to his cloth. Possibly he has been seeking a copy of Dante's *The Divine Comedy,* with the realisation that the earliest printed edition is far beyond his means. Unless he has taken the first copy to come his way he will have found that there is a bewildering variety of editions of Dante. For 80p or $2 he could have had an adequate late nineteenth-century edition in three small volumes, neatly printed with parallel texts in Italian and English. The expenditure of about £6 or $15 could have brought him one of several handsome editions; with luck he could have acquired a decayed but interesting sixteenth-century edition for under £50 or $130; he might have been offered the beautiful Nonesuch Press edition of 1928, bound in vellum, for less than £100 or $260. Important editions of books like *The Divine Comedy* have a certain investment value and, within limits, money paid for them is well spent. There can be slight gains even from cheap editions. If carefully marketed, almost any coherent assemblage of books should sell for more than the sum of the individual prices of its component volumes.

However, the intending collector should not fix his thoughts on financial gain. It is enough that he should be careful to avoid acquiring mere junk which his heirs and successors will have to consign to the bonfire or the salvage men. The real rewards are in collecting *per se* and the finding of treasures in unlikely as well as likely places. It is important that the collector should make friends with booksellers of the right type, including dealers in new books as well as those concerned with out-of-print, secondhand and antiquarian books. There are easier ways of making a fortune, so most booksellers are in the trade because they themselves love books. Of course there are sharks among them, but they are surprisingly few.

Secondhand bookshops are less in number than formerly, though there are possibly more dealers in secondhand books than ever. Instead of running shops, many of the clan work from private premises and sell only by post and appointment to view. This has advantages. Through the post, the collector who lives on the Isle of Mull, or in a remote corner of the Maine woods, can compete for scarce items on an almost equal footing with a rival whose home is in London or New York.

The collector should have his name in the files of several dealers to increase his chances of obtaining what he wants. Most mail order dealers issue lists or catalogues of books they have for sale. Some lists are barely-legible mimeographed sheets, while some catalogues are finely printed and lavishly illustrated. Both types should be studied, and this goes for the various grades in between. The mimeographed sheet may come from an informed but hard-up bookseller (like publicans who drink too much of their own beer, some booksellers ruin themselves by giving too much time to enjoying their own stock). It is more likely, however, that the poorly-produced list will come from an unschooled dealer who has little to offer the serious collector. None the less, it deserves attention. There is always the chance that it will contain a plum at a throw-away price.

The lush catalogue has probably been issued by a firm of high standing, with a name that is as good as a guarantee of integrity and accuracy. Every item it contains will be listed in detail and the report of condition, if colourful, will be fair. The only aspect that need worry the prospective buyer is the pricing. Big firms are just as reasonable as smaller men and are not given to making excessive profits. But their reputations depend on the range and quality of their stocks. To maintain these, they themselves must be prepared to pay top prices, so they rarely have bargains to offer.

Still unsure of himself and not yet addicted to any one author or subject, the beginner starts to gather his hundred best books. He does not want to pay highly for fine or rare editions until he has gained experience, yet has no wish to amass lumber. He will find a useful guide in *An English Library* by F. Seymour Smith, and discover that unless his tastes are exceedingly out-of-the-way, most of his favourites are obtainable in one or other of the various series, often called 'libraries', issued by important publishers. Among such series are Dent's *Everyman's Library* published in the United States by E. P. Dutton & Company, and the Oxford *World's Classics*. Many of the volumes in both series have special introductions written by important literary men, or other authorities. For example, the *Everyman* edition of Isaac Taylor's *Words and Places* has an introduction by Edward Thomas, a writer of the early part of this century, whose work is now highly regarded. Volumes of this kind, collected in good firsts, should more than retain their admittedly slight value over the years.

Budding bibliophiles must also keep an eye on new books. From time to time expensive limited editions of books, aimed directly at collectors, appear among the new publications, but there are ordinary first editions of major living authors to be considered as well. These should be grasped hot from the press

…y carry a fatal 'second impression before

…-soul collector spends a long apprenticeship in …alised buying. He soon becomes a journeyman in some special field. Everyone who claims to love English letters has read (or intends to read!) James Boswell's *Life of Samuel Johnson.* The reading of it has created many a Johnsonian, determined to obtain all he can by and about the great man. A badly-worn family copy of the *Life* is no longer good enough for him; he must have a better—but which? The ten-volume edition of 1859, edited by Croker and Wright, with its useful additional material, could be had in reasonable condition for about £10 ($26)—grade (i) in the Scale of Values, page 12—but a first edition could conceivably be picked up for £300 ($780)—grade (G). This may seem surprising, as there are records of firsts being sold for £1,400 ($3,640) in the salerooms, but price is largely governed by state and condition. There are several special points looked for in a first edition of the *Life of Johnson,* one or more of which is often lacking. Furthermore, most of the firsts which come on the market are bound in leather, but as first issued, the book was in two volumes, bound in impermanent paper-covered boards, and a copy in these boards is the most highly regarded.

Having bought the best copy he can afford, the Johnsonian still has a lifetime's work ahead. His idol was a more prolific writer than is commonly supposed. If first or early editions of all his books are sought, the dearest will most likely be the *Dictionary* and the *Lives of the English Poets,* but some of the others will be harder to come by.

If the collector is anxious for his books to grow in value over the years, it might be advisable for him to move into an area of collecting that is just beginning to be exploited and try to keep ahead of his rivals. If his inclinations are such that he must collect in a field where values are declining, he should be doubly careful of how he spends his money should try to choose the items least likely to drop in price.

Willy-nilly, the beginner will soon find himself involved the technicalities of book production. If his concern is with modern books he may get by with only a little knowledge; if his period lies anywhere between the beginning of printing in the fifteenth century and the early nineteenth century, he will have to give some time to the study of bibliography, which deals with the systematic listing and accurate description of books. Bibliography is really too wide a term. A mere list of books pertinent to a particular subject is also called a bibliography. It is a matter of regret that the English language possesses no such word as 'bibliology'. If it did, 'bibliography' could be used of book lists and their compilation, while 'bibliology' was reserved for the systematic analysis and description of books.

Books in the form that we know them pre-date the introduction of printing. Manuscript books, however, were often bound before being written, while printed books were, and are, invariably put through the presses, then bound. This may be stating the obvious, but there was a time when ordinary people had no idea how printed books were produced and were prepared to believe that printers were in league with the devil.

Basically, the making of a book consists of sewing together a number of sheets of paper of the same size and fitting the result with a hardwearing cover. Wooden boards (the words *beech* and *book* are said to be connected) were in early use, though covers of tough limp vellum may be as old. It is possible, but inconvenient, to make a book by sewing whole single sheets of paper together. The work is made easier if folded sheets are employed. When all paper was made by hand it was produced in sheets suitable for convenient handling. The largest books were made by folding these sheets in half and sewing them together. Smaller, but not necessarily thinner, books could be made by folding the sheets yet again, and so on down the line till a fat little book could be made from a single sheet folded several times.

A book composed of sheets folded once was called a *folio,* folded twice it was a *quarto,* three times an *octavo,* four times a *sextodecimo,* and five times a *tricesimosecundo.* These terms still obtain, but folio is often contracted to fo, quarto to 4to, octavo to 8vo, and the others are almost always written 16mo and 32mo (strictly 32do) and spoken of as 'sixteenmo' and 'thirty-twomo'. There are also 12mos and 24mos, achieved by particular methods of folding which are best understood by taking a sheet of paper, folding it once, folding it again longways in thirds, then making one more fold for 12mo and a further fold for 24mo. Each single sheet when folded makes a complete *gathering.* The *format* of a book: folio, quarto, or whatever, refers to the number of folds in a gathering and not to its actual size, since the original sheets, though matched for any given issue of a book, were not made to a single standard.

It is easy to visualise how a book in folio has to be printed. A single-fold gathering will give four pages which can be numbered 1, 2, 3, 4. To print on a single sheet for this sequence it will be necessary to set up the type for pages 1 and 4 together, as they are both on the same side of the whole sheet. The type for pages 2 and 3 must then be placed together for printing on the other side. If pages 1 and 4 are impressed in one printing and pages 2 and 3 in the next, the sequence will be correct when the sheet is folded.

Printing in quarto will be more complicated. If a sheet of paper is folded in half, then folded again, it will make four leaves in pairs, joined along the tops. If the eight resultant pages are numbered in order, then unfolded without the paper being cut, the outside of the sheet will show page 1 on the lower right, with page 4 above it, upside down, and page 8 on the lower left, with page 5 above, also upside down. The inside of the sheet will show 7 on the lower right, with 6 reversed above, and 2 on the lower left, with 3 reversed above. For printing both sides of a whole sheet in quarto, the pages of type will have to be arranged in the order explained. By similar experiments in folding and numbering, the arrangements for printing 8vo, 16mo and 32mo can also be adduced. For 12mo and 24mo, production methods varied. In earlier times it was usual to print a 12mo so that the sheets could be cut before sewing and double gatherings made of them. In the nineteenth century, the sheets were folded whole.

A bookbinder who had to fold and flatten a large number of sheets into gatherings for sewing together could hardly be blamed if he became confused. To help him keep the right order, every sheet was given a special mark called a signature. This was placed so that when the folds were made the mark would appear in the lower margin of the first page of each gathering. Quite often, the signature, with the right sequence of numbers added, was carried over several leaves. Usually the signature was a letter of the alphabet, with 'A' reserved for the gathering which contained the title of the book and other preliminary matter. This first gathering was likely to be folded differently from all the others. In older books, the letters J, U and W were not used and Z, too, was sometimes omitted. On the normal plan, the first gathering was A, the second gathering B, and so on. The first leaf of the first gathering would be marked A, or A_1, and if subsequent leaves were marked, they would be A_2, A_3, etc. Some printers preferred to use roman numerals and marked Ai, Aii, or Aj, Ajj. When there were more gatherings than available letters of the alphabet, a fresh start was made with double letters: AA, Aa, or aa. Rarely, the Greek alphabet was resorted to, and a few books are known with such signatures as § and ¶. Some modern books have numerals instead of letters. Many are devoid of either.

With a grasp of the system of signatures, it should be possible to tell the format of a book. A folio will have A on the first page, B on the fifth, C on the ninth, with this sequence continuing throughout. The quarto pattern will be A on the first page, B on the ninth, C on the seventeenth, and similarly to the end. In an octavo, the signature will change after every sixteenth page, in a 12mo, after every twenty-fourth. The same principles will apply to other formats. A whole gathering is often referred to as a signature, as: 'The book is an octavo, but has the last two signatures in fours'.

Apart from the possibility of the first gathering being atypical, other unexpected features may be met. During the nineteenth century, and perhaps earlier, 12mos were issued with three numbers of the signature of each gathering on every first, third and ninth page, in the order A_1, A_2 and A_3. Twelvemos are seldom produced today, but when they are, this strange order may still be used.

Another peculiarity arises when the single folded sheets of folios, instead of being sewn as individual gatherings, were printed so that they could be put together in groups of three sheets, folded to give six leaves. The sequence of the first gathering was then A_1, A_2 and A_3 on consecutive leaves, as might be expected, but the next leaf was signed A_4, so that the third sheet had in fact two signatures. From this the binder could see that his set of three sheets was complete and so pass on to the B gathering. This complication can be clarified by folding three sheets as folios and numbering them as described. Other anomalies which exist are less easily demonstrated, but they are hardly within the province of the beginner.

Sometimes the watermark—the maker's trade sign on the paper—is a guide to format. Until fairly recently, almost every sheet of paper supplied for printing had a watermark, put in the same place on each sheet: three-quarter-way across and halfway down. By plotting this position on a sheet of paper and folding according to the requirements of the various formats, it is possible to determine where and on what leaf the watermark will appear. Experts have refined this method to accomplish feats of detection, but they can be baffled when the watermark has been unconventionally placed, or omitted.

The beginner may resent involvement in such abstruse matters, but he is sure to meet references to signatures and formats as soon as he starts to receive booksellers' catalogues. Some dealers who should—and do—know better, use the terms folio, quarto and the rest to indicate size rather than format, but more of that anon. Once the format of a book is established, a good deal more can be found out. Old printers could be careless in numbering pages. It is possible for a book to be complete, but with the page numbers suddenly jumping from 166, say, to 187. If the format is known, the book can be tested for completeness and the gap in the pagination demonstrated.

Book production has always been subject to last-minute changes. Censorship, libel laws, or an author's cussedness have all brought about alterations to a book at a late stage in its journey to the buyer. If leaves are removed after printing and folding and others substituted, we have what are called cancels. For a long time, the word 'cancel' in this context could be confusing. There were no separate terms for the leaf which had to be removed and the leaf designed to take its place; both were cancels. Dr R. W. Chapman, an eminent bibliographer, came to the rescue in 1924 by inventing the term *folium cancellandum* for the leaf that has to be scrapped, and *folium cancellans* for its replacement. *Folium cancellandum* has now been shorted to *cancelland* and *folium cancellans* to *cancel*. Anybody who wants to talk of 'a cancel and cancelland' will notice the awkwardness of the terms, but such is the bookman's love of the grandiloquent that he will not accept 'cancel' (or cancel leaf) for the leaf to be removed and 'substitute' (or substitute leaf) for the replacement.

The substitution of a single leaf is easily noticed as it is usually pasted to the marginal stump of its predecessor. It may be harder to detect where two or more leaves have been replaced, but if the format and arrangement of signatures have been determined, the difficulty is not so great. The attitude of the collector who neither knows nor cares whether any of his books have cancels is understandable, but their absence or presence can make a great difference to the value.

Format inevitably gives a rough idea of size and little harm is done in describing large modern books as folios and quartos even if they are technically octavos; but this should not be done with old books. Early in the last century some books were issued in 8vo for the first edition, but in 12mo for the second. Certain 12mos of the period were of a size and shape comparable to those of a modern small 8vo, so if a bookseller describes such a 12mo as an 8vo, he may mislead his clients into thinking he has a first edition to offer.

Whatever their format, books vary in size according to the measurements of the individual sheets from which they have been made. There are large folios and small folios, large quartos and small quartos. However, it is only in dealing with octavos that the sizes are commonly given names. The most important are:

	royal 8vo	10in × 6¼in
	demy 8vo	8¾in × 5⅝in
	crown 8vo	7½in × 5in
	foolscap 8vo	6¾in × 4¼in

Modern octavo books do not necessarily conform to any of these, so when size has to be stated it is better to give actual measurements than to use this Procrustean nomenclature.

Once a book has been gathered and sewn, it still has to be

given a cover. Wooden boards soon gave place to pasteboard, which was more convenient and in certain circumstances more durable. From the fifteenth to the nineteenth centuries the standard permanent binding was in pasteboard covers overlaid with leather, vellum, or parchment. Unless they were also binders, printers delivered the completed sheets to a publisher-bookseller, who could sell the sheets as they were, have them sewn and given temporary covers, or arrange for them to be bound to his own or his customers' requirements.

Methods of binding varied in detail, but in general the sheets were folded into gatherings and pressed flat. They were then sewn along the spine—the part that normally shows when books are shelved—to five cords held taut and upright in a wooden frame. The number of cords could be more or less than five, but seldom was. Two or more blank leaves were sewn in at the front and back, or more often stuck on when the sewing was finished. The cords were cut from the frame so as to leave good loose ends on either side of the book, then the spine was glued and lightly hammered to give it a satisfactory roundness. The loose ends of cord were laced through holes made at the right places in the boards, tightened and glued down. Fraying the laced ends and smoothing them into the material of the boards was a refinement not always carried out. The leather, vellum, or parchment was cut to size and pared thinly along the edges. The inside of the leather or other material was then thickly soaked in paste all over and carefully laid on the spine and the outside covers, the pared edges then being folded and stuck down round the inner edges of the boards. The leather was pressed firmly against the spine and worked over the ridges of the cords to make attractive raised bands. The leather was turned over at the head and tail of the spine to form strong caps. The two outermost blank leaves were pasted down to the inner surfaces of the boards, one at the front and one at the back of the book. These leaves are the paste-down *endpapers* and their immediate blank neighbours are the free endpapers.

Books often have striped ridges inside the tops and tails of the spines. These are the head- and tail-bands, placed there for additional strength. Except in craftsman-bound books, modern headbands, if present, are stuck on. Until the eighteenth century they were made of strips of some tough material, such as vellum, and sewn to the book. The striped effect was given by using alternate colours of silken thread to cover the vellum strips and sew them down to the inner edges of the book. There are, of course, head- and tail-bands without stripes.

Once a book was bound it was titled on the spine and, perhaps, the front cover, and decorated. The titling could be done directly on the leather cover, or, when applied to the spine, on paper-thin leather labels called *titling-pieces.* The labels were applied blank to the spines and titled in position. Individual brass letters with wooden handles were heated and impressed in the right places, one by one, to form the required words. The impressions were covered with glair (prepared raw white of egg) over which gold leaf was laid. The letters were then reheated and applied again to the impressions already made. When the superfluous gold leaf was rubbed away, the gold titling remained.

Decoration was done in much the same way, using brass tools with designs cut on them in relief. When the tools were impressed without subsequent gilding, the book is said to be blind tooled. Large designs were built up from the impressions of several tools, or stamped from a metal block in one operation. Very occasionally, blind designs were applied freehand without heat, using a bone or ivory graver. Metal dies, hammered cold on the leather, were also used.

Books were also decorated by inlaying or overlaying with thin pieces of leather, though this was not done with vellum or parchment which, though more durable, is less tractable than leather. Overlaying, where the pieces of leather were pasted over the basic covering, was easier and cheaper than inlaying. Both methods were used to produce the panelled covers fashionable in the seventeenth and early eighteenth centuries. Silver or brass clasps were sometimes put on important books, and pieces of the same metals were used to reinforce and decorate the corners of the covers.

Gilding was a rather later development, but blind tooling and stamping goes back to the period of the *incunabula,* the term used for books produced in the earliest days of printing and generally accepted as covering the years up to 1500. The singular form, *incunabulum,* is seldom used, and *incunable* (singular) and *incunables* (plural) are now widely accepted.

Some bookbinders of the seventeenth century were grieved to find that in cutting skins of leather for covers they were left with pieces too small to cover a whole book, so they devised the *half binding* to use them up. Here the leather covers the spine and extends a little way over the boards while other triangular pieces give strength to the corners. The intervening area is covered in paper or cloth. Paper only was used for early half bindings. Though an invention of the late seventeenth century, this technique was not popular till nearly 100 years later. Books dated before about 1750 and described as being in contemporary half leather should be inspected with care. They may have been rebound at a later date. Quarter binding, where the leather is applied to the area of the spine only, without the protective triangles at the corners, is an even later development. A half binding where the allowance of leather is unusually generous is sometimes called a three-quarter binding.

A binder could finish his work and still leave the book *unopened,* that is, having the folds of its component gatherings still intact along the top and side. This should not be confused with the *uncut* condition, where the folds have been slit open, but the rough edges of the paper have not been trimmed. As both unopened and uncut books are likely to trap and retain dust, especially along their top edges, they were oftened trimmed and gilded at these vulnerable places; hence the descriptions *top edge gilt* (t.e.g.), *top and fore-edge gilt* (t. & f.e.g.) and *all edges gilt* (a.e.g.). The trimming was done with a special implement called a plough, which could be set to take off the minimum or maximum of paper. Binders who cared more for money than craftsmanship took off the maximum. The parings, when sold to papermakers, provided a useful perk. A heavily *trimmed* book with its resultant narrow margins is not desirable; when it is in the condition described as *shaved* —where the plough has eaten into the text—it is a disaster.

Books with flat spines instead of raised bands are a development of the eighteenth century. Before the sewing, grooves were sawn horizontally across the spines and the cords sunk into the grooves. The five-band convention was largely discarded; binders economised in time and money by sewing to three bands only. The smooth-back fashion was short lived, but when raised bands came back, binders continued to sew to three sunken cords. They then stuck five false bands to the spine and worked the leather over them.

In Georgian times it became usual for booksellers to offer their wares in temporary bindings of thin boards, covered with greyish-blue sugar paper, which is a coarse, laid variety, and backed with paper of a different colour. A printed label was stuck on the spine, also called the *backstrip*. When the customer bought the book, these makeshift covers were meant to be replaced by a permanent binding.

This practice persisted well into the nineteenth century, but in 1820 books began to appear with their boards covered in cloth instead of paper. These were still looked on as disposable, but within a few years cloth bindings were accepted as permanencies rather inferior to leather bindings.

Coeval with the rise of cloth was the beginning of casing instead of binding. Strictly speaking, a bound book is one where the cords to which the gatherings are sewn have been laced to the boards to make an integral whole. In casing, the gatherings are sewn to tapes, or sometimes to cords cut off close to the spine. A piece of mull (a kind of gauze) is glued along the sewn spine, with overlaps on either side. The case, consisting of cloth-covered boards with a flexible cloth spine, is made separately and the book is attached to the inside of the case by glueing down the overlaps of the mull and, where they exist, the short ends of tape. The endpapers are then brought over and pasted to the insides of the boards.

The first cloth covers were plain, but publishers soon saw that decoration would have an extra appeal. The first attempts were imitative of leather tooling, but there soon evolved a distinctive style of cloth decoration, making use of printed designs, plain and coloured. The designs of bookcloths can provide clues to the dating of editions and have been the subject of much research.

The arrival of cloth did not mean the end of boards. They became the accepted coverings for cheap editions and lost their austerity. Sugar-paper disappeared to be replaced by glossy paper, often decorated in colour. Under the influence of the arts and crafts movement, plain paper boards were revived at the end of last century. They were used for finely printed books in limited editions. Sugar-paper was again applied to the covers, but canvas or buckram was often used for the spines.

The Victorian age saw many novel experiments in book production. Wooden boards were brought back ('cedar from the Holy Land', 'oak from a tree felled by Mr Gladstone', etc); elaborate *papier maché* covers had their day; there were even books with their covers protected with wrought iron work. Sportsmen had books bound in the hide of some lately deceased favourite horse and big-game hunters had similar use made of the skins of lions, zebras and other wild animals.

Instead of being sewn, some books, not just pamphlets, were held together by metal staples. Saddest of all, it was found that books could be made up by trimming the gatherings into separate leaves, gripping these together in a press and sticking the backs with a *gutta-percha* or rubber solution. This method was favoured when thick paper, difficult to sew, was used. The average life of the dried solution was from fifty to sixty years, so that by now, most of the books produced by this method consist of a bundle of loose leaves spilling out from a pathetically impressive cover. The first of these Ozymandiases of the book world date from 1840; the last were put together not much later than 1900, by which time the transitory nature of the process had been revealed.

The dust-wrapper, or dust-jacket, was another innovation of last century. Dust-wrappers are known to have existed as early as 1832, but few examples have survived from before about 1885, as the first were only of plain paper, with or without the title of the book printed on the spine and front. Once they had served their purpose of keeping the book clean until it reached the customer they were discarded. By the beginning of the present century they had become almost universal and were illustrated to fit the contents, or carried printed information about the book. As knowledge about early wrappers is vague, collectors look for them only on twentieth-century books. It is often argued that because they are not truly parts of a book they should be ignored, yet books in dust-wrappers are always more eagerly hunted and fetch higher prices.

CHAPTER TWO

First Editions and their Problems

To non-collectors, 'first edition' has an almost mystical ring, describing, as they think, something which is always rare and valuable. The bibliophile approaches the term far less reverentially, realising that every book has run through a first edition, if no other, and that the only firsts of importance are those which are scarce and much in demand. For him, a first edition is desirable not because of fashion or commercial pressure, but because it brings him closer to a well-loved author's elbow than any other edition, or because it is the first appearance in print of some new statement about a subject he holds dear. The collector of illustrated or finely printed books is aware that first editions will be the crispest and clearest, having been produced before the plates and types have become worn. It is not just the first edition which is sought, but the first *state* of the first identifiable *issue* of the first *impression*. Later editions may have features which make them desirable, but such refined firsts will form the cornerstones of any worthwhile collection.

When a book has been set up in type, a certain number of copies may be printed and published and the type stored away. If the first printing, or first impression, sells well, another batch of copies may be run off without a great deal of trouble. This second printing is still officially of the first edition, but it is not what the collector wants. He wants his copy to be of the earlier printing, not of the second or any subsequent impression. Where not definitely stated to be so by the publishers, the later impressions often give themselves away by having corrections made to minor errors of fact, layout, or spelling, or by showing slight signs of wear on the type and illustrations. Sometimes in the course of the first printing an important mistake is noticed in the earliest copies. The machines are stopped, the correction is made and work resumes. As the mistake is not so serious as to call for the scrapping of the early copies, they are allowed to go forth like so many warty Cromwells, ready to find fame in the world of books as first issues. Their less maculate successors, though still of the first edition, are relegated to the ranks of the second issue.

The definition of a first issue as implied by the foregoing is not universally acceptable. Many bibliographers regard variations which have arisen from corrections made before the impression was ready for publication as denoting different *states* of the same issue. Only corrections made at the point of publication, or after the commencement of publication, are taken as signs of different issues. The distinction is quite clear in the case of some books, but obscure in the case of others.

It may be irrational of the collector not to rest content with a later issue, or with a reprint published immediately after the first impression and practically identical to it, but he is like a man journeying to the South Pole, who, if he can be shown the exact most southerly point of the earth, will choose to stand squarely on it rather than deviate by an inch. There are, however, occasions where the collector is willing to compromise. They will be described later, though it is as well to consider now the case of the man who cannot afford the fare to Antarctica so settles for an afternoon's southward bus ride—or the collector who cannot afford to spend a considerable fortune (at least £30,000—$78,000—for an imperfect copy) on a first edition of Chaucer's *Canterbury Tales,* so invests a small sum in a nice limited edition of 1946.

Now the position of the South Pole can be determined with reasonable accuracy by the use of modern scientific equipment. No such precise mechanical aids are available to the collector of books. He has to rely on the opinions of experts who may differ among themselves; he is not always clear as to the nature of the thing he pursues, since some books accorded the honour of first edition are not truly the printed firstlings of their author's mind. But in time he learns when to accept the rulings of the best authorities and when to trust his own judgement or follow his own inclinations. Ideally he wants his copy of a book to be the very first one published, with palpable evidence that it has been made up entirely from the first sheets printed and has gone through the bindery ahead of all its fellows. As he cannot have this outside of his dreams, he strives to get as near perfection as expert advice, common sense and financial resources will allow.

Desirable issues seldom fall like manna. Even the books described in subsequent chapters as being relatively common must be looked for with patience. Fortunately, the search need not always be in the dark. One of Richard Jefferies's earliest books is *The Scarlet Shawl.* Though not his best, it is one of his scarcest, yet the collector need have no difficulty in recognising the prime issue if it comes his way. The first edition was published by the firm of Tinsley Brothers in 1874. Anybody with a copy bearing that date can claim to have a first, but the matter does not end with that. Copies so dated can turn up in one of four different bindings, all in the original *publisher's cloth.* One is a bright blue cloth, one a red smooth cloth, one a red cloth with slight ridges running diagonally, and one is a red cloth finely grained. This last is on the earliest binding and is the one over which the collector rejoices—not before checking that it contains, as it ought, the first issue between the boards. The *points* by which this is known are: top edges uncut; a leaf of advertisements for Tinsley Brothers' two-shilling novels placed before the *half-title* (the leaf carrying nothing but a short title, coming immediately before the full title-page); a dedication leaf following the title-page, with TRAININ misprinted for TRAINING at line 7; at the end of the book, another leaf of advertisements for Tinsley Brothers' new novels etc.

The points of the first issue and the earliest binding have been settled by the work of Michael Sadleir, who compared various copies of the first edition, including the one at the British Museum, and reached definite conclusions. On the spine of the copy with the red cloth diagonally ridged, the name of the author is misspelt JEFFRIES. As this is the kind of error usually made at the outset and corrected later, it could suggest a first issue. But inside, the dedication is a cancel, with TRAINING correctly spelt, so this cancel betokens a later issue. The British Museum Library copy, in smooth red cloth, cannot be a first issue, since it has JEFFERIES correctly spelt on the spine, though stamped over the previous misspelling, which is not completely erased. Besides, the dedication in this copy also is a cancel. The blue cloth copy which Sadleir examined had the uncancelled dedication leaf, but despite this, other evidence led him to conclude it was the latest of all. The fine-grained red cloth copy remains as the earliest. If this illustrates how first issues can be established, it must be remembered that there are cases where the question of priority has never been satisfactorily settled, as will be seen when *The Posthumous Papers of the Pickwick Club* is discussed.

Over quite wide areas of collecting, problems of this kind are few. Either greater care is now taken in preparing books for the press, or printers are more reluctant to correct minor errors, but points of priority of issue less often arise in present-day books. Entire first editions show no variation in binding or in text. This simplifies matters for the collector of modern books. He feels safe in assuming that a book published in the past two decades is a satisfactory first if it carries no statement to the contrary—as 'second impression before publication,' 'second impression,' 'second printing,' 'second edition,' 'revised edition,' 'new impression,' 'new edition' etc. Caution is needed even here. Points have a way of lying hidden for years before emerging to discomfit the bibliophile.

Lady Audley's Secret by Mary Elizabeth Braddon, is one of the most notorious novels of last century—purely in the bibliographical sense. It first began to appear in print in *Robin Goodfellow*, a magazine edited by Charles Mackay. The first number of the magazine, with the first chapter of *Lady Audley*, was issued on 6 July 1861, but *Robin Goodfellow* was not a financial success and came to an end in September 1861, by which time only the first sixteen chapters of *Lady Audley* had appeared. The authoress had better luck with *The Sixpenny Magazine,* which took over the novel, made a fresh start with the first chapter and finished the serialisation in 1863. The first complete printing therefore spans *The Sixpenny Magazine* from Volume II to Volume IV. As soon as the serialisation had ended, the first edition in book form was issued in three volumes, dated 1862. The second edition, likewise in three volumes, followed hot on the heels of the first and is also dated 1862. There is little doubt that mixed sets, with the first two volumes in second editions and the third volume in the first, were also sold.

What does the collector do here? If he settles for the first edition in book form, ignoring all that went before, he is not very near to the authoress's original thoughts, as the book is different in many respects from the early *Robin Goodfellow* chapters and the complete *Sixpenny Magazine* serial. Yet if he collects the *Sixpenny Magazines* he is lumbered with much extraneous matter—and if he goes back to the sixteen chapters in *Robin Goodfellow* he has only a fragment. As it happens, he would do well in this case to go for the first complete printing in the *Sixpenny Magazine*. Finding all the requisite numbers will occupy a great deal of his time, but this is more likely to be achieved than the acquisition of a first edition in book form. *Lady Audley's Secret* is one of comparatively few Victorian three-volume novels really worthy of the booksellers' description, 'excessively rare in the first edition'. The likely saleroom price for a copy would be between £1,500 and £2,000 ($3,900 and $5,200).

Apart from this novel and one or two others, the collector of Victorian fiction disregards serial issues. Though the serial is usually the true first edition, he prefers convenience to logic and goes after the first edition in book form. It will cost much more but will take up far less shelf room. Anybody who has no objection to his library looking like a wastepaper depot could collect real first editions more cheaply than he who accepts them only in book form.

The bibliophile's normal avoidance of serials does not extend to certain novels and other works which were first issued in parts—notably several of the novels of Charles Dickens (1812-70). This author can indeed be regarded as the father of the *part issue*. Before his *Posthumous Papers of the Pickwick Club* was launched on the world, some quite insignificant stories, with or without illustrations, had been served up at the rate of one or two chapters a month, sewn in flimsy paper covers. They were no more than enlarged chapbooks, looked down on by booksellers and their customers alike. There was also a superior type of part issue for which some well-known artist would provide the illustrations while a literary hack supplied a brief text which more or less linked the illustrations together. In 1836, the publishing firm of Chapman & Hall engaged Robert Seymour to draw the pictures for one of these superior part issues. Seymour was well known as a sporting artist and the publishers expected to do well with the project. They engaged a young up-and-coming journalist to write the linking letterpress. Happily for literature, less so for Seymour, the journalist was Dickens. Almost from the start, he took the upper hand, so that the text became of more importance than the illustrations. Very soon, the already melancholic Seymour became so depressed that he killed himself, so another artist had to be found to replace him. A man called Buss produced a few illustrations which were used, but they were not satisfactory and the work of completing the illustrations fell to Hablot K. Browne, better known as Phiz.

In all, there were twenty parts issued in nineteen, the last number being a double one. As published, every number was scantily clothed in a flimsy paper wrapper, with some advertisement leaves between the wrapper and the illustrated text. Because of the two changes of illustrators and the increases in the numbers of copies printed as the work progressed, it is hard to decide what constitutes an authentic set of the first issues of *Pickwick* in parts. The Dickens bibliographers, J. C. Eckel—*The First Editions of the Writings of Charles Dickens*, revised edition 1932—and, more particularly, Thomas Hatton and A. H. Cleaver—*A Bibliography of the Periodical Works of Charles Dickens*, 1933, have gone far towards establishing the first issues, but some bibliographers still 'hae their doots'.

There are few known sets of the accepted first issue of *Pickwick* in parts, complete and in good condition, so only the wealthiest and most determined collector should aim so high. Good sets, bearing many, though not all, of the requisite stigmata, are still expensive, but within the reach of non-millionaire collectors. Those with little money to spare would be better advised to look for a good copy of the first edition in book form rather than accept a poor or defective set of the part issue. As is the case with many books of the period, the plates of *Pickwick* are liable to suffer badly from *foxing*, a bookseller's word for the condition of being marred with brown spots and blotches. A badly foxed first is hardly worth accepting as a free gift. A clean copy of a first in book form (dated 1837), rebound in one volume in full or half leather, might be worth anything upwards of £1.25 ($3), but should be considered as an example of Victorian binding rather than as a Dickens first edition. A copy of the first edition in original cloth and in suitable condition for a place in a serious collection would be in the (g) price grade (page 12) at least, moving much higher according to whether or not it carried the points of an early issue. In acquiring a first of *Pickwick*, the collector must do his bibliographical homework, or go to a thoroughly reliable dealer who will guarantee that any copy he may supply will be of an early issue.

There are booksellers for whom the date of 1837 on the title page is enough. At the sight of it they pencil 'first edition' on an endpaper together with a high price, leaving the customer to check for relevant points. They are not unscrupulous, but they want to make as much as they can from what, as far as they can tell, may be a valuable book. If somebody with superior knowledge is able to give them a true evaluation they will be prepared to accept it and fix a price accordingly.

The examples of *The Scarlet Shawl*, *Lady Audley's Secret* and *The Posthumous Papers of the Pickwick Club* illustrate some of the difficulties facing the first edition collector. Though selected from the area of nineteenth-century fiction, they could be parallelled in any field. There is no easy single formula for distinguishing first editions. In many cases it can be done only after years of patient study, or, more conveniently, by consulting the works of those who have already done the research.

Fortunately, reliable and reasonably detailed bibliographies, covering an enormous range of authors and subjects, have been published in the course of the last two centuries. The novice should find out which are appropriate to his needs and try to consult them. This is not always easy. Some advanced collectors and specialist booksellers growl in their mangers at beginners. They will write or talk knowingly about 'Wade 161' or 'Chubb 436', but will avoid revealing that the reference in each case is to a standard bibliography, Wade and Chubb being respectively Allan Wade's *W. B. Yeats Bibliography* and Thomas Chubb's *The Printed Maps in the Atlases of Great Britain and Ireland: A Bibliography, 1579-1870.*

Discovering the name of an appropriate bibliography is not in itself a means of gaining access to a copy. Many of these works were published in small limited editions and are out of print. As dealers look on bibliographies as the tools of their trade and established collectors guard their copies with their lives, these books seldom come on the market. Now, however, several of the most important old bibliographies are being reprinted by university departments or by firms with an interest in the antiquarian book trade. This is happening on both sides of the Atlantic. Watch should be kept for the announcements of reprints. Scarce bibliographies may sometimes be consulted through local public libraries and, despite the few tight-lipped exceptions, most booksellers will allow customers access to their working copies—under strict supervision, of course.

Anybody who wants to take a new path in book collecting must become his own bibliographer, but he need not wait till he has made himself an expert before he begins to acquire his books. If he has read this far, he will be able to avoid making gross blunders in his purchases and the inevitable errors can be regarded as the price that has to be paid for the acquisition of new knowledge. Where possible, he will write to publishers and librarians for particulars of the first editions of the books he seeks; he will studiously browse in bookshops and he will try to make contact with everybody who might be able to shed the smallest ray of light on the subject of his collection. The bibliographer, amateur or professional, is a kind of detective who seeks clues in every likely, and many unlikely places.

There are lumpers and splitters among bibliophiles. To the lumper, a first edition is a first edition and he does not worry very much about the complexities of states and issues. The splitter looks for refined gold twice gilded. His copy of a book not only must be earlier than any other, but must be in better condition. The lumper, with his eyes shut against all complexities, misses half the joy of collecting, but at least he enjoys the continual feast of a contented mind. The splitter, however, is doomed to a life of endless mental anguish. He pushes to extremes his search for points which will establish his copy as the only true and complete first. Genuine points have their value in establishing priority, but there are many which are not to be trusted. In the first edition of Joseph Conrad's novel *The Arrow of Gold* (1919), the title of the book is used as a running headline at the top of every page of the text. In some copies, the headline at page 67 reads THE RROW OF GOLD. The splitter seizes on this as evidence of first state, or first issue, arguing that the 'A' of ARROW must have been missing when printing started and put in later, when the mistake was discovered. This was accepted as a valid point at one time, but now it is fairly well established that the 'A' was in position when printing began, dropped out at a later stage, and was replaced. Copies with the 'A' missing can be regarded as no more than interesting variants. Similarly, some copies of the first edition of Samuel Johnson's *Marmor Norfolciense* are found with 'FINIS' absent from the last page. The splitters still argue about this, but it is generally accepted that the omission is the result of careless printing and cannot be taken as an indication of priority.

It must be emphasised that book collecting has no kinship

with the eccentricities of philately. Errors and misprints have no value except as indicators of priority or otherwise of an issue or edition.

Collecting variant copies of first or subsequent editions can become an end in itself, though it is a somewhat arid pursuit for a bibliophile who really reads his books. Surely it is enough that he should have one first edition of every book pertinent to his collection, provided it is in the best possible condition consonant with his means—and condition here includes completeness. Even the richest men in the world have little hope of buying certain early printed books in an absolutely complete condition, as no perfect copies are known to exist. Such rarities apart, completeness should be strenuously pursued. It is not too difficult to check for missing leaves in the text, but illustrations may present a more difficult problem. If they have been printed with the text and form part of the normal signatures, well and good, but if, as is quite usual, they have been printed separately and tipped or bound in, it may be hard to ascertain that they are all present. Where a list of illustrations is given there is no problem; where there is no list, the copy must be compared with a known complete copy, either by borrowing it, or by reading its description in a detailed bibliography. A missing free endpaper or fly-leaf need not be all-important before the era of cloth binding. The lack is always regrettable, but hardly detracts from completeness. For acceptance a leaf, other than one carrying an illustration, map, diagram etc, should be part of a gathering, with a signature, as explained in the previous chapter. This is rarely the case with an endpaper or fly-leaf. With cloth bindings, however, the goal is original condition, so absent leaves of any kind are a defect. Where called for, half-titles are a necessity. From about 1660, books issued in temporary covers or none at all, generally left the printer's with a short plain title on the leaf immediately preceding the title-page proper.

This was for protection and though often as not part of a signed gathering, it was not intended to be a permanent part of the book. Some bookbinders left them in when they bound, others disposed of them. Today, the careful collector insists that where it is known to have existed, the half-title should still be present. This equally applies to all other printed matter issued with the book—advertisements, errata slips etc.

Advertisements, mainly of other works from the same publisher, occasionally appear in seventeenth-century books, but are uncommon before about 1750. They are sometimes printed on a leaf placed before the title-page and included in the first signature; more often they occur on a leaf or leaves at the end where, in the earlier examples at least, they form an integral part of the book. By the beginning of the period of publishers' cloth, they can be on leaves bound in with the book, but not truly a part of it. They are rightly regarded as essential to a book's wholeness and may be taken as guides to priority of issue. On this latter point they are not entirely reliable. Where the advertisement leaves form a genuine part of the book, showing an appropriate signature, we can feel happy about some expert's ruling that the first issue has so many advertisement leaves, the second a different number and so on; but where the leaves are obviously a separate addition, there is always room for doubt. Nineteenth-century publishers were anxious to keep their advertisement lists up to date and so were liable to change them at any time. When copies of the first issue were being bound up, the binder was not interested in marrying the earliest copies of the book with the earliest lists of advertisements and indeed would be more inclined to scrap early lists altogether. Though necessary for completeness, advertisements are unreliable witnesses as to priority.

Sometimes errors are noticed in a book after it has been printed and are corrected on a piece of paper pasted in after binding. Such a paper is called an errata slip and is a frequent cause of headaches. Perhaps a large number of copies was issued before the correction was made, in which case a copy without the slip would be one of the earliest. But in these circumstances there is nothing easier than the manufacture of an early copy by the careful removal of the errata slip. If it is known that a certain book usually has an errata slip it is best to rejoice in a copy that has one and to lose no sleep over a copy in which it is lacking.

While a book in original sheets, unopened, uncut, unsewn and without covers is as near the primary state as it could be, it is rated below a copy of the same book which has been sewn and bound in the original boards or cloth. Binding or casing is an important part of wholeness.

In the strict sense, there is hardly such a thing as an original binding for a book of the seventeenth century or earlier. What is looked for is a contemporary binding, identifiable as of the same period as the book. From the eighteenth century until 1820, plain boards with paper labels on the back-strips are desirable, but copies bound in leather are not looked down upon and, where they are well-preserved examples of good craftsmanship, are sometimes to be preferred. From the time when publishers' cloth was developed to the present, rebinds in leather fall in esteem, again with the exception of the works of master craftsmen. The emphasis is on original binding.

Sometimes books are described as being in *binder's cloth*. This should not be taken to mean original cloth. It describes a book which has been rebound in cloth at some time. It is possible that a book of this description can be stripped of the cloth to reveal the original boards underneath, but the damage done in removing the cloth makes it an unrewarding operation. In any case, the re-covering in cloth will probably have necessitated the use of new endpapers and, with books of the nineteenth and twentieth centuries, original endpapers are desirable—some would say vital, but in these days of increasing demand and diminishing supply the collector must make up his own mind on that point.

Up to the present, first editions even in original bindings have been regarded with disfavour if they are *ex-library* copies, though if they date back to the days before cloth they have been grudgingly accepted. The prejudice stems largely from the practice of Mudie's Library, the most important of the old circulating libraries, of pasting an unsightly yellow label at the top of the outside cover of every book they made available to their borrowers. When such a book had outlived its usefulness it was sold cheaply and in many instances the new owner would have a go at the label with a penknife and succeed in scraping off part of it, leaving a mess even more disfiguring than the original label. With care and patience, these labels and fragments of labels can be removed, but faint traces will almost always remain, though they may be hard to detect. Some libraries used less disfiguring marks of identification, but the prejudice against Mudie's has extended to all such library copies. With the increasing scarcity of many collectors' items, however, the indications are that ex-library copies are becoming more acceptable.

A book from a private library, with its one-time owner's bookplate, is not regarded in the same light and is usually highly esteemed, especially, but not necessarily, if the former owner was a person of note. Bookplates are marks of *provenance* and should be honoured as such. Provenance is to books as pedigree is to the genealogist. Every true bibliophile thrills with pleasure when he sees, neatly written on an endpaper, a list of the names of the past owners of a copy of some rare work. If the book is now his, he can proudly add his name to the list. It is commoner, however, to find that the men of the past were strongly possessive and scattered their names liberally in all sorts of inappropriate places—on the title-page, at the beginning of the preface, on the blank sides of illustrations and so on. This kind of disfigurement is tolerated in books over 150 years old, but is frowned on in works of a later period. So it is with handwritten marginal notes, underlinings, textual emendations and end-of-chapter comments. If these are old they are accorded reverence as quaint messages from the past, if they are recent they are considered to be unwarranted arrogance, unless they can be proved to be in the hand of a person of eminence. A first edition of *Tom Jones,* heavily annotated in the handwriting of Dickens, or some other author who drew inspiration from it, would be quite a prize.

Manuscript inscriptions on one or other of the preliminary leaves of a book can be valuable marks of provenance, or serious flaws. Imagine how delightful it would be to possess an edition of Thomson's *The Seasons* with this authenticated inscription:

> To my dear friend John Keats in admiration and
> gratitude, from P. B. Shelley, Florence, 1820.

Imagine, too, how depressing to have an otherwise fine first of Milton's *Paradise Lost* with this ball-point inscription scrawled on the title-page:

> To Ada from Jess, with lots of love and candy floss,
> in memory of a happy holiday at Blackpool, 1968.

In another couple of centuries the second inscription might have period charm, but for the present it would be catastrophic.

Inscriptions on the title-page are acceptable if written by the author himself, for everybody loves an *association copy.* This is a term applied to a copy of a book associated with its author. A copy of Thackeray's *Henry Esmond* with the author's name and notes in it would be an association copy. Also so described could be a copy of Darwin's *Voyage of the Beagle* bearing the signature of Sir Charles Lyell, the geologist. It could be described as a Darwin association copy as the two men were friends, but it would more properly be a Lyell association item.

In their way, *signed copies* and *presentation copies* are association items, but for clarity the terms should be kept separate. A signed copy bears the author's signature without its having any other indication of a connection, and a presentation copy is one which states it has been given by the author to so-and-so. A presentation copy can express various degrees of intimacy. Lowest in the scale is one which is merely stamped 'Presentation copy', then comes 'with the author's compliments', perhaps in the author's hand, and next something like 'To W.M.T. from C.D.' where C.D. is recognisably the author's initials, written by himself. Beyond this stage, the individual must make his own scale of values. Is a copy of Yeats's *Countess Kathleen* of more value if it bears, in the author's writing, the legend, 'To F. from W.B.Y.' than if it is inscribed 'To Florence from William'? This is hair-splitting, but some bibliomanes will slice up strands of gossamer if they get the chance.

It should now be possible to summarise the most desirable condition in which the ordinary collector can hope to obtain his books, according to the period in which they were first published.

Books printed before 1501 : as nearly complete as possible, in contemporary bindings, with good provenance and, perhaps, with interesting marginal notes in a contemporary or near-contemporary hand.

Books from 1501 to 1701 : much as above, but with more emphasis on completeness and with contemporary bindings in really good condition.

Books from 1701 to 1820 : important changes were taking place during this period. In the earlier part, contemporary leather or vellum is desirable, but from about 1740 onwards, original boards should be looked for, as should half-titles, though the latter were introduced earlier. Boards, even in worn condition, become preferable to workaday leather from 1780 or thereby. Leather half-bindings, uncommon in the seventeenth century, now come into their own and in good condition hardly rank below full bindings.

Books from 1820 to 1901 : this period sees the beginning of publishers' cloth, though it is rare before 1830. It is also the period in which part issues came to the fore and plain boards gave way to decorated and pictorial boards. Where applicable, first editions in part-issue are the most acceptable, with original cloth in second place. As a rule first editions rebound in leather have little value, though some fine bindings are treasured for their own sake. The Victorian novel, as well as other important books, was frequently issued in three volumes and is often called a *three-decker* on this account. Some books of the period, having gutta-percha or stapled bindings, almost never show up in good condition.

Books from 1901 onwards : despite, or perhaps because of, the enormous number of books produced in this period it is the one which is most immediately rewarding to the beginner. There are still some hard problems on which he can sharpen his wits, but on the whole the task of identifying first editions is easier. The dust wrapper now becomes important and should be looked for. It should be remembered that first editions can now be acquired as they are published.

Though this summary applies primarily to first editions, it is applicable to other editions as well. If there is such a person as a determined second-edition collector he will find the details just as useful. They are also applicable to one-author collectors interested in acquiring every significant edition of works by their chosen favourite. This is different from collecting variant copies of the same edition and can be a rewarding aspect of bibliophily. Two names spring to mind in this field —Isaak Walton and Gilbert White. Many editions of Walton's *The Compleat Angler* have appeared since it was first published in 1653, some noteworthy for the extra material supplied by the various editors and some for the quality of the illustrations. The first edition of White's *Natural History of Selborne* is dated 1789 and has similarly been enriched at the hands of different editors in many editions.

CHAPTER THREE

General Literature to 1800

In the widest sense, 'literature' embraces everything that is written. As commonly used, it is a handy term for poetry, drama, fiction and that body of miscellaneous writing classed as *belles lettres*. Even in this narrower view, literature is still a vast domain, attracting the majority of bibliophiles. With so great a prospect before him, the collector of literature must cultivate single-mindedness. If his field is seventeenth-century prose, he ought not to go whoring after first editions of twentieth-century poetry, or nineteenth-century illustrated books. Chastity is equally desirable in other specialists. If they want to maintain contact with the work of other periods, they can buy it in paperbacks or cheap editions, or borrow from a public library. This will conserve precious time and money for the real pursuit. It is probably safe to say that the first edition assumes its greatest importance in this domain of literature, though it is true that the growing scarcity of some items, with a consequent rise in prices, has turned the attention of certain collectors to other desirable editions.

Quirks of fashion have devalued the works of some authors of the past hundred years and certain others may not maintain their high positions for ever, but collectors of books published up to the end of the eighteenth century are on pretty sure ground. Time has established a scale of values and in some cases prices have advanced spectacularly in the past fifty years. Just after World War I, a reasonable copy of Dryden's *Fables* in the first edition of 1700 would have cost about £2, or $8 at the exchange rate then prevailing. Today, a realistic price would be £36 ($94) or even more. At this rate of growth, the price should rise to £615 ($1,629) in the next half century. Such an increase, though possible, is unlikely. A levelling-out seems to be indicated here, though not a decline.

The period 'up to the end of the eighteenth century' could go back to 4004BC, the alleged year of the Creation. Postulants in bibliophily, however, should accept as their first year of grace AD1477, when William Caxton issued the first book printed in England. Its title, *The Dictes or Sayengis of the Philosophers,* is of academic interest only, as the few known copies of the original never reach salerooms or booksellers. A facsimile edition of 1877 is the best that can be hoped for.

The first considerable work of English literature to be printed was *The Canterbury Tales* by Geoffrey Chaucer (1340-1400), which came from Caxton's press in 1478. A beginner should think twice before making this one of his purchases, even if a copy were available. The price, as suggested in Chapter 2, might leave him short for further buying.

The Caxton *Canterbury Tales* is an *editio princeps,* which is the term for the first printed edition of a work which was already in existence as a manuscript book before the introduction of printing. It is also an incunable as defined in the first chapter and it is better to gain considerable experience before embarking on their collection, even if they are not so expensive as this one.

This does not rule out early authors for the tyro, only early editions. Caxton printed a second edition of *The Canterbury Tales* in 1482, Richard Pynson produced a third in 1492 and was followed by Wynkyn de Worde in 1498. Pynson and de Worde were pupils and successors of Caxton. There are no more Chaucer incunables, but the editions of the *Tales* by Francis Thynne (1532) and of Chaucer's works by John Stowe (1561) and Thomas Speght (1598) are just as scarce and almost as dear. It was not till 1721 that John Urry issued the first Chaucer in roman type—hitherto they had all been printed in black letter. Sadly, Urry spoilt the text by trying to modernise the language and rhythm. Copies of this edition would be in the price grade (g) to (f) (page 12), but students of Chaucer would do better with the five-volume edition prepared by Thomas Tyrwhitt and published 1775-8 (second edition in two volumes, 1798). It would cost no more than the Urry and is a landmark in Chaucerian scholarship. The best modern editions of Chaucer's works are those of A. W. Pollard, first published by Macmillan in 1898; of W. W. Skeat, first published by the Oxford University Press in 1894 and frequently reprinted; and of F. N. Robinson, also Oxford University Press, 1933 and later reprinted. These modern editions are not of outstanding interest to the advanced collector, but in a first printing each is a milestone in the progress of Chaucerian scholarship and should be valued as such. Similar editions of other old authors will be named in this and subsequent chapters.

The next English printed book of note is *Le morte Darthur reduced in to englysshe by syr Thomas Malory*, 1485, also from Caxton's press. Though translated from French writings, *Le Morte D'Arthur* is a distinctly English production which had a deep effect on subsequent literature and art. The first edition, two later editions by de Worde in 1498 and 1529, as well as the variants, *The Story of the Most Noble and Worthy Kynge Arthur*, printed by W. Copland in 1557, and *The Most Ancient and Famous History of Prince Arthur*, printed by W. Stansby for J. Bloom in 1634, are as far out of reach of the impecunious as are the early Chaucers. The first that comes within the scope of the ordinary collector is *Le Morte*

D'Arthur, two volumes, 1817, edited by Robert Southey. It is not adjudged as being of great merit and is grade (h). The three-volume edition of 1889-91, edited by H. Oskar Sommer, with an essay by Andrew Lang, is much better and might be grade (g). In 1947, modern scholarship produced the three-volume Oxford English Texts edition, originally priced at £8 ($32 at the time) and now worth double in sterling. Little is known about Sir Thomas Malory (*fl* 1470), who wrote the work, but it is believed he did so in prison.

The Vision of Pierce Plowman is attributed to William Langland, a contemporary of Chaucer. It must have been written before 1400, but the *editio princeps* did not appear until 1550. Copies, when available, would be grade (E) or higher. For ordinary purposes, the two-volume edition of 1886, edited by W. W. Skeat, ought to be discoverable in grade (i).

Apart from the ancient Gaelic bards, Scotland's first important poet was the Aberdonian, John Barbour (1316-95). His epic, *The Bruce*, predates *The Canterbury Tales*, but had to wait until 1616 for its first printing, by A. Hart, at Edinburgh. The best modern edition is that of the Scottish Text Society, in two volumes, edited by Skeat and published in 1894. It should be available for about £6 ($16). Other good editions which may be ferreted out are the three-volume edition by J. Pinkerton, Edinburgh, 1790, and John Jamieson's two-volume edition, Edinburgh, 1820.

The greatest poets of the Middle Scots period were Robert Henryson (1430-1506), William Dunbar (1460-1420) and Gawin Douglas (1474-1522). Though all three looked to Chaucer as their master, they were not imitators but original poets. Only Dunbar saw any of his poems in print. The printers were Walter Chepman and Andro Myllar, who set up the first Scottish press in Edinburgh in 1507 and, the following year, produced Dunbar's *The Ballade of Lord Barnard Stew-*

art, The Flyting of Dunbar and Kennedy, and *The Twa Mariit Wemen and the Wedo,* all as separate items. First editions of these three poems are unobtainable except by theft from the National Library of Scotland, but the titles should easily be found in *The Poems of William Dunbar,* edited by W. M. Mackenzie, Edinburgh, 1932, reprinted London, 1950. Other editions are those of 1834-66, in three volumes, edited by David Laing, and of 1893, in three volumes, edited by Dr Small for the Scottish Text Society.

Robert Henryson's first work to be printed (by Chepman and Myllar) was *The Traitie of Orpheus,* probably in 1508. His *The Testament of Cresseid* followed in 1593, printed by H. Charteris, Edinburgh. The first collected edition of his *Poems and Fables* did not appear until 1865, edited by David Laing and published at Edinburgh. Subsequent editions are by G. G. Smith, for the Scottish Text Society, three volumes, 1906-14, and W. M. Metcalfe and T. D. Robb, 1917.

Gawin (Gavin) Douglas's first printed poem was *The Palis of Honoure,* from the London press of William Copland about 1553, the year in which Copland also printed the first edition of Douglas's verse translation of Virgil's *Aeneid.* If a copy of this book were to become available, it would be in grade (D) at least. The Edinburgh edition of 1710, printed by Symson and Freebairn, should be (g), as should the four-volume edition of Douglas's works, edited by John Small, Edinburgh, 1874.

The more important contemporary English poets were Alexander Barclay (d 1552), the satirist and self-confessed doggerel-writer, and England's first two sonneteers, Sir Thomas Wyatt (d 1542) and Henry Howard, Earl of Surrey (d 1547). Between 1557 and 1574, Richard Tottel or Tottell printed seven editions of the songs and sonnets of Wyatt and Surrey. Another edition came from J. Windet in 1585 and another from R. Robinson in 1587. All nine are (A), for every one is different, with poems by other contributors as well, including Lord Vaux and Nicholas Grimold. The entire collection is sometimes known as *Tottel's Miscellany* and was reprinted as such in 1717 and 1795. The reprints should be (g), or a little above. Wyatt is well served in the collection of his poems edited by Kenneth Muir and published by Routledge in 1949, but there is no recent authoritative edition of Surrey.

Wyatt and Surrey heralded a great upsurge of English letters. Sir Philip Sidney (1554-86) was a devotee of the sonnet, but no satisfactory complete edition of his works appeared until 1962, when his poems, edited by W. A. Ringler, were issued in the *Oxford English Texts* series—a collector's piece for the future. Early (never first) editions of his *Countesse of Pembroke's Arcadia* turn up at the important book auctions, where they have not as yet risen above (i).

Sidney's greatest contemporary poet was Edmund Spenser (1552-99), author of *The Shepheard's Calender,* 1579, and *The Faerie Queene,* the first three books of which appeared in 1590. Early editions of Spencer are not for the humble, who should look for the ten-volume edition of 1880-2, edited by Dr A. B. Grosart, grade (g). No other non-dramatic poet of this period measures up to Spenser. Perhaps the younger Michael Drayton (1563-1631) comes nearest. His best work is found in *Ideas mirrour. Amours in quaterzains,* 1594, but *Poly-Olbion or a chorographicall description of Great Britain,* two volumes, 1612-22, is a favourite with collectors who can afford grade (D) books.

Of the prose written in Spenser's day and earlier, little falls into our category of literature. Sir Thomas More's *Utopia* should be admitted, since it was the ancestor of such diverse books as *Gulliver's Travels* and *Erewhon.* More (1478-1535) wrote *Utopia* in Latin and had it published at Louvain in 1516. The first edition is rare, as is the first English translation, *A fruteful and pleasant worke of the best state in a pub-*

lyque weale and the new yle called Utopia, by Ralphe Robynson, 1551. Even the edition of this translation by the Rev T. F. Dibdin, in two volumes, 1808, is uncommon and would be (g).

The English theatre achieved its first full flowering in the sixteenth century. Thomas Norton (1532-84) and Thomas Sackville, Earl of Dorset (1536-1608), collaborated in writing *Gorboduc,* the first tragedy of importance in the English language, published in 1561. It is most easily obtained in Dent's two-volume *Everyman* edition of minor Elizabethan drama.

Comedy was also cultivated in the same period. The first landmarks are Nicholas Udall's *Ralph Roister Doister,* probably 1566, and *Gammer Gurton's Needle,* 1575. The only copy of the original *Roister Doister,* in Eton College Library, lacks the title-page, though the name of the work and its author have been authenticated from other sources. Several copies of *A ryght pithy, pleasaunt and merie comedie; intytuled Gammer gurtons nedle* are known in the 1575 edition. Its author is now accepted as being William Stevenson, a jovial cleric. Apart from the reprint of the first edition made in 1818 and now (f), *Ralph Roister Doister* is found in the *Everyman* minor Elizabethan drama. *Gammer Gurton's Needle* is given in the second volume of Robert Dodsley's *Select Collection of Old Plays*—twelve volumes in the first edition of 1744, but fifteen in the re-edited edition of 1874-6. While a complete set of Dodsley in either edition would be (d), odd volumes should be found at less than £1.25 ($3). A reprint of the nineteenth-century edition was published in 1963 at £35 (then $100).

After Udall, poet-dramatists come thick and fast until Elizabethan drama reached its peak with William Shakespeare (1564-1616). It is impossible in a book of this scope to deal adequately with Shakespeare and what has been written about him, or to give much advice on a truly representative collection. There might be worse ideas for the Shakespeare student than to start with a one-volume edition of the works, such as *The Oxford Shakespeare,* in print, then acquire facsimiles of the original editions—say Helge Kökeritz's facsimile of the 1623 First Folio and Sir Walter Greg's facsimiles of the earliest quartos. These are publications of the Oxford University Press.

For further acquisitions, the best guides would be the standard Shakespeare bibliographies: William Jaggard's *Shakespeare Bibliography,* Stratford-on-Avon, 1911 (reprint, 1913), and *A Shakespeare Bibliography* by W. Ebisch and L. L. Schuecking, Oxford, 1931, with supplement, 1937. Both would be (h).

The complexities of Elizabethan and Jacobean drama are so great that for further information the reader had best refer to *English Theatrical Literature 1559-1900,* published by the Society for Theatrical Research in 1970. This book is based on Robert W. Lowe's *A Bibliographical Account of English Theatrical Literature,* 1888, but has been revised by J. F. Arnott and J. W. Robinson to include material which has come to light since the original work was published. The book is, of course, invaluable to students of later drama.

Among Shakespeare's younger contemporaries and immediate successors were the metaphysical poets, first so designated by John Dryden. The epithet is nowadays associated with the poets' mystical aspects, but was originally intended as a jibe at their fanciful language. John Donne (1573-1631) is the chief metaphysician, but in his own time much of his verse circulated in manuscript, so the collector of rare first editions is well-nigh defeated from the start. There is, however, *Poems, with elegies on the author's death,* 1633, to be looked for in grade (E), apart from Donne's sermons and devotional works, highly prized by collectors of theology. The most dependable text of the poems is probably that of Sir Herbert Grierson's edition, two volumes, Oxford, 1912.

George Herbert (1593-1633) is another important metaphysical poet, most of whose verse is contained in a single book, *The Temple*, published in the year of his death. Early editions might be (b), with the actual first (G). Richard Crashaw (1612-49), Abraham Cowley (1618-67), Henry Vaughan (1622-95) and Francis Quarles (1592-1644) are also grouped as metaphysicals. The last named is a favourite with collectors of old illustrated books. His *Emblems*, 1635, is a series of verses each based on a text from the Bible and followed by an epigram, illustrated by a wood engraving.

George Wither (1588-1667) produced a similar *Collection of Emblems ancient and Modern* in the same year. Really good first editions of these emblem books would be in the (G) and (F) ranges.

Robert Herrick (1591-1674), one of the sweetest of English lyricists, links the metaphysicals and the Cavalier poets. His chief work is *Hesperides*, 1648, rare enough to be worth £1,000 ($2,600) in a first edition, but included in Humbert Wolfe's four-volume edition of Herrick, Cresset Press, 1928, and now (h). The true Cavalier poets were Thomas Carew (1598-1639), Edmund Waller (1606-87), Sir John Suckling (1609-42) and Richard Lovelace (1618-58). Their first editions are (H), but other early editions would cost considerably less and most of their poems are in the *Everyman* edition of *Minor Poets of the Seventeenth Century*.

Andrew Marvell (1622-78) is sometimes grouped with the Cavalier poets, but he was on the other side and wrote poems in honour of Oliver Cromwell. The first collection of his works was *Miscellaneous Poems*, 1681, an edition with an error of pagination, skipping from page 116 to 131, and probably (G).

Part of Marvell's fame rests on his having been secretary to

John Milton (1608-74). As would be expected, first editions of Milton's major poems are much desired. His *Paradise Lost*, 1667, in the first state of the first edition, could sell for £3,000 ($7,800), though worn copies in the later states might be worth no more than a tenth of this amount. None of Milton's other works is quite so highly prized, but none is cheap. Milton was also a pamphleteer. Items like his *Discourse shewing in what state the three kingdomes are in at this present*, 1641, though only of four leaves, would be grade (d). The best modern edition of his poems is the two-volume *Poetical Works*, edited by Helen Darbishire, Oxford, 1952-5.

A watershed in the history of books has already been passed. In 1926 there appeared one of the great works of English bibliography: *A Short-Title Catalogue of Books Printed in England, Scotland, & Ireland And of English Books Printed Abroad 1475-1640*, compiled by A. W. Pollard and G. R. Redgrave, with the help of others. Not every extant book from that period was recorded, but it is plain that the compilers' hope was not in vain that their errors and omissions would not exceed five per cent. The work is usually known as the STC and the books it lists range from Caxton's translation of Le Fevre, *hEre begynneth the volume intituled the recuyell of the historyes of Troy*, printed by Caxton himself at Bruges in (probably) 1475, up to the many volumes published in 1640. Some collectors specialise in STC books, whatever their subject.

The beginner has already been advised not to concentrate on early books, yet he ought to be aware of them and have some idea of their cash value. If he thinks he has made a find while searching for later editions of fifteenth- to seventeenth-century authors, the STC will be his best general guide to authenticity. In time he may acquire his own copy; from the outset he should know where one may be consulted.

Pollard and Redgrave's work was magnificently continued by Donald Wing of the Yale University Library, who compiled *A Short-Title Catalogue of Books Printed in England, Scotland, Ireland, Wales and British America, and of English Books Printed in Other Countries 1641-1700.* The first three volumes were published at New York in 1945-51 and the index volume at Charlottesville, 1955. This massive bibliography is referred to as *Wing* for short and, covering a period of expansion in printing and publishing, it contains far more entries than the STC.

During the *Wing* era, the greatest developments were in prose. Francis Bacon (1561-1626) and Robert Burton (1577-1640) had already helped to set new standards. They will be dealt with in a later chapter. However, *The Pilgrim's Progress* by John Bunyan (1628-88) should be considered now because of its effect on later writing.

Though it is an all-time best seller, copies of the first edition, 1678, in anything like acceptable condition are very rare, as can be gauged from the fact that in 1947, when a well-documented copy—known as the Warner copy, from one of its previous owners—was put up for sale by Sotheby's, the London auctioneers, it made £4,400 (about $12,570 at the rate then prevailing). If a comparable copy, in a contemporary binding and with only minor defects, was auctioned today, the price would be considerably higher. There are many fine editions of this book to tempt the collector, and also thousands of tired copies of worthless editions which depress booksellers' cheapest shelves.

The works of John Dryden (1631-1700) could hardly be more different from those of Bunyan, the tinker-pastor. Dryden was a scholar and classicist whose verse set the fashion for a hundred years. The beginner might feel safe in starting a Dryden collection for some of his first editions range between (i) and (d). He would have to buy cautiously, however, and seek guidance from Hugh Macdonald's *John Dryden: A Bibliography of Early Editions, and of Drydeniana,* Oxford, 1939.

Dryden wrote some plays which are too wearisome for production today. In Victorian and Edwardian days, the plays of Dryden's contemporaries and immediate successors were also unacceptable, not because of tediousness, but because their wit and humour were considered coarse. Nevertheless, there has always been a demand for first editions of the so-called Restoration dramatists. Victorian gentlemen paid well for them and placed them in the darker recesses of their libraries. The leading Restoration playwrights, most of whose best work dates from the reigns of William and Mary (1689-1702) and Anne (1702-14), are Aphra Behn (1650-89), Colley Cibber (1671-1757), William Congreve (1670-1729), Sir George Etherege (1634-91), George Farquhar (1678-1707), Thomas Otway (1652-85), Sir John Vanbrugh (1664-1726) and William Wycherley (1640-1716). As an indication of prices, the first collected edition of the plays of Cibber is (I) and firsts of individual plays range from (f) to (a).

Single plays of this period are often sold as 'disbound'—a term which officially means that they have been plucked out of larger miscellaneous volumes. For some of the plays the term should sometimes be 'unbound' for there are cases where they were first issued without an outer binding.

Milton and Dryden apart, there are no giants among the poets of the *Wing* period, though several are above average height, including Sir John Denham (1615-69), John Oldham (1653-83), Matthew Prior (1664-1721), Thomas Stanley (1625-78) and Thomas Traherne (1637-74). Traherne was known only as a writer of religious works until his poems were discovered at the beginning of the present century by Bertram Dobell, a scholarly bookseller, who edited and published Traherne's *Poems* in 1903 and *Centuries of Meditation* (prose) in 1908. Ill-informed collectors cannot believe these are true firsts and keep on looking for non-existent seventeenth-century copies. Though scarce, the Dobell editions may be reasonably priced when found, but some booksellers have already rated them (g).

After 1700, the bookman's world expands. No single bibliography could encompass all the English-language books of the eighteenth century. This means the fledgeling collector can begin to spread his wings, even if they get a bit singed. There are still plenty of good literary items of the century waiting to be winkled out. When they appear at important metropolitan or provincial sales they usually command fat prices and, at even fatter, find their way into the catalogues of high-class booksellers. If time is of less account than money, the aspiring eighteenth-century enthusiast can attend the remoter and least-publicised house sales in the hope of picking up odd lots of books of the period at no great cost. He will, of course, make suitable preparatory studies. He will know, for example, that the first collected edition of *The Spectator* was published between 1712 and 1715 and should be in eight volumes. Though the set of part issues, 1711-12 is the true first, the 1712-15 edition is a high enough aim for the beginner. If he buys it in any grade below (f) he will have done well.

The novice at sales must not 'buy blind'. He must check every promising book for condition during the viewing time before the sale. Here even the experienced buyer may err. Few people can remember the collation of every book within their field and defects which would be noted in the catalogues of important sales may not be given in the list of a small sale. This is just one of the hazards the bargain-hunter must run.

The rise of the novel belongs to the eighteenth century. Some school textbooks date the beginning of the English novel from the first publication, in 1719, of *Robinson Crusoe*, by Daniel Defoe (1661-1731). But Defoe was a shocking fibber and passed off *Robinson Crusoe* as a true story. None the less, the old fraud wrote a masterpiece and an authentic first edition which includes *The Further Adventures* would certainly be worth £3,500 ($9,100) in good condition. None of Defoe's other works is in quite the same class—a first of *The Life of Captain Singleton*, 1720, would probably be (a). As Defoe was a prolific writer of pamphlets, examples of his work in this direction are still obtainable. Some are (e), but a few can cost much more.

Though it is a very different book, *Gulliver's Travels*, 1726, is associated in the minds of many with *Robinson Crusoe*. Jonathan Swift (1667-1745), the author, was one of the world's great satirists and a master of English prose. A good copy of the first edition of *Travels into several Remote Nations by Lemuel Gulliver* may be (D) and should be capable of being classed as 'Teerink AA'. This esotericism denotes first issue and is a reference to *A Bibliography of the Writings in Prose and Verse of Jonathan Swift, D.D.* by H. Teerink, first edition published at The Hague, 1937, and second edition, edited by A. H. Scouten, at Philadelphia, 1963.

The great English novelists of the eighteenth century are Henry Fielding (1707-54), Samuel Richardson (1689-1761) and the Irish-born Lawrence Sterne (1713-68), alongside whom must be set the Scot, Tobias Smollett (1721-71). With these, prices may appear puzzling. A set of the nine volumes of the first of Sterne's *Tristram Shandy*, 1760-7, may make £1,000 ($2,600) at auction while the six volumes of Fielding's far greater *Tom Jones*, 1749, in comparable condition, may be grade (G). The difference is in comparative scarcity; more copies of the Fielding novel having been printed than of the Sterne. Merit, however, influences the price of *Tom Jones* as compared with the same author's *Joseph Andrews*, 1742. There is little to choose as to scarcity, but all considerations being equal as regards condition etc, *Tom Jones* will probably be priced a little higher. Fielding's *Amelia*, 1751, is the least valuable of his firsts—perhaps (a). It is the commonest Fielding of all. *Tom Jones* was so successful that in anticipation of an immediate demand for a new book from the same pen, Strahan, the publisher, had 5,000 copies of *Amelia* printed—one of the largest first editions of the century.

No such high hopes were entertained by Rivington and Osborne when they began publication in 1740 of Richardson's *Pamela.* The first edition was small, which makes it worth anything up to £1,400 ($3,640) today. With *Pamela,* Richardson became famous throughout Europe. He had taken the novel out of the bawdyhouse and tavern into the drawing-room. His later novels, *Clarissa Harlowe,* 1747-8, and *Sir Charles Grandison,* 1753-4 were equally successful, but being printed in greater numbers, more copies have survived, so they are priced considerably below *Pamela,* without being within easy reach of the collector with little money.

Sterne's *Tristram Shandy* first rolled from the presses in 1760, but further volumes continued to appear at intervals until the ninth and last was published in 1767. Because it is a multi-volumed work, issued over several years, complete sets of the first edition are hard to find. A dedicated Sternean might build up a set by acquiring cheap odd volumes over a long period. The final cost could be low, but the result would probably be unsatisfactory. It is unlikely that the bindings would match and the volumes might be of differing heights.

Joseph Andrews, Fielding's first novel, began as a satire on *Pamela,* but soon the author went his own way, pausing in the parlour or tarrying in the tavern, but keeping his characters, as real as those of Richardson's, on the move, as did Cervantes with Don Quixote and Sancho Panza. A similar pattern was repeated in *Tom Jones,* where Fielding acknowledges his debt to Cervantes. The idea was taken up by other authors and influenced the English novel for a long time. It is obfuscated in Tobias Smollett's earlier novels, *Peregrine Pickle,* 1751, and *Roderick Random,* 1748, but is clear in *Sir Launcelot Greaves,* 1762, and *Humphrey Clinker,* 1771. Significantly,

Smollett published a translation of *Don Quixote* in 1755—grade (g). The scarcest of Smollett's novels is *Sir Launcelot Greaves,* which might cost (G), while the others might vary from (f) to (I).

Many minor novelists took their cues from the masters. Richard Graves (1715-1804) produced *The Spiritual Quixote* in 1772 and Charlotte Lennox (1720-1804) had her *The Female Quixote* published in 1752. Other novelists of the period included Henry's sister, Sarah Fielding (1710-68) with *David Simple,* 1744, Thomas Amory (1691-1788) with *John Buncle,* 1756, Henry Brooke (1703-83) with *The Fool of Quality,* 1766, and Mrs Elizabeth Inchbald (1753-1821) with *The Simple Story,* 1791. A collection of such minor works would provide a survey of the manners and mental attitudes of the eighteenth century, but good firsts would find an average in grade (b).

As he wrote only one novel, Oliver Goldsmith (1728-74) cannot be classed as a great novelist, but his *The Vicar of Wakefield,* 1766, is a masterpiece, deservedly prized by collectors, who will pay up to grade (D) for a first issue of the first edition. Novices must beware of mistaking the Dublin edition of 1766 for the genuine article. The Dublin edition was pirated and is of no value save as a curiosity. Goldsmith's friend, Dr Johnson, did not rise to the heights with his one novel, *The Prince of Abissinia,* 1759, now usually called *Rasselas.* As Johnsonians need it, it is in some demand in (c).

When Horace Walpole (1717-97), an amateur of antiquarianism, wrote *The Castle of Otranto* in 1765, he started a craze for the Gothic novel, a kind of eighteenth-century shocker, full of ghostly ruins and screams in the night. His best-known followers are Ann Radcliffe (1764-1823) with *The Mysteries of Udolpho,* 1794, Matthew Gregory Lewis (1775-1818) with *The Monk,* 1794, Mary Shelley (1797-1851) with *Frankenstein,* 1818, and Charles R. Maturin (1782-1824) with *Melmoth the Wanderer,* 1820. Scarcity and her connection with the poet make Mrs Shelley's book the dearest (H), and Walpole's pioneer work is scarcely less. The others should be (a).

Though they published their work in the nineteenth century, Maturin and Mrs Shelley were carrying on the eighteenth-century tradition. In *Frankenstein*, however, Mrs Shelley also anticipated the rise of science fiction. In this she had a predecessor, Robert Paltock (1697-1767), whose *The Life and Adventures of Peter Wilkins*, 1751, has a kinship with the fantasies of Jules Verne. Science fiction enthusiasts may think twice before adding a first of this book to their collection. It would be (I).

The fantastic orientalism of William Beckford (1759-1844) inspired his *Vathek*, a gloomy tale in an *Arabian Nights* setting. Beckford wrote it in French, but a Dr Samuel Henley got possession of the manuscript and translated it into English. It was in this translation that the book first appeared at the end of 1876. The French original was published in Paris and Lausanne the following year. Beckford disapproved of Henley's version and tried to suppress it. For a time high prices were paid for it as a great rarity, but as copies continued to turn up, it became obvious that Beckford had not been successful. Today, *Vathek* is becoming really scarce and is (a) in the English version and at least (H) in the French.

When respectable oldtime bibliophiles died, their prudent executors would check their libraries and quietly remove certain items for unceremonious cremation. Thus perished many a first edition of John Cleland's *Memoirs of a Woman of Pleasure*, two volumes, 1748, a book better known to us as *Fanny Hill*. The first edition is a rarity, still liable to be sold *sub mensa*, so its present value is hardly known.

Reference has already been made to *The Spectator*, a new venture in journalism, begun by its chief contributors, Joseph Addison (1672-1719) and Sir Richard Steele (1672-1729). It ran from March 1711 to December 1712 and popularised the

POEMS,

CHIEFLY IN THE

SCOTTISH DIALECT,

BY

ROBERT BURNS.

THE Simple Bard, unbroke by rules of Art,
He pours the wild effuſions of the heart:
And if inſpir'd, 'tis Nature's pow'rs inſpire;
Her's all the melting thrill, and her's the kindling fire.

ANONYMOUS.

KILMARNOCK:
PRINTED BY JOHN WILSON.

M,DCC,LXXXVI.

Page 65 *The Burnsite's dream possession: a facsimile of the title-page of the Kilmarnock edition—the first of Robert Burns' poems*

Page 66 *A popular Victorian yellowback: the front cover of Arthur Sketchley's* Mrs Brown and King Cetewayo, *one of the 'Mrs Brown' series, given as No 34 by Sadleir, but the number '33' can be seen at the bottom left of this copy*

Page 67 *The evolution of the dustwrapper: wrappers of two Rider Haggard first editions showing the quick development from plain for* Benita *in 1906, to fully illustrated for* Marie *in 1912*

Page 68 *A steel engraving from Edward J. Eyre's* Journal of Expeditions of Discovery into Central Australia*, 2 vols, 1845. Typical of many illustrations in travel books of the period, this picture is*

light essay, which continued to flourish thereafter. Goldsmith was a master of the medium and many of his best essays are in *The Citizen of the World*, two volumes, 1762. Prices for this book fluctuate from (d) up to (G) and the variations cannot be explained entirely by differences in condition.

Dr Johnson practised the essay, but his great gift to English language and literature was his *Dictionary of the English Language*, two volumes, folio, 1755. For good or ill, this was the book above all others which standardised modern English spelling. Really good copies are (D) or (C), but a student of the eighteenth century might pick up a defective, but still interesting, copy for less.

The two greatest British poets of the eighteenth century could hardly have been more dissimilar. One was a withdrawn, waspish little man, unprepossessing, but educated and urbane. The other was an extrovert, well-built and handsome, but ill-schooled and rustic.

Alexander Pope (1688-1744), the first of the two, was quite prolific and collectors can still build a nice selection of his commoner firsts without spending a fortune. The first collected edition of his works, 1717, in a good contemporary binding, should be (d) and small items, such as *Of the Characters of Women*, 1735, might be (g). During most of the present century, Pope has been rather neglected, but interest may be reviving, so intending collectors should not delay.

Robert Burns (1759-96), the other member of the incongruous pair, published less than Pope. *Poems, Chiefly in the Scottish Dialect* was brought out at Kilmarnock in 1786, and this is the edition that every Burnsite dreams of owning. As the original binding was of thin paper, the mortality rate has been high. Only a few copies in original condition exist. It is hardly surprising that a really good rebound copy would be worth at least £2,000 ($5,200). The second edition of Burns's poems was published at Edinburgh in 1787 and is far commoner than the Kilmarnock edition. In the first issue of the Edinburgh edition, 'stinking' is written for 'skinking' in *To a Haggis* on page 263. The first issue of the Edinburgh edition is (H) and the second issue (d).

Later editions of Burns are less valuable. Prices have never risen very high for two items containing the first printings of many of Burns's best songs: George Thomson's *A Select Collection of Original Scottish Airs for the Voice*, Edinburgh, 1799-1818, and James Johnson's *Scots Musical Museum*, Edinburgh, 1787-97. Burns has also been credited with the authorship, or part-authorship of the *Merry Muses of Caledonia*, a collection of bawdy Scots songs, published with no place or date given, but presumably at Dumfries in 1800. No author's name appears. The *Merry Muses* was reprinted privately in 1827 and this is the only old edition which ever comes on the market, at grade (g). There is a full discussion of the authorship of the book by J. DeLancey Ferguson in *The Merry Muses of Caledonia*, edited by James Barke and Sydney Goodsir Smith, 1965.

The standard collectors' reference book on Burns is James Gibson's *The Bibliography of Robert Burns*, Kilmarnock, 1881, but a new bibliography of Burns and Burnsiana is overdue.

William Cowper (1731-1800) and Thomas Gray (1716-71) are next in importance as poets. Cowper did not produce a large number of separate editions of his poems, so he presents the collector with no great undertaking. In the first issue of the first edition of his *Poems*, 1782, however, there are no cancels and there is a preface. Later issues have cancels at E_6 and E_{16} and the preface is suppressed. Prices might be between (G) and (I) according to issue. Apart from the exiguous firsts, there are several later editions of Cowper worth collecting.

Gray was a considerable poet whose popular fame rests on his *Elegy Wrote in a Country Church Yard* [*sic*], first published in 1751. The earliest issue of the first edition illustrates how a collector's point, though detracting from the literary merit of a book, can add to its cash value. The phrase, 'kindred spirit', was one of Gray's gifts to the English language. It occurs in the *Elegy* at the fourth line of the twenty-fourth verse. It is not found in the first issue, where its place is taken by the feebler 'hidden spirit', yet the collector intent on priority will pay about four times as much, perhaps £700 ($1,820), for the unmemorable version as for the other.

The eighteenth century furnishes the collector with a whole army of lesser poets. James Thomson (1700-48), who wrote *Rule, Britannia!* as well as two long poems, *The Castle of Indolence*, 1748, and *The Seasons*, 1726-30; and William Collins (1721-59), are among the best, but that man-of-all-letters, Oliver Goldsmith, must also be ranked with them. Thomas Chatterton (1752-70), the unhappy prodigy who passed off his work as being by a fifteenth-century poet, Thomas Rowley, deserves a mention, as do John Gay (1685-1752) and John Dyer (1699-1758).

Poetry flourished as never before. Three particularly dreary versifiers enjoyed a popularity which lasted into the next century: James Beattie (1735-1803) who wrote *The Minstrel*, 1771-4, Robert Blair (1699-1746) whose *magnum opus* was *The Grave*, 1743, and Edward Young (1683-1765), who gave us *The Complaint, or Night Thoughts*, 1742-5. Their works are more fun to collect than read. Firsts of Blair and Young are of far less value than the later editions illustrated by William Blake. Thomas Tickell (1686-1740), Richard Savage (1697-1743) and Stephen Duck (1705-56) make an interesting trio when their surnames are put together.

Firsts of these minor poets would be between (h) and (f), but hawkeyed seekers may still pick them up for considerably less. One way of acquiring their works is to look for them in John Bell's *The Poets of Great Britain, from Chaucer to*

Churchill, Edinburgh, 1777-92. The complete set consists of 109 volumes, usually described as 12mos, but actually 18mos. A set would certainly be (I) or (H) in the salerooms, but odd volumes might be dug out in bookshops at 80p ($2) each. There are rather similar later collections of poetry, but they lack the period feel and smell of the Bells.

Drama in the eighteenth century was largely a matter of bombast and ostrich plumes—the latter being the accepted headwear for tragediennes. Some of the comedies of the time are enjoyable, but most of the tragedies—and many survive as firsts—are dull. Even Sheridan, who ridiculed the overblown tragedies in *The Critic*, 1779, was as boring as his contemporaries when he adapted Kotzebue's *Die Spanier in Peru* as *Pizarro*, 1799.

Much of the drama of this period is collected for its historical rather than its literary interest. It is a field not yet denuded of material. Unbound copies of individual plays were sold to audiences during the run of the play and may now appear with added paper covers. Sometimes the covers are pasted on, sometimes the book or booklet has been resewn to include the added covers. The stickler for original condition can have an endless debate with himself as to whether resewing contravenes the rules.

Names to look for are John Gay (1685-1732), George Lillo (1693-1739), Edward Moore (1712-57), Henry Fielding, David Garrick, the actor (1717-79), Samuel Foote (1720-77) and Arthur Murphy (1727-1805). Helpful books for the collector are *A History of Early Eighteenth Century Drama*, Cambridge, 1925, and *A History of Late Eighteenth Century Drama*, Cambridge, 1927, both by Allardyce Nicoll. If it was more generally available, *Some Account of the English Stage*, 1660-1830, ten volumes, Bath, 1832, would be recommended. It was the life's work of the Rev John Genest (1764-1839) and was hopefully offered for sale at five guineas (£5.25) the set.

There were few buyers, even when the price was reduced to 30s (£1.50). It is scarce today and is (H).

The literary man may settle for collecting only the two great dramatists of the century, Oliver Goldsmith (*hic et ubique!*), and Richard Brinsley Sheridan (1751-1816). Goldsmith's fame in this department of letters rests on *She Stoops to Conquer*, 1773, and *The Good Natur'd Man*, 1768. First editions of these are (a). Considering their popularity in his own times, Sheridan firsts are rather scarce. *The School for Scandal*, undated, but published at Dublin in 1780, is the Sheridan high spot. Only a rash prophet would suggest a price for the next copy, acceptable in all its parts, which may be offered for sale. The other Sheridans would be priced much as the Goldsmiths.

CHAPTER FOUR

General Literature from 1801

On 1 January 1801, the world's great age did not begin anew. Nevertheless, this date provides a convenient mark for the commencement of the Romantic Revival, which, at our distance, seems to belong to the early nineteenth century. The collector and the literary scholar (he ought to be the same person, but often is not) knows that the revival began earlier, but would be prepared to peg it to the new century.

In their enthusiasm for its fresh lyricism, our immediate predecessors glossed over certain absurdities in the new romantic literature. They would smile at the oriental extravagances of the Brighton Pavilion, but swallow them whole in Coleridge's *Kubla Khan*; they would frown at the revived Gothic of a Pugin church, but wallow in the archaisms of the *Ancient Mariner*. As we now see things in a different perspective, the collector of neo-romantic literature must view his position afresh. The chief writers of this period were truly great, so there is no danger of the established collector having his books seriously devalued, yet the beginner may be pleased to find that the prices of the items he would like are not accelerating so fiercely as in the recent past.

Before becoming too sanguine, however, he should remember that sheer scarcity helps to maintain the prices of books which have any intrinsic merit. Robert Southey (1774-1843),

Poet Laureate and brother-in-law of Coleridge, is among the least regarded of the romantics, but certain of his books will always be highly priced. The seldom-seen *Omniana*, 1812, in two volumes, original boards, might cost (e) in the Scale of Values, page 12; the two volumes of his *Annual Anthology*, Bristol, 1799-1800, could rise to (I) in similar condition. Southey had nearly 1,400 volumes of his own library covered in flowery chintz and titled on the spine with distinctive paper labels. These he called his 'Cottonian Library'. Not every old book covered in chintz is from this source, but anybody who found one that was and could establish its provenance would have a rare treasure.

Southey, William Wordsworth (1770-1850) and Samuel Taylor Coleridge (1772-1834) formed the trio known as the Lake Poets. Several others were associated with them, particularly Thomas De Quincey (1785-1859), Charles Lamb (1775-1834) and, through Lamb, Charles Lloyd (1775-1839). Lloyd, a Quaker from Birmingham, is relegated to the footnotes in histories of English literature, but his name can still raise a little stir in the salerooms. The first edition of Coleridge's *Poems on Various Subjects*, Bristol, 1796, contained four poems by Lamb as well. The next edition, in 1797, had an extension to the title, reading: 'to which are now added poems by Charles Lamb and Charles Lloyd'. The following year, Lamb and Lloyd together produced *Blank Verse*, a small collection of their poems.

The Coleridge and Lamb poems of 1796 would probably be (H), in boards, the second edition (I) and the Lamb and Lloyd *Blank Verse* (a). Yet a really good first of Lloyd's own individual *Poems on Various Subjects*, Carlisle, no date, but 1795, could well be (G). However, as this is not a well-known book, there may be a number of copies which have never been brought out into the open, waiting for the lucky hunter. If he finds one, he should check for the needful misprints at pages

26, 47 and 57, and hope that the original boards are still firm.

Coleridge's great collaboration with Wordsworth produced the *Lyrical Ballads*, 12mo, Bristol, 1798. Whatever changes in fashion may lie ahead, it will remain a treasured book. The first issue is priced right out of the ordinary collector's reach and even the second issue is (G). There is little hope of picking up bargains in this book or in any other Coleridge and Wordsworth firsts. A rebound copy of Coleridge's *Christabel; Kubla Khan*, 1816, in fairly good condition, might be (f), but in fine condition in original wrappers would be (G), so a reasonable rebind of Wordsworth's *The Excursion*, 1814, could be (h), but a really good copy of his *An Evening Walk*, 1793, could be (A).

In the face of such prices, it should comfort beginners to know that Coleridgeana and Wordsworthiana—writings by and particularly about these authors—still provide a happy hunting ground for modest collectors. In 1968, a bookseller in Cheltenham, England, produced a remarkably fine catalogue on the Romantic Revival. It contained 947 items, almost every one an English first edition, yet the average cost per item was less than £5 ($13). Even allowing for price increases since that time, such a catalogue, if issued today, would still bring the cost of worthy material within the reach of every collector.

George Gordon, Lord Byron (1788-1824), John Keats (1795-1821) and Percy Bysshe Shelley (1792-1822) are the next trio of romantic poets to be considered. Byron regarded himself as a classicist rather than a romantic. Though something of a radical, he never quite uncurled his aristocratic lip, and his poetry contains more sardonic wit than warm human sympathy. Nonetheless, his verse enjoyed great popularity in his lifetime. For this reason, several Byron first and early editions are relatively common—a complete set of *Don Juan*, sixteen cantos, 1819-24, may be only (e); on the other hand, a choice copy of *The Waltz; An Apostrophic Hymn*, 1813, written by

Byron under the pseudonym of Horace Hornem, could cost about £1,500 ($3,900). This work failed to catch the public eye and the poet repudiated it.

Keats, who burnt himself out with hectic creative energy, epitomises the Romantic Revival. His first book, *Poems,* was published in 1817, with Shelley's help, but proved a failure. Today it would be grade (G). His next publication, the following year, was *Endymion.* This is even more prized—the first issue of the first edition, identified by an erratum leaf of one line of print, would certainly be (E). *Endymion* was savaged by the critics of *Blackwood* and *The Quarterly.* However, *Lamia and Other Poems,* 1820, the last of Keats's works to be published before his death, was highly praised in the *Edinburgh Review.* As a first, this collection would be (G). Keats first editions are even more elusive than the prices suggest.

The death of Keats led his friend, Shelley, to write and publish *Adonais, An Elegy on the Death of John Keats,* in 1821. This is one of the greatest poems in the English language and grading the first edition as (H) is like defacing Michelangelo's 'David' with an outsize price label. But the collector must learn that fine feelings hardly exist in the marketplace. Shelley's unactable drama, *Prometheus Bound,* 1820, has 'miscellaneous' misspelt as 'miscellaneus' on the contents page of the first issue of the first edition. The presence of this point doubles the value over the second issue, to put it in grade (H), or possibly higher. These examples show the kind of expenditure the Shelley collector faces, but there is in grade (g) the first acceptable collected edition of Shelley's *Poetical Works,* four volumes, 1839. This was the first authorised edition, edited by Mrs Shelley. Earlier unauthorised editions are almost worthless.

The upsurge of interest by Irishmen in their literary figures is extending to Tom Moore (1779-1852), who did almost as much for non-Gaelic Irish song as Burns did for Lowland Scots song. A first of Moore's *Irish Melodies*, 1821, may be (e), but the trend is upwards. His first volume of poetry was published pseudonymously in 1801 as *The Poetical Works of Thomas Little*. It is an uncommon book, probably (I). Only Moore's *Lalla Rookh*, 1817, shows no sign of increasing in value and is still a drug on the market.

George Crabbe (1754-1832) stands outside the Romantic Revival, but his early classicism developed into a highly individual realism, best seen in *The Borough*, 1810, which could be (g) or (f). Sir Walter Scott (1771-1832) was once a popular poet. His romances, *The Lay of the Last Minstrel*, 1805, *Marmion*, 1808, *The Lady of the Lake*, 1810, etc are dreich and dreary reading for modern readers, though they brought new colour to European literature in their time. Occasionally a bookseller will chance his arm by offering a first edition of one of Scott's poems at a fancy price, but many provincial dealers would be pleased to dispose of their copies at no more than £5 ($13).

Charles Lamb, already considered as a poet, is better known as an essayist. Indeed he was the virtual inventor of the light essay in which the writer says nothing in particular, but says it very well. Lamb wrote many of his essays for the *London Magazine* under the name of Elia and the first collection in book form was published at London as *Elia. Essays Which Have Appeared under That Signature in the London Magazine*, 1823. Keen Elians have put this first in grade (I)—rather high, perhaps, since modern critics have been carving up Lamb. His second collection, *Last Essays of Elia*, was published at London in 1833. This volume and the 1823 *Elia*, uniformly rebound, are sometimes sold together as the two first editions. Here there lies a problem. The 1833 London edition of the *Last Essays* is not truly the first, for the collection was published at Philadelphia, Pennsylvania, in 1823.

Ought the collector to go for uniformity and disregard the earlier alien, or should he make a strict point of priority? This problem arises with other authors as well as Lamb and the debate among bibliophiles continues.

One of the most desired Lamb items is *The King and Queen of Hearts*. As first published in 1805, this is a little 16mo, issued in blue printed wrappers and containing fifteen illustrations. It is very scarce, but the American composer, Jerome Kern (1885-1945), possessed a copy that, as far as is known, is unique. It has the date, 1805, printed on the wrapper, and this has been found on no other. When the Kern copy was sold at New York in 1946 it fetched $1,000 (then equivalent to £250). The finder of a similar copy today could expect its value to be $2,600 (£1,000) if not more.

William Hazlitt (1778-1830), Thomas De Quincey (1785-1859) and James Henry Leigh Hunt (1784-1859) may be considered together. All three were essayists and miscellaneous writers and extremely talented. A considerable body of their writings could be acquired in firsts fairly cheaply—between grades (i) and (b). Issues of their works are often determined by the number and dating of advertisements in the various volumes so reference must be made to the appropriate bibliographies.

Sooner or later, the collector will have to contend with Thomas J. Wise, whose baleful influence on bibliophily was at its height at the beginning of the present century. Wise, who began his working life as a London clerk, developed a taste for collecting books. In his young day, the unchangeable bookman pursued the unreadable book: if it was old, it was good, if it was modern it was despised.

Not having much money, Wise had to hunt on foot, as it were, where others could ride. In doing so, he found his quarry right at hand. In a few years he had not only formed an enviable collection of then modern authors, but was profitably encouraging others to do the same. He stressed the importance of condition and popularised systematic bibliography. Soon he was the accepted authority on nineteenth-century English books and compiled scholarly works on several authors.

Despite his love of books, he was a vain and venal man. He had a facility for discovering rare editions and when they were not to be discovered, he manufactured them and became a master forger. Though he made money from his fake treasures, there is little doubt that vanity also was a spur which pricked him to the production of items which set collectors agog from Bakersfield, California, to Broadstairs, Kent. His forgeries were of authentic works. He never tried to write new material in an established author's style.

Hardly a collectable poet of the nineteenth century escaped his attentions, from Tennyson to Swinburne. His acknowledged masterpiece is the reputed Reading edition of *Sonnets by E. B. B.*, supposedly 1847, by Elizabeth Barrett Browning (1806-61). This is itself so fine and rare that £700 ($1,820) was paid for a copy at Sotheby's in 1967—a greater amount than any genuine first edition of Mrs Browning's works has ever made. Wise forgeries are not spurned by collectors and such is their value that forgers have forged some of the forgeries. Incredible as it may seem, a few of these spurious efforts have knowingly been sold at prices rivalling those of the true Wise forgeries.

John Carter and Graham Pollard, two of England's most accomplished bibliographers, finally blew the gaff on Wise in 1934 with the publication of their joint book, *An Enquiry into the Nature of Certain 19th Century Pamphlets.* No direct accusations were made, but the finger was clearly pointed at Wise, by that time a frail old man. He died peacefully in 1937.

Since Wise's day, some of his chosen victims have not advanced in popularity. The only genuine Elizabeth Barrett

Browning items in much demand today are her first book, *Essay on Mind*, 1826, and the first edition of her *Poems*, 1844, in two volumes, with eight pages of advertisements dated 1 June 1844, at the beginning of volume 1, and an additional leaf at the end. These two items are each (H).

With Robert Browning (1812-89), the position is much the same. The Wise forgeries are about as valuable as the genuine firsts. A single-volume edition of *Bells and Pomegranates*, 1841-6, may be (I), but his late firsts, usually bound in maroon cloth and published by Smith, Elder & Co, may be found at 80p ($2.10). These husband and wife poets provide a cheap and interesting subject for the beginner to collect. Ironically, he will have to turn for help to Wise, whose bibliographies of the Brownings are still standard.

Alfred, Lord Tennyson (1809-92) is placed much as the Brownings. The Wise forgery of *Morte D'Arthur, Dora and Other Idylls*, allegedly 1842, is perhaps the dearest Tennyson book, in grade (F), while the genuine first issue of *In Memoriam*, 1850 (with 'the' for 'thee' on page 2, line 13, and 'baseness' for 'bareness' on page 198, line 3), may only be (g). The commonest Tennyson firsts are at present worth little more than those of the Brownings, but interest is reawakening. Once again, the collector's guide is Wise's Tennyson bibliography.

As with the Brownings and Tennyson, so with most of the other English poets of the Victorian period—most have a few books which are costly and several which are cheap, though they may be hard to track down.

The nineteenth century also saw the rise of the American poets, with William Cullen Bryant (1794-1878) in the van. Bryant's first book, *Poems*, 1821, published at Cambridge, Mass, is highly regarded and may be (F). Other Bryant items, however, are commoner. A first issue of his *A Forest Hymn*, no date, but 1860, should be (i) to (h). John Greenleaf Whittier (1807-92), the Quaker poet, can be collected inexpensively save for his *Snowbound*, 1866, in the first issue, which has the last page of the text numbered '52' (it is unnumbered in the second issue). This should be (F). A first issue of *The Song of Hiawatha*, 1855, by Henry Wadsworth Longfellow (1807-82), would be in the same grade. His *The Belfry of Bruges*, 1845-6, in original wrappers, might be (e), but his other firsts should be cheaper.

Though American, these three poets belong partly to the English tradition. The first issue of *The Song of Hiawatha* has the American form of the past tense of 'dive' in line 7, page 96. Longfellow quickly amended this, so the second issue has the English 'dived' instead of the American 'dove'.

It is unlikely that Walt Whitman (1819-92) would have been as eager to make this change. His is a much more strongly American voice. A few Whitman items are within reach of the indigent, but most are dear. The slim *Leaves of Grass*, first issue (with no extra pages of press notices), 1855, is (E). Later editions—not mere reprints—do not decline much in value, for Whitman kept adding poems until the original 94 page quarto had swollen to nearly 400 pages in the eighth edition.

Although Emily Dickinson (1830-86) belongs to much the same period as Whitman, very little of her poetry appeared during her lifetime. It was not until the publication of the three series of her *Poems* at Boston, Mass, in 1890-91-96, that a proper appraisal of her genius could be made. Much of her verse is tinged with mysticism and has a surprisingly modern ring, yet collectors seem still to blow hot and cold over her books. The three series of *Poems* together may be grade (H), or they may sometimes be obtainable more cheaply. Her *Masque of Poets*, Boston, 1878, published while she was still alive, is barely grade (g).

None but the experienced and well-heeled should attempt

the collection of first editions of the poetry of Edgar Allan Poe (1809-49). Their bibliography is complicated and they are desperately expensive. Only twelve copies of his *Tamerlane and Other Poems,* 12mo, Boston, Mass, 1827, are known to exist, so a copy of this unpretentious book in paper wrappers is likely to cost $30,000 (£11,550).

If poetry throve in the nineteenth century, the novel boomed. There were no great names at the beginning, but Maria Edgeworth (1767-1849) bridged two centuries with *Castle Rackrent,* 1800, and *Belinda,* three volumes, 1801. Both are mainly of interest to literary historians, but in fine original condition might be (a).

Greatness was not far off. In 1811, *Sense and Sensibility,* three volumes, by Jane Austen (1775-1817), appeared. Sir Walter Scott published his first novel, *Waverley,* in 1814. Both authors are justly esteemed, but Jane Austen is the more popular today. A good first of *Waverley* in boards might be worth £120 ($312), but the value of *Sense and Sensibility* in like condition would be nearer £300 ($780). In the early twenties, the *Waverley* might have been £50 ($200 old rate) and the *Sense and Sensibility* £25 ($100 old rate).

The other Jane Austen novels have much the same value, but the rest of Scott's novels are much cheaper than *Waverley,* not because of modern preferences, but because Scott was an immediate popular success and his subsequent novels were published in first editions large enough to ensure that they are still common. In her day, Jane Austen's readership was much smaller. By diligent pursuit and the payment on average of £18 to £20 a copy ($45-$50), a Scott collector could gain over the years a complete set of the Waverley Novels in very good firsts.

For much the same average expenditure, most of the novels of Charles Dickens (1812-70) could be acquired, but this would soar if the part issues were sought, the great hurdles being

Pickwick (already described) and *Great Expectations,* 1861, which was not issued in parts, but is very elusive and is in the (I) class at least. William Makepeace Thackeray (1811-63) is another novelist who could be collected for much the same average cost. With him, the great stumbling-block would be *Vanity Fair,* 1847-8.

There are impressive leather-bound first editions of this novel in grade (i). The perfectionist, however, would require a first issue in the original 19/20 parts. In April 1915, a fine set from the library of General Brayton Ives was sold in New York for $990 (£198 at that time). The same set—or one so like it as to make no difference—was again sold in New York in April 1947, for $2,500 (then £625). Allowing for the general upward trend in prices, this set should now be approaching $4,000 (£1,500) in value.

First editions of the other Victorian 'greats' may be dearer on average than those of Dickens and Thackeray, who were best-selling novelists. Firsts of the Brontë sisters, Charlotte (1816-55), Emily (1818-48) and Anne (1820-49) would probably be grade (e) or above, as would those of George Eliot (Mary Ann Cross, born Evans, 1819-80). Anthony Trollope (1815-82) is now accepted as a major writer and his firsts would average out in grade (d).

The later Victorians of note, Thomas Hardy (1840-1928), George Meredith (1828-1909) and R. L. Stevenson (1850-94), are now commanding greater attention than formerly, so Hardy firsts are grade (f) and Meredith and Stevenson firsts (h). In the cases of all three, prices vary greatly for different items and the few specially desirable books raise the average.

In pursuing Victorian fiction, the real joy lies with the books of minor authors. Here, Michael Sadleir was the pioneer collector and the authoritative book on the subject is his *XIX Century Fiction, A Bibliographical Record Based on His Own Collection,* two volumes, Constable & Co Ltd, London, and

University of California Press, Los Angeles, 1951. This magnificent work gives details of the books in Sadleir's private collection, with some added information on books that he had been unable to find. The illustrations of some of his choice items are provocative of bibliomanic lust, and also illustrated and definitively named for the first time are the various types of cloth favoured by Victorian binders.

There are apparently 3,761 items listed, but the real total is 2,861, for the numbering skips from 2,009 to 3,000 in the midst of descriptions of the novels of W. Clark Russell. Professor Robert Lee Wolff of Harvard University drew attention to this slip in *The Book Collector*, volume 14, number 3, 1965. Such an error in no way detracts from the value of *XIX Century Fiction*. New information which has come to light since the book was compiled might have been ignored but for Sadleir's pioneering.

In describing the *Mrs Brown* series by 'Arthur Sketchley' (George Rose, d 1882), enormously popular as yellowbacks less than a hundred years ago, Sadleir expresses the hope that his is a correct and comprehensive survey. From copies subsequently examined, his information is shown not to be quite accurate. He dates *Mrs Brown on Cetewayo* as 1879, but this is obviously wrong. Cetewayo, the African chief, did not come to England until 1882. He also gives this title as number 34 in the series, but some copies are numbered 33. His number for *Mrs Brown on Home Rule* is 36 and for *Mrs Brown on Jumbo* 35, but these are numbered 31 and 32 respectively on some copies. Only the most temerarious bibliographer would dare to lay down the law here, so Mrs Brown is still snarled up.

Sadleir's collection is now surpassed by that of Professor Lee Wolff, who has over 6,000 items. To cover the entire fictional output of the period he reckons he would require about 36,000 more. This is a vast area for the collector to explore, but if he sets off on the route already charted by Sadleir, he will be safe until he has gained enough experience to go his own way.

Some nineteenth-century firsts are now almost unobtainable in a condition fit for the collector's shelves. Only the individual can decide whether it is better to accept a first which is a ruin, or make do with a fine second edition. More and more, the frustrated *aficionado* is turning to entries like this, from a bookseller's catalogue of the seventies:

> 'OUIDA' (Louise de la Ramée): *Under two Flags*, 1st one-vol. edn., 1869 ... An excellent substitute for the virtually unobtainable three-decker first £2.50

It is hardly possible to give useful guidance on prices for the books which Sadleir lists. Competition is fierce and a prize like J. Sheridan Le Fanu's *Guy Deverell*, three volumes, 1865, may cost £150 ($390) in the saleroom, while the obscure Mrs J. C. Bateman's *The Netherwoods of Otterpool*, three volumes, published anonymously, 1858, may be waiting in a junk shop at well under £1—say $2. Certain booksellers apply a kind of Morton's fork to Victorian fiction. If a novel is listed in Sadleir it deserves to be priced high; if it is not in Sadleir it must be rare and so worthy of an extortionate price. There are many valuable novels NIS (not in Sadleir), but the cachet has been given to some dreary Sunday school tract of the 1860s and a deal of money asked for it. This is not so much sharp practice as stupidity, and serve the collector right who is taken in.

There is much to be said for breaking away from Sadleir. As Lee Wolff puts it: 'The advantage of indiscriminate acquisition is that discrimination can come later, in the reading.' He then asks what should govern selection. 'If George Augustus Sala (Sadleir), why not Edmund Yates (NIS)? If Captain Chamier (S), why not G. R. Gleig (NIS)?' Yet he, no less than Sadleir, has neglected Stevenson and the early Kipling, and, curiously, he has not delved deep into the minor American novelists, hardly touched by Sadleir, whose main concern was with books published in Britain. Here, surely is an avenue worth more intensive exploration.

American collectors naturally pursue their major writers of fiction, so that Poe's prose is as hopelessly out of reach of the ordinary collector as is his poetry. A first of Nathaniel Hawthorne's (1804-64) *The Scarlet Letter*, 1850, would be (b). The novels of Stephen Crane (1871-1900) are mostly grade (g), though his rare *Maggie: A Girl of the Streets*, New York, 1893, 'by Johnston Smith', would be grade (B). Henry James (1843-1916) firsts are probably (f) on average and those of 'Mark Twain' (Samuel Langhorne Clemens—1835-1910) and J. Fenimore Cooper (1789-1851) are only a little less. Bret Harte (1839-1902), Ambrose Bierce (1838-1914) and Herman Melville (1819-91) have their following, while *Uncle Tom's Cabin*, 1851-2, by Harriet Beecher Stowe (1811-96) is still sufficiently in demand to be (H).

But who has as yet seriously collected the works of William G. Simms (1806-70), Sylvester Judd (1813-53), Josiah G. Holland (1819-81), Maria S. Cummins (1827-66) and others who would certainly have been bagged by Sadleir had they been English writers? A section of Sadleir's collection was given over to yellowbacks—cheap editions of novels (and sometimes non-fiction) published in England in garish pictorial boards, throughout the second half of the nineteenth century. They have equivalents in America—for example, Harper's 'Black and White' series—which are not yet widely collected.

The last decades of the century brought changes. The expansion of education generated an indiscriminate demand for books. Some of the meanest-looking publications of all time belong to this period. It was an era of crude commercialism, leading to the escapist aestheticism of poets like D. G. Rossetti (1828-82) and A. C. Swinburne (1837-1909), and the pessimism of James Thomson ('B.V.') (1834-82). Swinburne in particular declined in favour in the twentieth century, but interest in him and the others may be reviving. Swinburne's *Atalanta in Calydon,* 1865, has always held its own and is now grade (g), but even his other works show a slight upward trend. The first collected edition of Rossetti's *Poems,* 1870, may be (e) in fine condition, and Thomson's *City of Dreadful Night,* 1880, (g).

Three widely different writers typify the literary and social conflicts of the last years of the Victorian era: Oscar Wilde (1854-1900), Bernard Shaw (1856-1950) and Rudyard Kipling (1865-1936). Wilde was not just a precious hothouse plant. The brittle wit of his epigrams, often containing a shrewd criticism of late-Victorian society, is found at its best in such plays as *The Importance of Being Ernest,* and *An Ideal Husband,* both first published in 1899 and probably (h). Though some of Wilde's firsts are scarce, they work out at an average just below (h).

Bernard Shaw used his wit to attack the institutions of his times. His plays and prefaces show his mastery of direct English, but he is not popular with collectors, except in signed copies. Some of his earliest writings may go to £8 ($20) unsigned, but most of his plays, in good first editions, are not too hard to find at under £1 ($2.60) a copy.

Shaw may have been opinionated and wrong-headed, but his works can still be seen, heard or read with delight by all save the stuffiest of ultra-English stuffed shirts. For them, Kipling is the man. There is no escaping his jingoism. He believed the English were the salt of the earth, with the Irish and Scots as mustard and pepper, though he took an American wife. He was also a born storyteller, with brilliant flashes of psychological insight, and a freedom from the longwindedness of many of his contemporaries. Most Kipling firsts can be acquired as cheaply as can Shaw's and a few special items rise to (h). As might be expected, the dearest item is a Wise forgery, *The White Man's Burden*, 1899, in grade (b).

Authors do not conveniently stop writing at the end of one century to clear the decks for a fresh crew in the next. A collection of twentieth-century literature must comprehend works by writers who spanned the two periods. Apart from Shaw and Kipling already mentioned, they include Sir J. M. Barrie (1860-1937), Robert Bridges (1844-1930), George Moore (1852-1933) and George Russell ('AE') (1867-1935). None of these should prove expensive to buy—ordinary firsts should not rise above £8 ($20). From this period onwards, signed limited editions come to the fore and have a value much above ordinary first editions. The suggested values throughout this chapter are based on ordinary, unlimited, unsigned firsts.

Joseph Conrad (Teodor Josef Konrad Korzeniowski, 1857-1924), E. Arnold Bennett (1867-1931) and H. G. Wells (1866-1946) are typical writers of the first part of the new century. All are accepted as worthwhile writers too, but such are collectors' foibles that most of their first editions can be had for very little. Collectors who buy for prestige rather than enjoyment may part with up to £100 ($260) for Conrad's *'Twixt Land and Sea Tales,* 1912, in a fine first, but will ignore the same author's *The Rescue,* 1920, at under £2 ($5). So, also, with Bennett, whose *Old Wives' Tale,* 1908, might cost over £50 ($130) as a first, but whose other equally readable novels are available below grade (i). Wells is the worst case of all. Apart from his early science fiction and two books which he wrote about playing with toy soldiers and the like, booksellers can hardly give away his first editions. It is just possible that interest will swing towards these three in the future, but investor-collectors should not bank on that.

Once the century was under way, literature began to take new directions. James Joyce (1883-1941), brought out *The Day of the Rabblement* in Dublin in 1901. This book, really little more than a pamphlet, is Joyce's rarest work and is grade

(E). In the same year, George Douglas Brown (as George Douglas) wrote *The House with the Green Shutters* in which, with his opening paragraph, he emptied a pail of slops over the gooey Scottish novelists of the kailyaird school. An undervalued book, it may be had as a fine first edition for £8 ($20) despite its scarcity.

Change was manifest by 1911, the publication date of *The White Peacock* by David Herbert Lawrence (1885-1930). Like most of Lawrence's novels, it is conventional in form. As an innovator, Lawrence is more notable for the things he said than how he said them. The Lawrence collector should think in terms of paying an average of £20 ($52) an item, though the actual price range will be between £4 ($10) and £40 ($104).

Early twentieth-century fiction awaits its Sadleir to collect and classify the works of the minor novelists. If Sadleir could rejoice in Rhoda Broughton and H. S. Merriman, surely Ethel M. Dell and P. C. Wren also deserve a champion. Perhaps some beginner will lay the basis of a *XX Century Fiction* bibliography now, while prices of the 'minors' are low—only he must not be too hopeful of finishing up with a valuable collection.

So far, attention is still focussed on the bigger names of the twentieth century. The prices of many of their firsts are difficult to assess as supplies dry up and the demand grows greater. Joyce's *Ulysses* in the Egoist Press edition, Paris, 1922, is certainly (I) and everything else of his is moving up. An average grading of (h) is hardly safe for the novels of Virginia Woolf (1882-1941) in view of a recent resurgence of interest in her work. Many of the American novelists average (i) for their firsts, including Theodore Dreiser, F. Scott Fitzgerald and Edna St Vincent Millay. Even the works of Ernest Hemingway, whose assertive masculinity appeals to wide sections of the American public, have not moved out of reach of the ordinary collector.

E. M. Forster, whose *A Passage to India*, 1924, is one of the great novels of the century, is an author whose body of writing is small and so can be collected in entirety on a modest budget, though the time when *A Passage to India* could be had as a first for under £20 ($52) is gone. Copies are hard to come by and the price increases every time one appears.

The novels of a whole range of authors may still be acquired for anything between £4 ($10) and £20 ($50). These authors include Aldous Huxley (though his *Brave New World*, 1932, may go higher), Richard Aldington, Sinclair Lewis and Edith Wharton. Irishmen at home and abroad are happy with grade (i) for James Stephens' *The Crock of Gold*, 1912, and comparable novels by others of their fellow-countrymen. But the philistine Scots are unenthusiastic collectors of their modern writers so that the great trilogy by James Leslie Mitchell (as Lewis Grassic Gibbon): *Sunset Song*, 1932, *Cloud Howe*, 1933, and *Grey Granite*, 1934, can be had for less than £4 ($10) a volume.

Some oddities among twentieth-century fiction are attractive. The writings of Frederick Rolfe (Baron Corvo) come under this heading and are now (h) or (g), though the first issue of *Hadrian the Seventh*, 1904, with the thirty-two-page catalogue at the end, is even dearer. If not an oddity, Ronald Firbank was a highly individual writer. His high spot is *Odette d'Antrevernes*, in wrappers, 1905, in grade (h).

The novice may even yet discover another Amanda McKittrick Ros, whose novels, as Angus Wilson has written (*The Spectator*, 3 December 1954), 'have probably given more dishonourable pleasure than any works in the English language'. The only editions of Mrs Ros's novels than can be looked for with confidence today are the reprint of the 1897 Belfast edition of *Irene Iddesleigh*, 1,250 copies, Nonesuch Press, 1926, and the 1935 edition of *Delina Delaney*, Chatto & Windus.

The delight of these comes mainly from the author's idiosyncratic handling of language and naive use of incredible situations. When the eponymous heroine of *Delina Delaney* first visits Columba Castle:

> The different shades of a lustrous lounge seemed to spurn at her in sparkling silence; the embossed seats of brilliant brilliancy that rested quietly here and there throughout the room almost taunted her girlish timidity with their blooming laugh of rosebud scorn.

When Lord Gifford examines the corpse of the villainess, Lady Mattie, Mrs Ros, in all seriousness, makes him exclaim:

> O God, it is true! This is my cousin, Lady Mattie Maynard! She had six toes on her right foot!

The beginner has already been advised to collect new first editions of living authors as soon as they are published. He would be unwise, however, to interest himself in current firsts primarily in the hope of financial gain. The darlings of one decade may become the outcasts of the next. In the twenties, while the author was alive, prices of the first editions of John Galsworthy were spectacularly high. Today, with few exceptions, they are low. Sir James Barrie is another who has suffered eclipse. A first edition of his *Tommy and Grizel*, 1900, cost 35s in 1930, more, in real terms than its decimal equivalent today of £1.75 ($4.55). Yet many booksellers would now be delighted to sell a copy for 40p ($1).

Our century has seen a steady decline in the ordinary reader's interest in poetry, yet it has been an age of remarkable poets. The four greatest are probably W. B. Yeats, T. S. Eliot, Ezra Pound and C. M. Grieve. Of the four, Yeats and Eliot maintain the most consistently high standards. Yeat's mannered dreaminess rarely dissolves into whimsy and Eliot's obsession with desiccation seldom turns to aridity. Pound and Grieve (better known under his pseudonym, Hugh MacDiarmid), magnificent at their best, can weary with the dull hum of the axes they so often grind. Those who would collect these poets are seeking the best and must pay. The dearest are Eliot and Yeats, some of whose works in ordinary firsts are grade (a), but there are signs that Pound and MacDiarmid are advancing in the same direction.

With £60 or $150 available, it should be possible to obtain the one significant book of Gerard Manley Hopkins (1844-89), who, though a nineteenth-century poet, did not become known until his *Poems,* edited by Robert Bridges, was published in 1918. Since that date, Hopkins's effect on English poetry has been all-pervading. Among those acknowledging their debt to him are W. H. Auden, Stephen Spender and C. Day Lewis, the present Poet Laureate. Of the three, Auden is closest in stature to Eliot, as is reflected in the prices of his works.

During his formative years, the American poet, Robert Frost, lived in England where his first obtainable book of poems was published—*A Boy's Will,* 1913. The first issue is (G). Though Frost shares Hemingway's insistence on masculinity, he is a nature poet of the highest order who had a vitalising effect on Edward Thomas (1878-1917), an almost major English poet, hard to collect, but not dear in ordinary first editions—perhaps averaging £6 ($15). Thomas was one of several fine poets killed in World War I.

The best of these was Wilfred Owen (1893-1918). His *Poems,* edited by Siegfried Sassoon, was first published in 1920 and is (f). Sassoon was himself a poet of the 1914-18 war. His *Counter Attack,* 1918, would have a value of about £8 ($20). Rupert Brooke (1887-1915) is the legendary World War I poet. His most celebrated book is *1914 and Other Poems,* 1915, but the rarest is *Lithuania,* Chicago, 1915. A copy in the original wrappers sold in New York for $6,750 (£2,700) in 1968. Robert Graves began as a poet of World War I, but has continued to produce work of an impressive quality. His early firsts are in (e) grade on average.

By the end of the nineteenth century the distinctively American poetic voice had fully matured. Edwin A. Robinson (1869-1935), the poet of Tilbury Town, is typical of the period. His early *Children of the Night*, Boston, 1897, is grade (I), or perhaps (E) in the limited edition on vellum, published at the same time. His other works do not rise so high and should be in the (h) to (g) range. This would also be the grading for the works of Carl Sandburg (1878-1967), though his near contemporary, William Carlos Williams (1883-1963) has risen in esteem and most of his books are grade (c), while his *Al Que Quirere!*, Boston, 1917, is (a). For some strange reason, that fine poet, Vachel Lindsay (1879-1931), is not a first favourite with collectors and should be available in grade (h).

Dylan Thomas (1914-53), who started to write verse in the thirties, became something of a legend in the period after World War II. While he had considerable talent, it is doubtful if future generations will accord him quite the position he holds today, when his *18 Poems*, first issue, first edition, 1934, is grade (I).

Other important poets of the first half of the century include Edwin Muir (1887-1959), Walter De la Mare (1873-1956) and John Masefield (1878-1966). Roy Campbell (1901-57) also wrote verse. Sir John Betjeman, still productive, is not, perhaps, a great poet, but his verse is wonderfully evocative of England and the English scene. Among younger writers there are almost as many different schools of poetry as there are poets Some show great promise, others seem merely to be making private noises in public. Time will tell which are worthy of the bibliophile's work.

His suicide at Minneapolis focussed attention on John Berryman (1914-1972), a poet whose best work has been considered as good as that of T. S. Eliot. As often happens when a writer dies tragically, collectors who have hitherto ignored them suddenly become aware of his books and fiercely compete for copies. Berryman's ***Homage to Mistress Bradstreet***, 1956, has moved up to grade (g) and his other works show a trend in the same direction.

CHAPTER FIVE

Fine Books and Illustration

Once a collector has gathered together a reasonable number of books, he may still have an uneasy feeling of dissatisfaction. In his way, he has done moderately well, yet everything is rather impersonal. His ordinary first editions have brought him near to his favourite authors, but not near enough. This is when he begins to think of presentation copies, signed copies and limited editions associated with their progenitors.

Since the late nineteenth century, the extra desirability of books with their authors' signatures has been emphasised by the leading bibliophiles (and, one suspects, by the leading booksellers). Gradually the difference in price between ordinary first editions and those that are signed has increased. Where there is an additional personal inscription, the gap has yawned even wider.

In July 1969, two copies of the first edition of Dylan Thomas's *Collected Poems*, 1952, were sold at Sotheby's. One copy, unsigned and without inscription, sold for £7 ($17.50); the other, inscribed 'for Mother & Dad with love from Dylan, Laugharne, November 1952', fetched £420 ($1,050). It is difficult enough to estimate the cost of an ordinary book which is out of print and in demand; it is almost impossible to do so for a copy that is inscribed and/or signed. In the case of the Thomas, the price increased sixtyfold, but no general rule can be deduced from this. The collector must let his heart and his pocket fight the matter out between them in arriving at the figure he is prepared to pay.

It was with an eye on the requirements of collectors that the production of limited first editions, signed by their authors, developed in the eighties and nineties of last century. The practice is, of course, much older. An edition of the *De Rerum Naturae* of Lucretius, published at Leyden in 1725, carries a notice, signed by the editor and printer, that only 800 copies were printed. A poem, *The Rival Lapdog and the Tale*, printed for W. Smith and G. Greg, 1730, would appear to be the first English book in a numbered and signed edition.

From the end of the nineteenth century onwards, signed limited editions are often printed on superior paper and specially bound. They may also be large-paper copies, which means that while the text takes up the same space as in ordinary copies, the pages have much bigger margins. This is an affectation which grew out of the tastes of a vanished race of bibliophiles. When books of an earlier age left the printers, they had been given wide margins so that once the binder got to work on them, he could trim them down with the plough (see Chapter 1) without cutting into the text. Generally speaking, the best bookbinders did the least trimming, so bibliophiles preferred copies with good margins, particularly in the case of books published in the sixteenth and seventeenth centuries by the Elzevirs, a family of Dutch printers. A 'tall Elzevir' became a byword among bookcollectors. In his book, *The Library*, 1881, Andrew Lang wrote: 'In Elzevirs a line's breadth of margin is often worth a hundred pounds... No Elzevir is valuable unless it be clean and large in the margins.' Niggardly margins are unpleasing to the eye, but those that are excessively wide are no better; yet there are still special editions produced where generosity in this respect is not related to artistic proportioning.

The bindings of some limited editions of the late nineteenth and early twentieth centuries are also unsatisfactory. While the ordinary editions were cased in honest cloth, their betters were decked in boards covered with sugar paper and given undyed canvas spines. This looks impressive, but wears badly. The canvas, usually with a fragile paper titling-piece, discolours easily and the sugar paper soon becomes rubbed and scored.

Limited editions were especially popular in the twenties. The most clueless of poetasters would have their meretricious verses issued at their own expense, with a printed note on a flyleaf stating that this was the first edition, limited to *x* copies, signed by the author. A misguided collector could amass these cheaply and end up with nothing that he, or anybody else, would ever want to read.

Contemporaneous with the development of the limited edition was the rise of the private press. Normally, books from a private press are printed without the use of elaborate machinery, the type being set by hand. The owners of the press may also print for commercial publishers, but their main concern is to produce whatsoever books they choose, as finely and beautifully as they can. The owners may or may not be the actual printers and binders as well. Some so-called private presses are really publishers who supervise the production of fine books without themselves doing any printing. Private press work is almost invariably in limited editions, as it is hardly practical to adapt hand printing to large-scale production.

The first British private press of note was the Strawberry Hill Press, started by Horace Walpole in 1757. The most desirable work of this press is the 1757 edition of the *Odes* of Thomas Gray, whom Walpole patronised. In original condition, this book would be grade (G) in the Scale of Values (page 12). Other early private presses were the Lee Priory Press, founded in 1812 by Sir Samuel Egerton Brydges (1762-1837) and the Auchinleck Press, begun in 1815 by Sir Alexander Boswell (1775-1822), son of James Boswell, the biographer of Samuel Johnson. The most obsessive bibliomaniac of all time, Sir Thomas Phillips (1792-1872), began his Middle Hill Press in 1822. Though his printers produced some worthy books and pamphlets, the craftsmanship was not always of a high standard. The products of the Daniel Press, founded in 1845, were better, but the beginning of the modern private press was in 1891. In that year, William Morris launched the Kelmscott Press, which set new standards of excellence in English book production. Nowhere is this seen to better advantage than the Kelmscott edition of Chaucer, with designs by Sir Edward Burne-Jones, published in 1896. The edition was limited to 425, with forty-six copies bound in princely style by T. J. Cobden-Sanderson at the Doves Bindery. These latter are now worth more than £2,000 ($5,200) a copy. Cobden-Sanderson joined with Emery Walker to form the Doves Press in 1899 and produced more beautiful books, in a specially-designed type. The partnership lasted until World War I. When it was broken, Cobden-Sanderson—in a fit of pique, some say—threw the lovely Doves Press type into the River Thames, whence it has never been recovered.

The Eragny Press was founded in 1894 and in 1895, C. H. St J. Hornby set up the Ashendene Press, which turned out magnificent work until the thirties of this century. The Vale Press was started in 1896, and in 1898, C. R. Ashbee, founder of the Guild of Handicraft, a community of craftsmen, developed the Essex House Press as part of the Guild's activities. Ashbee designed a curious type, called Endeavour, for his press. It heavily exaggerates the characteristics of the Kelmscott types, but is surprisingly effective in the right context.

Other famous private presses of later foundation are the Shakespeare Head, Nonesuch, Gregynog and Alcuin, with the

Golden Cockerel (1921) as the best known of all. Most of them have done great service to Spenser, Shakespeare, Milton, Bunyan, Keats, Shelley and writers of like calibre. As illustrators, Eric Gill and Robert Gibbings gave a unique quality to the Golden Cockerel productions and were followed by Russell Flint and Buckland Wright, whose bosomy ladies effectively decorate the later Golden Cockerels.

In America, the Grolier Club of New York played a major role in the revival and development of fine printing and binding. This unique association of dedicated book-lovers and publishers was founded in 1884 with a membership limited to one hundred (later enlarged). It aimed to collect and exhibit the best works of the past while issuing new books to serve as types of the best that modern skill and taste would do. There was no Morris or Cobden-Sanderson to produce masterpieces for the club. Nevertheless, the early publications achieved a distinction of style and quality which had a galvanic effect on commercial book production. As it was the club's first publication, the 1884 reprint of *A Decree of Starre-Chamber 1637*, commands attention in the bibliophilic world and is likely to be grade (f), but it was the third publication, in 1886, which showed what the club could achieve. This was an edition of Washington Irving's *History of New York . . . by Diedrich Knickerbocker*, with illustrations by George H. Boughton, Howard Pyle and Will H. Drake. Even better was the Grolier edition of Bishop de Bury's *Philobiblon*, 1889. Both it and the Irving would be unlikely acquisitions under the (I) grade. Later products of the club have been of particular interest to bibliophiles and include the Geoffrey Keynes *Bibliography of William Blake*, 1921, grade (b) and Luther S. Livingston's *Franklin and His Press at Passy*, 1914, grade (c).

The Grabhorn Press of San Francisco is an outstanding example of an American private press at least indirectly influenced by the Grolier Club. Typography is a subject dear to the hearts of the principals of this press and the student of printing no less than the bibliophile should look out for such Grabhorn products as *Nineteenth Century Type...cast by United States Founders now in the Cases of the Grabhorn Press*, 1959, and *The Compleat Jane Grabhorn: A Hodge-Podge of Typographical Ephemera*, 1968, both (g). The Grabhorn Press has issued many notable books of a different sort, such as the fine 1930 edition of Whitman's *Leaves of Grass* (H).

The collector of private press books must be prepared to pay high for his acquisitions. The Ashendene *Don Quixote*, a large folio of 1913, of which 145 copies were printed, would be grade (G) and might even topple into grade (F); the special Doves Press version of Milton's *Areopagitica*, twenty-five copies on vellum, 1907, would be (H); the Golden Cockerel *Endymion*, by Keats, (g) or (f), and the Gregynog's famous *Shaw Gives Himself Away*, 1939, (a). Some lesser productions of these presses are not so expensive, but none is cheap.

Fine printing characterises the work of the best private presses. Unhappily, this is a feature for which the bulk of ordinary British book production has not been distinguished. The early English and Scottish printers never reached the standards of their masters on the continent of Europe. Typographically, the first folio edition of the plays of Shakespeare, 1623, is a disgrace to the great dramatist. The same could be said of the early editions of many of our important writers. John Day (1522-84) was the outstanding printer of his time. It is a matter for regret that the work by which he is best known, the first English edition of John Foxe's *History of the Acts and Monuments of the Church* (Foxe's *Book of Martyrs*), 1563, grade (E) or more, was printed before he had cast his improved roman and italic types in the 1570s.

Nobody of great note appears on the scene until William Caslon (1692-1766), who began by engraving designs on guns.

Between 1720 and the year of his death, he cut many founts of type of different kinds. His roman and italic were good enough to be sought after by foreign printers. The edition of the works of John Selden, printed by Caslon in 1726, is probably the best example of his craftsmanship.

After Caslon, the next important name is that of John Baskerville (1706-75), who served many trades until he turned to printing in his mid-forties. He looked at the whole craft, concerning himself with the quality of paper and ink as well as layout and choice of type. The types he cut were better than anything that had previously been achieved in England. His *Virgil* of 1758 was the first of several masterpieces. It may be only grade (h) in ordinary leather, but some copies were specially bound and can be (H). Baskerville Bibles, produced in the 1760s and 1770s, are among the few eighteenth-century Bibles which have any value—perhaps (f) or (e).

The Foulis brothers, Robert (1707-76) and Andrew (1712-75), of Glasgow, were the first producers of fine books in Scotland. Their printer, Alexander Wilson, designed types rather similar to those of Baskerville, giving the books from the Foulis press a dignity unique in Scottish printing. The Foulis *Horace*, 1744, and *Homer*, four volumes, folio, 1756-8, are outstanding productions. A fine set of the *Homer* would be (H), but one or two minor Foulis productions should be available in grade (i).

John Bell (1745-1831) was not a publisher of the first rank. He made an important contribution to European typography, however, when he published his edition of Shakespeare, 1773-5. It was the first considerable work to dispense with the long 's' which so closely resembles an 'f'. There seems to be no foundation for the theory that he decided on the change because the misreading of 'f' for 's' was liable to produce embarrassment in one of Shakespeare's songs.

At the close of the eighteenth century, the difference between the thick and thin strokes of printed letters became greater and led to the development of what are called modern face types, with the contrast very strongly marked. McKerrow (*An Introduction to Bibliography*, 1927) suggests 1815 as the date when modern face became really common and declares that the period 1815-44 was perhaps the worst of all from the point of view of type design.

In 1844, Mrs Hannah Mary Rathbone had a book published anonymously by the Chiswick Press: *So Much of the Diary of Lady Willoughby as Relates to Her Domestic History, & to the Eventful Period of the Reign of Charles the First.* It was written in the archaic language that the title suggests. Wishing to maintain the illusion of antiquity, Charles Whittingham, principal of the Chiswick Press, had a special fount of type cut for the book. He chose Caslon's type as his model, retaining the long 's', and was so pleased with the result that he used this revived Caslon again in the same year to print an edition of Juvenal for the publisher, William Pickering (1796-1854). Pickering, most of whose books were printed by Whittingham, approved of the new type, so it was used again and again—to particularly good effect in Pickering's edition of Milton, 8 vols, 1851. *Lady Willoughby's Diary*, with a second volume published in 1848, may cost £10 ($26) and the Juvenal would be in the same grade. The Milton could be (h), but frequently appears in a fine binding which adds considerably to the price. The name of the Chiswick Press has continued to be linked with fine printing up to the present.

After Whittingham, types in Caslon style took over from the thick-and-thin modern faces in many areas of book production. Though it may be confusing, revived Caslon and similar types are referred to as old-face and old-style despite the fact they superseded modern faces. Between the times of Whittingham and Morris, satisfactory developments in book production were few.

Printing in more than one colour goes back to the earliest days. In Germany, Johann Fust and Peter Schoeffer printed a psalter at Mainz. It is the first book to carry a date (1457) and is also the first book with colour printing. This was confined to initial capital letters, executed in red and blue. The letters were cut on wood, and either two blocks were used, one inked in blue for the letter and one in red for the surrounding decoration, or a single block was employed with the two different coloured inks applied to the appropriate areas at the same time.

Probably a two-block system was used for the first English book printed with added colour—*The book of Hawking, hunting and blasing of arms,* St Albans, 1486, said to be by Dame Juliana Bernes or Berners. The coloured illustrations are of coats of arms. A facsimile reproduction of this book, edited by William Blades, was published in 1901 and copies might be in grade (h). Notwithstanding this early venture, colour printing was little used until the eighteenth century, though black and white illustrations were common.

As with printing, the story of the English illustrated book in the early stages is uninspiring. Illustrations were almost invariably printed from wood blocks and if some are not entirely without artistic merit and others possessed of a quaint charm, none is a work of genius.

The art of reproducing illustrations from engravings on copper plates was known in the first half of the fifteenth century, but was hardly used in English books before the middle of the seventeenth. Wenceslaus Hollar (1607-77) was a Bohemian who lived in England after the restoration of Charles II. He produced illustrated books which are now highly valued —his *Animals of the Chace,* 30 etchings, 1646-7 may be grade (H). He was followed by David Loggan, famous for his bird's-eye views of the ancient English universities: *Cantabrigia Illustrata,* no date, but 1688, and *Oxonia Illustrata,* 1685. Really fine copies may be worth the (F) grade, but specimens in which the plates are only slightly foxed might be found in (H). Both books are still suffering at the hands of breakers who sell the individual plates at inflated prices.

The first great English book illustrator is William Hogarth (1697-1764). He did a series of engravings for the three parts of *Hudibras,* a long satirical poem by Samuel Butler (1612-80). The first editions of the parts appeared in 1663-64-78, but the first Hogarth edition was 1726. It has been neglected by collectors and should be grade (h), or even (i). Hogarth's other important series of book illustrations was for an edition of *Don Quixote.* This also has been unaccountably cold-shouldered and can be found in grade (i).

Hogarth's inclination towards caricature was developed by many of his successors, but a more refined influence came from Hubert-François Bourguignon (1699-1773), whose *nom-de-guerre* was Gravelot. A Parisian, he lived in London for fifteen years and illustrated many English books, including a 12mo edition of Dryden's *Dramatick Works,* 6 vols, 1735, and, with F. Hayman, the mixed sixth and third edition of Richardson's *Pamela,* 4 vols, 12mo, 1742. Gravelot's elegant style is never insipid.

Although Francis Hayman (1708-1776) was a friend of Hogarth's, his work more closely resembles that of Gravelot, with an added English robustness. His engravings may be found in Smollett's *The Adventures of Roderick Random,* 2nd edition, 2 vols, 12mo, 1748, and Christopher Smart's *Poems on Several Occasions,* 4to, 1752, as well as in other books of the time. As a first edition, the Christopher Smart would be (f) at least; but Hayman illustrations are to be found in quite cheap items of the period. There is a delightful rococo touch to the engravings of Anthony Walker (1726-65). He contributed headpieces and vignettes to several publications, but his work is at its best in his seven illustrations for William Somerville's poem, *The Chace,* in the fourth edition of 1757 (i).

The spirit of Hogarth is manifest in the work of Thomas Rowlandson (1756-1827). When the German-English publisher, Rudolf Ackermann (1764-1834) projected his *Microcosm of London,* three large volumes of coloured illustrations of public buildings and places, he commissioned an architect, A. C. Pugin (1762-1832), to draw the buildings and Rowlandson to supply the foreground figures. The arrangement worked well. The dignity of Pugin is balanced—some might say overbalanced—by the liveliness of Rowlandson. *The Microcosm,* published 1806-8, is eagerly pursued, too often by breakers, and is (E). Rowlandson's most popular work is his series of coloured aquatints for the *Tours of Doctor Syntax,* three long poems by William Combe (1741-1823), who is not otherwise remembered. The three tours were first published in 1812-20-21 and ran into many editions, with the Rowlandson illustrations. A good set of the three firsts would be (I), but later sets, still with the coloured aquatints, might be had for a sum in the (f) or (g) grades. As was the normal practice at the time, colouring for the Rowlandson books was supplied by hand. The colour-printing improvements referred to earlier were still to come.

Rowlandson's mantle fell on George Cruikshank (1792-1878). Most people know him as the illustrator of Dickens's *Oliver Twist,* but he was a prolific artist whose work spans many years. No better examples of his book illustrations are to be found than those in the English translation of *German Popular Stories* by the Brothers Grimm, published in two volumes, 1823-6, with twenty Cruikshank plates. Together, the volumes are probably (d), if free from the foxing which so often disfigures them. Cruikshank collectors can start more humbly. There are plenty of books with his illustrations to be had under £2 ($5).

Hablot K. Browne (1815-82), who usually signed himself Phiz, was Dickens's chief illustrator. His work has a Hogarthian element of grotesque, but lacks Cruikshank's fierce concentration. He worked for many others besides Dickens and his illustrations are easily found in Victorian novels of differing standards. John Leech (1817-64), who did the plates for Dickens's *A Christmas Carol,* 1843, had a similar style and also illustrated G. A'Beckett's laboured *Comic History of England,* two volumes, 1847, and *Comic History of Rome,* no date, but 1852. The hand-coloured plates rather than the text make these collectors' pieces in grade (h).

After Cruikshank, Browne and Leech, the guts went out of book illustration, as can be seen by comparing the original illustrations for Dickens's *Our Mutual Friend,* 1864-5, by Marcus Stone, with those of *Oliver Twist* or *David Copperfield.* Samuel Palmer (1805-81) did some good work, but is more famous in other artistic fields, as is Birket Foster, who produced some pleasant rustic pictures for equally pleasant rustic books.

The great era of topographical steel engraving was the first half of the nineteenth century. Francis Grose (1731-91) made a tour of England and Wales in the latter part of the eighteenth century and as a result published his *Antiquities of England and Wales,* 1773-87, lavishly illustrated with copper engravings of old churches and other buildings. A tour of Scotland in 1789 brought him the friendship of Burns (they were both fond of the bottle) and produced *The Antiquities of Scotland.* He died while working on a similar book for Ireland, but it was duly produced in the year of his death. A complete set of the *Antiquities,* in ten volumes, should be (d).

Grose's success set a pattern frequently followed in the next century, further encouraged by the invention of steel engraving, which was capable of giving finer gradations of tone than was copper. Between 1803 and 1814, John Britton (1771-1857) and E. W. Brayley (1773-1854) issued *The Beauties of England and Wales* in eighteen volumes full of topographical engravings. Though cheap at one time, a complete set must now be graded (I) as the number of copies has been seriously reduced by the breakers. Britton alone produced several other books of the same kind. William Beattie and W. H. Bartlett were associated with similar works covering Scotland, Switzerland and other parts of Europe. Between 1845 and 1852, R. W. Billings (1813-74) published his *Baronial and Ecclesiastical Antiquities of Scotland* in four volumes, which would be no bad bargain if they were in the (f) grade. One of the most highly desired books of topographical illustrations is William Daniell's and Richard Ayton's *Voyage Round Great Britain*, eight volumes, 1814-25, containing 308 hand-coloured aquatints. It is another work which has fallen foul of the breakers and is now certainly worth £1,700 ($5,420) when complete and clean.

The two greatest names in English book illustration are those of William Blake (1757-1827) and Thomas Bewick (1753-1828). Blake was poet, artist, engraver and mystic all in one. If his draughtsmanship was sometimes defective, this was more than compensated by the visionary power which shines through everything he did. Only those who have seen the originals can fully appreciate the enchanting beauty of his *Songs of Innocence*, 1789, or the grandeur of his twenty-one *Illustrations to the Book of Job*, prepared and published when he was an old man—1826. Original editions of Blake's major works are above the £1,000 ($2,600) mark. Even coloured facsimiles, produced at various times, are hardly to be had below grade (f). Copies of Blair's *The Grave*, 1808, and Young's *The Complaint, or Night Thoughts*, 1797, with Blake illustrations, may be graded (d) and (G) respectively.

Thomas Bewick was a more mundane person than Blake, though there is nothing cloddish in the execution of his celebrated woodcuts, despite the earthy nature of some of the subjects. Apart from his *British Birds* and *Quadrupeds*, his best-known book is his edition of Aesop's *Fables*, Newcastle, 1818. A reasonable copy might be had in grade (g). Not every woodcut in the Aesop is the work of Bewick, for he had several pupils who learnt to engrave in the Bewick style and worked with him before spreading their wings and setting up for themselves. None of them ever developed the same feeling for the medium that the master possessed in such measure. Bewick, and alleged Bewick, plates are to be found in many books of the late eighteenth and early nineteenth centuries. They are among the cheap finds that still await the dilligent hunter.

Bewick confined himself to black-and-white, convinced, nevertheless, that satisfactory colour-printing from wood was a possibility. It was left to George Baxter (1804-67) to show how it could be done. Three-colour printing from metal plates was practised by James Le Blon as far back as 1720, but his was a laborious and expensive process, scarcely applicable to ordinary book illustration. Baxter, following up experiments by others, tried to print from wood blocks using a watercolour medium. After further experimentation, he adopted oil colours and found them more satisfactory. He then combined the use of metal plates for the basic drawing with wood blocks for the areas of colour.

His first important achievements in book illustration were two coloured prints in *The Feathered Tribes of the British Islands*, 1834, by Robert Mudie. He followed up with a little more book work, but later concentrated on producing individual prints. He granted licences to other firms to use his process, one of them being Kronheim & Co of London, who did much colour printing for books, sometimes by cruder processes than Baxter's.

If the Mudie is too expensive in grade (h), pleasure can be more cheaply bought in collecting less important books with Baxter, Kronheim or sometimes Le Blond (no connection with the Le Blon mentioned earlier) coloured illustrations.

While Baxter was conducting his experiments, others were attempting to produce illustrations in full colour by lithography, in which the prints are taken from a special type of stone. At first it was difficult for lithographers to get subtle gradations of tone, but this was no disadvantage as far as Owen Jones (1809-74) was concerned. He was interested in reproducing flat designs in colour, so chromolithography, as colour lithography is called, suited his purposes admirably. Jones, who became superintendent of works for the 1851 Exhibition in London, worked in association, and sometimes in collaboration, with H. Noel Humphreys (1810-79) to produce many beautiful illuminated books, some of them bound in carved wood, some in charmingly absurd *papier maché*.

The great Humphreys-Jones work is *Illuminated Books of the Middle Ages*, 1849, magnificently coloured and gilded, and definitely (H) in top condition. Jones's *Grammar of Ornament*, 1865, may be only (h), and later editions, liable to be loose within their covers because of perished gutta-percha bindings, should be available around £8 ($20). Later refinements of chromolithographic technique made possible the reproduction of many handsome colour plates in the better books of about a hundred years ago. In some methods of lithography where oil colours were used (oleolithography), the oils took a very long time to dry. This caused the illustrations to be sticky after they were bound into the book with the result that they adhered firmly to the neighbouring leaves of text. Collectors should beware of this and inspect all such books very carefully. If text and illustration are stuck together there is no known way of separating them without doing irreparable damage.

Randolph Caldecott (1846-86) was an artist who often availed himself of the opportunities of colour printing. Between 1878 and 1885 he produced a series of sixteen picture books for children, full of bright illustrations. A good complete set would be (f) and will probably rise higher. He had something of John Leech's zest, but was altogether more genial. His characters are all sleek-headed men and such as sleep o' nights. When Caldecott died he had just begun to illustrate a series of books for Macmillan, the publisher. His work was continued and developed by Hugh Thomson, an artist who delighted in the costumes and settings of the Regency. His illustrations have more grace than vigour and are to be seen at their most charming in more than one Macmillan edition of Jane Austen.

Though the development of book illustration in America followed much the same lines as it did in Britain, there are some divergences. F. O. C. Darley (1822-88) was the counterpart of Hablot Browne, but his younger contemporaries and immediate successors lost no vigour when they illustrated the life and events around them. Winslow Homer (1836-1910) was, among greater things, an early pictorial journalist. His folio of two portraits and sixteen tinted lithographs, *Proceedings at the Reception in Honor of George Peabody*, Boston, Mass, 1856, is a fair sample of his work in this sphere and is grade (g). The sense of history in the making was well maintained by Frederic Remington (1861-1949) who followed. His *Pony Tracks*, New York, 1895, is only one of several books which he produced before and after the turn of the century, all of them collected and still not too hard to find in the (g) to (b) grades. Howard Pyle (1853-1911) and E. A. Abbey (1852-1911) were contemporaries of the Scottish Hugh Thomson and drew in a similar idiom. One of Pyle's most successful books was *The Merry Adventures of Robin Hood*, New York, 1883. Here the subject gave full scope for his talents and the book is justifiably grade (g). The folio edition of Goldsmith's *She Stoops to Conquer*, New York, 1887, with drawings by Abbey, is not now so highly regarded and should be grade (i) until those who appreciate its elegant illustrations become aware of its merits. For the present, the Hugh Thomson *She Stoops to Conquer* takes precedence.

Working at the same time as Thomson was Aubrey Beardsley (1872-98), whose cool passion is in such striking contrast to Thomson's elegant artificiality. Beardsley accomplished much in his short life, beginning with his illustrations in the Pre-Raphaelite manner for an edition of Malory in 1893-4 (now in grade (I) when in the original twelve parts) and ending with some illustrations for Ben Jonson's *Volpone,* 1898, grade (g). As an interpreter of end-of-century decadence through skilful economy of line combined with a wealth of two-dimensional decoration, Beardsley had no equal. His work is sure to become much more valuable in the years ahead.

Sir Max Beerbohm, a product of the same age, was a clever penman in a quite different way. His caricatures of the great people of his day are never savage, but always amusingly to the point. He was much more than a cartoonist and apart from his books of drawings he produced many essays, short stories and a bizarre novel, *Zuleika Dobson,* 1911. No wonder Bernard Shaw dubbed him 'the incomparable Max'. His books of drawings are in grades (i) and (h), but a fine first of *Zuleika Dobson* would be (f).

Towards the end of last century, when it became possible to reproduce line drawings without their first having to be cut on wood, encouragement was given to a new race of topographical illustrators, among the best of whom were E. H. New and F. L. Griggs. New was an Evesham man, brought up in the shadow of the Cotswolds. Something of the mellowness of Cotswold stone is apparent in his fine drawings.

F. L. Griggs was born and spent his early years in Hertfordshire, but he, too, fell under the Cotswold spell and made his home in Chipping Campden, loveliest of the small Cotswold towns. He trained as an architect, but in taking to pen-and-ink drawing he was influenced by Samuel Palmer. His illustrations can be seen in such books as a 1902 edition of *The Sensitive Plant* by P. B. Shelley, *A Book of Cottages and Little Houses* by C. R. Ashbee, 1906, and *The Villages of England* by A. K. Wickham, 1932. As Griggs is not yet widely collected, most of the books he illustrated may be found below the £2 ($5) mark. The important exceptions at present are *Ernest Gimson: His Life and Work,* Shakespeare Head Press, 1924, and *Campden,* same publisher, 1938, both of which are grade (f) and rising.

In the twenties, when Griggs was turning from book illustration to the production of some of the finest etchings of the century, a new school of wood-engravers was springing up, led by Eric Gill, Robert Gibbings, John Farleigh, Joan Hassall and others. They brought a different emphasis to the technique of white line on black first devised by Bewick. English wood-engraved illustration reached a peak in the thirties, but has declined since then. No other form of engraving marries so well with clean, well-defined type. However hard they strain after effect, the illustrators and typographers of today seem incapable of turning out books with the unassertive dignity of those of that heyday of wood engraving.

Though the best examples from the period were issued in limited editions by the Golden Cockerel Press and are costly, there are plenty for the modest collector to work on. A first edition of Bernard Shaw's *The Adventures of the Black Girl in Her Search for God,* 1932, should cost no more than £2 ($5) in brilliant condition. It contains some of John Farleigh's most impressive work. Unfortunately, it was issued in paper boards which have not stood the test of time. It would be a mistake to pay much more than 80p ($2) for a copy worn at the spine.

Line drawing is the basis of much modern illustration and has many competent exponents. One of the most pleasing contributors to this art was John Minton, who would undoubtedly have developed his technique had he lived. He is easily and cheaply collected as most of the books he illustrated are still found on the ordinary shelves of ordinary secondhand booksellers. They include H. E. Bates's *The Country Heart*, 1949 (not later editions), Reginald Arkell's *Old Herbaceous*, 1950, and Elizabeth David's *French Country Cooking*, 1951.

An earlier and highly individualistic exponent of the line drawing was Jessie Marion King (1876-1949). She was a disciple of Charles Rennie Mackintosh (1868-1928), the great Scottish Art Nouveau architect and designer. Her illustrations are sometimes excessively sentimental, but all have the weird charm of the Art Nouveau. In describing himself as a lover of 'Jessie at her dottiest', Sir John Betjeman is referring to her technique of sprinkling her drawings with tiny leaves, pebbles, blossoms, or anything which would display her Hopkins-like love of dappled things. The essential Jessie King is to be found in *The Defence of Guenevere and Other Poems* by William Morris, London and New York, 1904, for which she did the illustrations and designed the cloth binding. Much of her work was done for quite obscure little books. Few people other than her keen fans know of *The Legends of Flowers* by Mantegazza, translated by Mrs Kennedy, published at Edinburgh and London, 1908, with a coloured frontispiece by Walter Crane and decorations throughout by Jessie King. This is the sort of charming item that rewards those who do not collect entirely from booksellers' posted lists. At present no Jessie King items are likely to be above grade (i), but interest in her work is growing.

A really inviting private library is one where a variety of books is immediately apparent. There are rows of modern volumes, immaculate in their dustwrappers, books of last century in cloth which still looks fresh, some items in original boards, mostly protected in cases, and some rather battered books of all periods, well, rather than badly, worn—for much-used books wear differently from neglected books. There will also be some books more or less handsomely bound in leather.

In recent years, leatherbound books have been bought indiscriminately for their decorative qualities, but it is only those who are out of touch with the market who imagine that such 'library furniture' can still be had for a few pence a yard. Today, any sort of rubbishy literature sells at a high price if it is contained within attractive calf or morocco leather. In the face of inflation of this sort, the serious collector of fine craftsman bindings has now to pay a small fortune for the items he wants. Beginners are well advised to steer clear of this branch of bibliography—it is full of boobytraps.

However, it is possible to secure some pleasing leather or half-leather bindings of the eighteenth and nineteenth centuries, pleasant to look at and containing readable matter, within grade (i). A few of these bindings may have binders' tickets on the front paste-down endpapers—little labels with legends like 'Bound by LYON, *WIGAN*'. These present a challenge to the inquiring mind, so the zealous collector can enjoy himself by consulting old trade directories and pestering local librarians to gain more information about those old bookbinders.

Since most of his books will already have a bearing on the history of publishers' cloth, a collector whose chosen period is the nineteenth century may care to become an amateur of cloth bindings in addition to following his main line. The earliest authentic examples of original cloth bindings are probably on some volumes of Pickering's Diamond Classics, issued in calico about 1822.

Brander Matthews, in his *Bookbindings, Old and New*, London and New York, 1896, states: 'I have among my Sheridaniana the third edition of Dr Watkins's "Memoirs of the Public and Private Life of the Right Honourable Richard Brinsley Sheridan", printed for Henry Colburn in 1818, and both volumes are clad in glazed calico... The date of the biography is that of the binding.' Despite this statement, the matter is open to doubt. Brander Matthews's copy may have lain unbound in the publisher's warehouse for several years before being sent forth in calico. John Carter has studied the subject of cloth bindings from many angles and has consulted the records kept by publishers of the early nineteenth century. He refuses to date the introduction of cloth farther back than 1820, declaring that 'inferences of early date drawn from books themselves can only be made with extreme caution'—*Publishers' Cloth, 1820-1900*, New York and London, 1935.

Anybody with a real interest in fine bindings will not be content to treat the matter purely as ancient history. The paper dustwrapper has largely destroyed the incentive that gave us brightly designed covers on ordinary books, but there are still craftsmen at work who can clothe books in leather and gold as well as could any of their predecessors. It should be the duty and the pleasure of the true bibliophile to have at least one of his books bound by a capable binder. A fine morocco or calf binding will be expensive, but if the work is entrusted to the right man, it will be a thing of beauty and a joy for ever—or for at least three hundred years.

CHAPTER SIX

Adventure, Detection and Children's Books

The universal love of a good story made inevitable the creation of the novel. For many years the reading public was prepared to wait more or less patiently while the novelist put down his knitting, as it were, and digressed on the beauties of scenery, the vanity of human wishes, or almost anything else that came into his head. Later, authors became aware that some of their readers did not welcome digressions, but wanted the strands of narrative to be kept on the move to produce a compact, well-knit whole. So began the 'rattling good yarn'.

The development of the adventure novel was no sudden thing and no dates can be given. The shape of things to come may be discerned in *Lorna Doone* by R. D. Blackmore (1825-1900). This novel has plenty of action, even if some parts of it move as slowly as a Devonshire farm waggon. The first edition, published in 1869 in three volumes, was accepted as no more than a good average historical novel, yet the terseness of the writing at the 'exciting bits' must have had an effect, for from the date of its first appearance, the English novel of adventure becomes less long-winded. He who wants to read *Lorna Doone* in his own copy of the first edition must expect it to be in the (H) grade of the Scale of Values (page 12).

Probably the development of the railways encouraged the short direct novel of adventure. Bookstalls were quite early established at the larger railway stations, where intending passengers could buy books to while away their journeys. Many of the novels sold were reprints of the bulky bestsellers of the period, but not all of these were suitable for railway journeys. With a growing demand for fairly short, light novels, authors arose to satisfy it. The first efforts were, for the most part, poorly written, but the style gradually moved up in the world.

By the 1880s, the rattling good yarn had truly emerged. The appropriately named *Dawn* by H. Rider Haggard (1856-1925), was published in 1884 and his *King Solomon's Mines* appeared the following year. *She* and *Allan Quatermain* date from 1887 and thereafter the Rider Haggard output was well maintained. The bibliography of several of this author's novels is quite complicated and first editions are moving upwards from the (h) and (g) grades. At the same time, R. L. Stevenson, and particularly Rudyard Kipling, were writing their tales of adventure in crisp, direct English of a high order.

A further phase was reached in 1894 with *The Prisoner of Zenda* by Anthony Hope (Sir Anthony Hope Hawkins, 1863-1933). This was the original Ruritanian romance, for the author invented the kingdom of Ruritania for this novel. He repeated his success with the sequel, *Rupert of Henzau,* in 1898, leaving the stage ready set for a host of imitative stories. *Rupert of Henzau* is fairly easy to identify in a first edition, but *The Prisoner of Zenda* should have the mis-spelling 'imposter' on line 7 of page 112, the misprint 'hree' for 'three' on the last line of page 296, and there should be only seventeen titles in the list of books advertised at the end. Both novels have much the same value as firsts, being grade (h).

With *Monsieur Beaucaire,* New York, 1900, Booth Tarkington developed another type of historical romance, still popular. It derives from Alexandre Dumas, *père,* but cuts the corners. One of its most important subsequent practitioners was Baroness Orczy (1865-1847) with her Scarlet Pimpernel novels: *The Scarlet Pimpernel*, 1905; *I Will Repay*, 1906; *Eldorado*, 1913; *Sir Percy Hits Back*, 1927. The Booth Tarkington novel may be grade (h), but the Orczys might be below grade (i).

Though his early work has affinities with Stevenson and Kipling, John Buchan (1875-1940) soon developed a stiff-upper-lipped style of his own, emergent in *Prester John*, 1910, and fully developed in the Richard Hannay novels: *The Thirty-Nine Steps*, 1915; *Greenmantle*, 1916; *Mr Standfast*, 1919. These are only a few from Buchan's large output, now popular with collectors, but still quite cheap of acquisition, perhaps at under £4 ($10) for good copies of most first editions.

Since Rousseau's day, the noble savage has had many literary manifestations. In 1914 he was given a Nietzschean twist by Edgar Rice Burroughs, who created a wild white superman as hero of *Tarzan of the Apes*. Though not a work of great literary merit, the book is a favourite with collectors of popular fiction and the first edition is moving from grade (i) to grade (h). Perhaps mention should be made of the phenomenally successful *Ben Hur*, New York, 1880, by General Lew Wallace (1827-1905). This novel brought together religion and adventure as never before. However, first editions are not rare and sell for unspectacular prices in grade (i).

The picaresque novel, which flourished in the eighteenth century, is well exemplified in the works of Smollett and can be regarded as a form of adventure fiction even if it is hardly within the 'rattling good yarn' classification. Captain Frederick Marryat (1792-1848) however, came near to writing such yarns. Whether he is regarded as a mainstream author or as a purveyor of adventure makes no difference to the challenge he offers to the collector. In 1951, Sadleir wrote that several of Marryat's firsts were almost undiscoverable in any condition. Since then the position has worsened and pious hope more than anything else prevents collectors from writing off such rarities as *The Naval Officer,* three volumes, 1839, as being absolutely unavailable. If a copy of this book, complete in original boards and in good condition, were auctioned in any of the well-known salerooms it would probably rise well above grade (A). Of Marryat's works, *Diary of a Blasé,* Philadelphia, 1836, *Jacob Faithful,* Philadelphia and Baltimore, 1834, *Peter Simple,* Philadelphia and Baltimore, 1833-4, and *Stories of the Sea,* New York, 1836, were first published in America, so the first English editions take second place.

In his two novels of the sea, Michael Scott (1789-1835) shows some literary kinship with Marryat. Both novels were first published anonymously, *Tom Cringle's Log,* two volumes, Edinburgh and London, 1833, and *The Cruise of the Midge,* two volumes, Edinburgh and London, 1836. As a first edition, each occurs in two different bindings, of which the priority has never been fully established. Good copies should be (b).

This summing-up only touches the fringe of adventure fiction and its collection, but should give some idea of its many possibilities.

Detective stories may be so crammed with adventure that the books in which they are contained are likely to crack at the joints, but they are usually placed in a class of their own. The first acknowledged detective story is Edgar Allan Poe's *The Murders in the Rue Morgue,* 1841. This masterpiece of its kind—and as fabulously expensive as other Poe items—did not set an immediate fashion in America.

Soon the detective story was being independently created in England. London's real-life detective force came into being in 1845, when twelve police officers were seconded for plain-clothes work. Five years later, Dickens, as the good journalist he was, wrote about the force in his magazine, *Household Words,* but did not at once grasp the fictional possibilities. In

1852, however, Mr Bucket, the detective, appeared in Dickens' *Bleak House*, which, nevertheless, cannot be greeted as England's first detective novel as the main interest does not centre on a crime and its solution. Towards the end of the fifties, there came a spate of railway yellowbacks dealing with the reminiscences of former detectives, authentic and otherwise. The first of these recorded by Sadleir in *XIX Century Fiction* is *Recollections of a Detective Police Officer*, 1856, by 'Waters' (William Russell, alias 'Lieut Warneford'). Sadleir lists many similar books from that year onwards.

The first English full-length detective novel of consequence was *The Moonstone*, three volumes, 1868, by Wilkie Collins (1824-89). Naturally, the first edition is assiduously hunted down. The first issue, distinguished by the misprint 'treachesrouly' on page 129 of volume two, is firmly in grade (H). After Collins' success, the detective novel of quality became established in England. Dickens's *The Mystery of Edwin Drood*, 1870, would no doubt have resolved itself into a first-rate example had the author lived to complete it.

It took some time for the form to recross the Atlantic. Allan Pinkerton (1819-84) helped to establish it by publishing at Chicago in 1874 *The Expressman and the Detective*, for which he drew on his own experiences as a private agent. This book is grade (g). Within three years, the American output of detective fiction was rivalling the English. In 1878, America produced the first woman crime writer, Anna Katherine Green, with her *The Leavenworth Case*. Unless some later author borrowed her name, this lady had a long literary career. A novel under the same writer's name, *The Step on the Stair*, was published at New York in 1923. In 1879, another woman took to the detective medium. *Shadowed by Three* by Lawrence L. Lynch, was published at Chicago in that year. The masculine ring to the author's name is false; Lawrence L. Lynch was the pseudonym of Mrs M. van Deventer. The works mentioned in this paragraph should all fall within grade (g).

Early efforts lack the refinements of the best modern whodunnits. The man who brought a new dimension to the detective novel was Sir Arthur Conan Doyle (1859-1930), creator of Sherlock Holmes. Holmes came on the scene by the back door, for his first adventure appeared between the pages of *Beeton's Christmas Annual 1887*, among a great deal of unmemorable prose and verse. This annual is grade (E) only because it contains the first printing of the first Holmes story, *A Study in Scarlet*. The next year, this appeared as a book, in wrappers. The first edition in book form is as scarce as the annual and is also (E). None of the other Holmes books commands so high a price. Some of the others could be graded thus: *The Adventures of Sherlock Holmes*, 1892 (e); The *Memoirs of Sherlock Holmes*, 1894, (h); *The Hound of the Baskervilles*, 1902, (i).

Fergus W. Hume (d 1932) also contributed to the whodunnit revolution by writing *The Mystery of a Hansom Cab*, first published at Melbourne in 1887. The 5,000 copies of this paperbound edition were sold out in three weeks and a second edition was equally successful. Hume then parted with the rights to a syndicate called 'The Hansom Cab Publishing Company' which took the book to London, where the first English edition of 25,000 copies, in black and white pictorial wrappers, was issued in 1888. As Hume had no connection with the syndicate, all he received for the English and American rights was £50. He came to London in 1889 and after 500,000 copies of the original editions had been issued he brought out a revised edition (Jarrold & Sons, no date) which sold very well and can sometimes be found on bargain shelves at little cost. Though it is not regarded as a collector's item it is important in that the author's preface gives the true history of the book for the first time.

One of the mysteries of this mystery is that no copies of the first Melbourne edition or of the first London edition ever appear on the market. The earliest known London edition is marked 'seventy-fifth thousand' and is grade (g). It has been suggested that this seventy-fifth thousand is in fact the first London edition and that 'seventy-fifth thousand' was printed on it to boost sales—but this cannot be proved.

The success of Sherlock Holmes encouraged the appearance of whole packs of eccentric criminal investigators, but the public had to wait till 1907 before a sleuth appeared who could have discussed crime with Holmes as an equal. He was R. Austin Freeman's Dr Thorndyke, who made his debut in *The Red Thumb Mark,* first published in black paper wrappers and in black cloth, the front cover in both styles bearing a thumbprint in red. In either form, copies are desperately scarce and it would be difficult to predict the price of the next copy to come to light.

The twentieth century saw an enormous growth in the popularity of detective fiction. G. K. Chesterton (1874-1936) struck a new note in 1911 with *The Innocence of Father Brown,* grade (h). This would also be the rating of *Trent's Last Case,* 1913, by E. C. Bentley (1875-1956). This novel is so good that devotees naturally look for other Trent cases. Some were published in the *Strand* magazine during 1914, but did not appear in book form until 1928, in *Great Short Stories of Mystery, Detection and Horror,* edited by Dorothy Sayers (1893-1957). In 1936 there appeared the full-length *Trent's Own Case,* by Bentley and H. Warner Allen. Because it was not published until long after the other Trent stories, it is often overlooked. Though not common as a first, it might be had for under £5 ($13).

Although her aristocratic amateur detective, Lord Peter Wimsey, is rather *démodé* in the 1970s, Dorothy Sayers was a brilliant writer in the medium and is now attracting the attention of collectors, though her firsts should not cost above £4

($10). The first Peter Wimsey novel was *Whose Body?* published at New York (before the first English edition) in 1923. Her nearest rival among the many women in the field is the astonishingly prolific Agatha Christie, whose *The Mysterious Affair at Styles*, 1920, was also first published at New York, and who is still writing in 1972. Few Agatha Christie novels are scarce as firsts and so provide good quarry for the collector with little money to spare.

From being an intellectual exercise tricked out with thrills and occasional horrors, the detective story has recently become more of a study in violence. This change should be observed by collectors, who must decide for themselves whether the bulk of detective fiction from the fifties onwards should be placed in the same category as the older whodunnits.

Though they were not specifically addressed to a juvenile market, almost all the adventure novels mentioned above and several of the detective stories can be enjoyed by older children. So too can certain other novels, hard to classify, but best considered as fairy tales written from an adult angle. Among these may be named *Vice Versa*, 1882, and *The Brass Bottle*, 1900, by F. Anstey (Thomas Anstey Guthrie, 1856-1934); *The Sword in the Stone*, 1939, and *Mistress Masham's Repose*, 1947, by T. H. White (1906-62) and J. R. R. Tolkien's Hobbit stories, comprising *The Hobbit, or There and Back Again*, 1937; *The Fellowship of the Ring*, 1954; *The Two Towers*, 1954, and *The Return of the King*, 1955. The type of adult, or semi-adult, fantasy which is found in these books is considered to be out of keeping with the present age, so they may be the representatives of a dying genre and worth collecting on that account if on no other. None would be really expensive in first editions (the Hobbit books may be creeping towards grade (i)), but they may show a big rise in the years ahead.

Some kindly folk, adult and juvenile, still applaud at performances of *Peter Pan* when asked to demonstrate their belief in fairies—but nobody is fooled. Belief, agnosticism even, have gone. The *sidh*, the little people, the trolls, nymphs and fauns have been smothered in petrol fumes and poisoned by pesticides; the glades where they danced have been dug up by bulldozers. Their places have been usurped by venomous Venereans (genteely called Venusians by non-classicists), aerial octopodes, predatory parsnips and other unromantic things from outer space. The evil deeds of these repulsive imaginings are recorded in the swelling corpus of science fiction, early examples of which are now pursued by an army of collectors. Such is their vogue that while the social novels of H. G. Wells are neglected, the first issue of the first edition of Wells' *The Time Machine*, 1895, and the earliest edition of *The First Men on the Moon* have been elevated into grade (g).

Had the monsters of SF been known to Mrs Sarah Trimmer (1741-1810), she would have dealt with them far more effectively than any spacegun-packing hero. It was a crime in her eyes to expose children to the evils of fantasy. She described *Cinderella* as one of the worst stories for children ever written, depicting the vilest of human passions—jealousy, vanity, and a love of dress. She was expressing the view of many serious-minded people of her generation. Fairy stories to them were pernicious rubbish printed on vulgar broadsides and chap-books and hawked from door to door by low persons. The idea that children should be allowed to read books which were not improving and instructive was repugnant.

In her children's book, *The History of the Robins*, 1786, Mrs Trimmer showed what she considered to be suitable to the juvenile mind. Birds are allowed to converse as humans, but only for the purpose of instilling moral lessons, as when Mother Robin reproves her young with, 'Are these the sentiments that subsist in a family which ought to be bound together by love and kindness? Which of you has cause to reproach either your father or me with partiality? Do we not, with the exactest equality, distribute the fruits of our labours among you?'

As a period piece, *The History of the Robins*, even in grade (h), would be a welcome addition to the library of a collector of children's books, but it would hardly be acceptable fare for a modern child. So with almost all juvenile literature of the eighteenth century. Dr John Aikin (1747-1822) and his sister, Mrs Anna Letitia Barbauld (1743-1825) combined to write *Evenings at Home; or, The Juvenile Budget Opened*, three volumes, 12mo, 1793-4. Despite the cosy title, this turns out to be another attempt at edification, consisting largely of dialogues between an earnest tutor and his two pupils. The tutor has a crafty way of luring the boys off on country walks to lower their resistance, then pumping them full of knowledge. 'When you have cooled yourself,' he tells them on one occasion, 'you may drink out of that clear brook. In the meantime we will read a little out of a book I have in my pocket.' This is the kind of tactic often repeated. *Evenings at Home* is another work collected for its curiosity value and is in the same price grade as the Mrs Trimmer.

Maria Hack (1777-1844) was a kindly Quaker lady with an abhorrence of fiction. Her four-volume book, *Winter Evenings; or, Tales of Travellers*, 1818, should cost about the same as the two previous curiosities, but it achieved a genuinely comfortable family atmosphere. It also was cast in dialogue form, with a mother telling stories of travel to her two children for the improvement of their minds. When little Lucy asks why almost all the pretty books she reads are about things that never happen, Mamma supposes that people who write books for children think that they will be better pleased with fiction than with truth.

Lucy. They are mistaken then, Mamma.

Mamma. I am glad you think so, my dear Lucy: I wish you may always be distinguished for the love of truth.

Despite the criticisms found in these educative works, fiction specially written for children hardly existed, and there was almost no light verse other than the nursery rhymes of oral tradition. Isaac Watts (1674-1748) with his *Divine Songs for Children,* 1715, moralised for the benefit of boys and girls and left for present-day collectors a book in grade (e)—first or early edition. In 1804, Ann (1782-1866) and Jane (1783-1824) Taylor followed Watts's example with *Original Poems for Infant Minds,* and *Rhymes for the Nursery,* 1806, the latter containing 'Twinkle, Twinkle, Little Star'. Both books might be grade (h) as first editions, but are liable to rise.

The liberators came in the middle of the nineteenth century in the persons of W. M. Thackeray, Edward Lear (1821-88) and Charles Lutwidge Dodgson (1832-98). The first to strike his blow for juvenile freedom was Lear, with the publication of *A Book of Nonsense,* in 1846. The first edition did not bear Lear's name, but was attributed to Derry Down Derry. This edition of Lear is truly rare and it would probably mislead if any price were suggested. Early editions in good condition are hard enough to find and may be grade (f). Lear's later books, *More Nonsense,* 1872, and *Laughable Lyrics,* 1877, are equally devoid of 'improvement'. Presumably Lear had a wider public, ready to assimilate larger printings, when these last two books were published, for they are not so scarce as firsts, though still desirable enough to be in grade (f).

Thackeray broke with the moralising tradition in *The Rose and the Ring,* 1855, by adapting the theatrical tradition of burlesque (in the English, not the American sense) to a children's book. As is only right in a fairy story, virtue is rewarded and vice is punished, but the amusing characters are not a bit goody-goody. An acceptable first edition in the original pictorial boards should not be above grade (h).

Charles Lutwidge Dodgson, universally known as Lewis Carroll, was the greatest liberator of all. More clearly than any of his contemporaries he grasped that children could be written to as though they were sentient beings and not treated as amorphous lumps of protoplasm to be terrorised or moralised into shape. He entered the children's dream world and saw with their eyes. He mocked the pious rubbish which had been presented to the young in the name of literature; for Carroll must have realised what he was about when he wrote his parodies. In *Alice's Adventures in Wonderland*, 1865, but 1866, Watts's song about 'How doth the little busy bee?' becomes 'How doth the little crocodile?' and the Taylor sisters' 'Twinkle, twinkle, little star' is transformed by the Mad Hatter to 'Twinkle, twinkle, little bat'.

One of the grimmest children's books of all time appeared in 1828. It was called *The Child's Guide to Knowledge: Being a Collection of Useful and Familiar Questions and Answers on Every-Day Subjects, Adapted for Young Persons, and Arranged in the Most Simple and Easy Language*, by A Lady. In the course of its long innings the work was 'considerably improved'. By 1873 it had reached its forty-seventh edition and a new edition appeared in 1880 'with considerable additions by Barbara R. Bartlett'. The original authoress was a Mrs R. Ward, about whom little is known, but it is clear she was a down-to-earth lady. In the original preface she explains:

> It has not been thought advisable to introduce any woodcuts or engravings, which might take off the attention of children, for whom this little book is professedly designed; and the authoress trusts that the simplicity of the language in which the information is conveyed renders *picture* illustration unnecessary; she believes, indeed, that they would not add to, but rather detract from the usefulness of the work.

The long catechism begins by asking 'What is the World?' and answering 'The earth we live on.' The next question is, 'Who made it?' with the answer 'The great and good God.' Then follows:

Q. Are there not many things in it you would like to know about?
A. Yes, very much.
Q. Pray then, what is bread made of?
A. Flour.
Q. What is flour?
A. Wheat ground into powder by the miller.

So the interrogation continues, page after unrelieved page. Lewis Carroll must have known this work. Probably he had had to learn the answers by heart when he was a child. If so, he took his revenge in *Through the Looking-Glass*, 1872. In chapter nine, Alice has to endure an examination by the Red and the White Queens, who want to know if she can answer useful questions. By putting Q. for the Queens' questions and A. for Alice's answers, this dialogue results:

Q. How is bread made?
A. I know that! You take some flour—
Q. Where do you pick the flower? In a garden or in the hedges?
A. Well, it isn't *picked* at all, it's ground—
Q. How many acres of ground? You mustn't leave out so many things.

Tracing such connections between different books is one of the bibliophile's delights and helps to explain why a first edition of a tiresome book like *The Child's Guide* may be in grade (g), along with a first of *Through the Looking Glass*, which, though in greater demand, is far less scarce.

The case of *Alice in Wonderland* is different from that of *The Looking Glass*. The true first edition of *Wonderland* is as scarce as hens' teeth. No sooner was it published than the author had the copies recalled, as he was dissatisfied with the printing and presentation. It is not known how many copies escaped the recall, but they were very few. When found, a copy is one of the plums of bibliophily. It would be unremarkable for a copy of the true first edition to change hands at over

£6,000 ($15,600). The best the ordinary collector can hope for is a copy of the second edition, 1866, generally known as the first published edition. Complete and in good order it would be grade (b).

John Ruskin (1819-1900) wrote an imitation Grimm's fairy tale, *The King of the Golden River*, 1851, which is less tendentious than most children's stories of the time. A first edition might be had for under £6 ($15), which is a lot less than would have to be paid for firsts of Nathaniel Hawthorne's *Wonder Book for Girls and Boys*, 1852 (reddish cloth covers), and *Tanglewood Tales*, 1853 (with advertisements dated August 1853). These are grade (f).

Influenced by his friend, Lewis Carroll, George Macdonald (1824-1905) produced *Dealings with the Fairies*, 1867, *The Princess and the Goblin*, 1872, and *The Princess and Curdie*, 1883. Though pleasant works, they are slightly marred by the whimsical preciousness which so often afflicts Anglo-Scots in writing for children. The Macdonalds should be collectable as firsts at less than £6 ($15) a copy.

Meanwhile, the mind-improvers were fighting a rearguard action. Margaret Gatty (1806-73) published her *Parables from Nature* between 1855 and 1871. These were after the style of Mrs Trimmer's *History of the Robins*, but more relaxed. Charlotte Yonge (1823-1901) wrote a series of pleasantly uplifting novels for children, beginning with *The Heir of Redclyffe* in 1853. Her first editions are likewise well below the £6 ($15) level, except for *The Instructive Picture Book*, 1857. This rather overrated work has coloured plates and is grade (e) at least.

Juliana Horatia Ewing (1841-85) struck an uneasy balance between edification and amusement. Her *The Brownies and Other Tales*, 1870, provided the myth on which the junior branch of the Girl Guides is founded; her *Jackanapes*, 1883, enjoyed a popularity above its deserts. Most of her books were attractively produced in pictorial boards and are interesting to collect if bought cheap—say under £2 ($5).

Louisa M. Alcott (1832-88) deserves the attention she receives from collectors on both sides of the Atlantic. *Little Women*, 1868; *Good Wives**, 1869; and *Little Men*, 1871, may be sentimental, but they are still among the best books ever written for older children—or older girls at any rate. The least valued by collectors is *Little Men*, grade (g). The others are grade (f), or possibly (e) if in superlative condition.

Captain Thomas Mayne Reid (1818-83), son of an Irish Presbyterian minister, American citizen and English gentleman, epitomised the romantic hero of Victorian boys' fiction —a field in which he himself was prolific. As a rebel against life in the manse, he was packed off to America where he had a varied career as schoolmaster, actor and journalist. In 1847 he volunteered for service with the American army in the Mexican War. He served with distinction and resigned at the end of the fighting with the rank of captain. After further adventures he came to England where his first novel, *The Rifle Rangers*, was published in two volumes in 1850. Thereafter he devoted himself to writing, returning to America for a time, but ending his days in England. Some of his work was aimed at adults, but most was written for boys. Changing fashion and his habit of holding up the action to expatiate on natural history have put him out of favour, but his books and magazine stories offer good hunting in the (i) to (e) grades.

Mayne Reid's influence on boys' fiction is noticeable in some of the American Dime Novels of the sixties and seventies of last century. These were published by Irwin P. Beadle & Co, New York, and enjoyed a wide circulation throughout the USA. They were issued twice a month, in paper wrappers,

**Good Wives* is the title commonly given to the second part of *Little Women*, published in 1869, but not used for the first edition and still unfamiliar in the United States.

and were not without a certain distinction in their writing. Authors included Edward S. Ellis (1840-1916) and Horatio Alger (1832-99). Runs of the early Dime Novels are now eagerly pursued and the value of some individual numbers has increased two hundredfold since their publication.

Possibly because it has a ring of forthright honesty, Frank was once a popular name for the heroes of boys' stories. Under the pseudonym of Harry Castlemon, Charles A. Fosdick (1842-1915) wrote a series of 'Frank' books, such as *Frank before Vicksburg*, Philadelphia, 1865, and *Frank Nelson in the Forecastle*, Philadelphia, 1876. Gilbert Patten (1866-1945), who wrote as Burt L. Standish, had a less martial Frank as his hero. His Frank Merriwell was an upright athletic schoolboy, featured in *Frank Merriwell's Daring*, New York, 1908, *Frank Merriwell's Victories*, New York, 1910, and many others, still read by American boys. All these 'Frank' items should be found between grades (i) and (h).

In a different way, Kate Greenaway (1846-1901) was also a liberator. The illustrations of children which she drew for her own books and those of others captivated late-Victorian mothers and encouraged them to dress their young offspring in sensible, loosefitting clothes somewhat in Regency style. Most of the Greenaway books were painstakingly printed in colours by Edmund Evans and no collection of children's books is complete without at least one example. They can be found in grades (i), (h) and (g). Walter Crane wrote and illustrated books for children in a manner rather similar to that of Kate Greenaway. His *Flora's Feast*, 1889, and *Queen Summer*, 1891, are grade (i).

The Greenaway-Crane period was also that of Andrew Lang (1844-1912). He wrote some original stories for the young, but is better known as editor of a series of fairy books, named from the colours of their bindings. Lang rifled the world's stores of folk-tales for his collections, so if his florid style does not suit every modern child, his garnered material is invaluable to the folklorist. *The Blue Fairy Book*, 1889, was the first, followed by the *Red*, 1890, *Green*, 1892, *Yellow*, 1894, *Pink*, 1897, *Grey*, 1900, *Violet*, 1901, *Crimson*, 1903, *Brown*, 1904, *Orange*, 1906, *Olive*, 1907, and *Lilac*, 1910. There were other books in the series, not necessarily collections of fairy stories. Perhaps an average of £4 ($10) a volume would be a fair price.

Lang was one of several Anglo-Scottish writers for children, working in the nineteenth and early twentieth centuries. He was but a mild sufferer from the whimsicality which afflicted his fellows. J. M. Barrie (1860-1937) had it in full measure. This did not prevent his play, *Peter Pan* (first produced 1904) from being an enormous success. When *Peter Pan and Wendy*, the story of the play, was published in 1911 it met with almost equal success. As Barrie is out of favour now, a first of the book ought not to cost much above £2 ($5). However, *Peter Pan in Kensington Gardens*, 1906, extracted from *The Little White Bird*, 1902, is a different story in every sense. Illustrated by Arthur Rackman, it would be grade (i) in the ordinary edition, but grade (a) in the limited edition, signed by the artist.

Kenneth Grahame (1858-1932), another Anglo-Scot, published *The Golden Age* in 1895. Though about children, it is hardly a children's book. *Dream Days*, 1899, is better and contains *The Reluctant Dragon*. But best is his *The Wind in the Willows*, 1908, which is grade (f).

The last of the Anglo-Scots worthy of mention is A. A. Milne (1882-1956), who dramatised *The Wind in the Willows* as *Toad of Toad Hall*, in 1929. He is best remembered for the Pooh books: *Winnie-the-Pooh*, 1926, and *The House at Pooh Corner*, 1928. When clean, in dust-wrappers, they are grade (i). Milne's first book of children's poems, *When We Were Very Young*, 1924, is scarce as a first and is grade (g).

Edith Nesbit (Mrs Hubert Bland—1858-1924) had ambitions to be a poet, but found her vocation in juvenile fiction.

Her first major work was *The Treasure Seekers,* 1899, which introduced the Bastable family. Their adventures continued in *The Would-be-Goods,* 1901; *The New Treasure Seekers,* 1905, and *Oswald Bastable—and Others,* also 1905. The Bastables have many surprising adventures, but are never involved with the supernatural as are E. Nesbit's other family, the children (no surname given) in *Five Children and It,* 1902; *The Phoenix and the Carpet,* 1904, and *The Story of the Amulet,* 1906. Interest in all the Nesbit books—she wrote many—is growing, but good copies of firsts might still be available under £4 ($10).

Very young children were catered for as never before with the appearance of the Peter Rabbit books by Beatrix Potter (1866-1943). The first was *The Tale of Peter Rabbit,* and a whole series followed, ending with *Cecily Parsley's Nursery Rhymes* in 1929. They were charmingly illustrated by the author and most of the titles are still in print in Britain. First editions, ordinary and limited, are hard to find in acceptable condition and some of the ordinary ones may cost £6 ($15). *The Fairy Caravan,* 1929; *Sister Anne,* US edition, 1932, and *Wag-by-the-Wall,* 1944, followed the main series, but are not so good.

Arthur Rackham's work as an illustrator of children's books and others still enjoys a high reputation. Imposing volumes full of well-reproduced coloured plates by him were specially issued for the Christmas gift market for many years. The would-be connoisseur could buy limited signed editions bound in vellum, with perishable silk ties. Rackhams are much in vogue and dangerously high prices are being asked for them. The most desirable are now approaching grade (H). Clever illustrator though he was, Rackham is not in the Blake or Bewick class, so those investing for posterity should buy with care.

CHAPTER SEVEN

Biography, History, Travel

Every schoolgirl knows (or if she does not, her English teacher should be a candidate for expulsion) that Mrs Elizabeth C. Gaskell (1810-65) wrote one of the best biographies in our language. A novelist herself, she became friendly with Charlotte Brontë and when Charlotte died in 1855, Mrs Gaskell began work on *The Life of Charlotte Brontë*, published in two volumes in 1857. The first edition (Scale of Values grade (e) at least in the original dark brown cloth with wavy graining), and the second, which followed almost immediately, contain material which was suppressed in the later editions. Even to this day, publishers have been reluctant to reprint the full text of the first edition.

Someone who is specialising in the works of a particular writer will also want to acquire appropriate biographical items. He will find, however, that few authors have been as well served as Charlotte Brontë, though one woman writer is as well known from her biography as from her own works: Mary Wollstonecraft (1759-97), wife of William Godwin and mother-in-law of Shelley. Mary Wollstonecraft, a leader of the Women's Lib of her day, was almost as radical as the present-day members of the movement. Godwin wrote his wife's biography and had it published in 1798 under the title of *Memoirs of the Author of 'A Vindication of the Rights of Woman'*. A good first in original boards could hardly be found below grade (e). Some recent editions were published as *A Memoir of Mary Wollstonecraft.*

Sufficient reference has already been made to the most famous biography of all, *The Life of Samuel Johnson,* by James Boswell (1740-95). It is often forgotten that Johnson had a previous biographer in Sir John Hawkins (1719-89), whom Johnson appointed as his literary executor. Hawkins's *Life of Samuel Johnson* was published in 1786, five years before Boswell's. It is a less monumental work, but contains some of Johnson's *obiter dicta,* including his refreshing pronouncement that a tavern chair is the throne of human felicity. Though collectors compete less eagerly for the Hawkins version than the Boswell, it would be good value for money in grade (e).

Johnson himself was an important biographer. His *Lives of the English Poets,* though full of Johnsonian prejudice, is a great piece of literary criticism as well as a useful summary of the careers of fifty-two poets. The true first edition was published at Dublin in three volumes, 1779-81, but it is rated no higher than the first London edition, the four volumes of which were all issued in 1781. Good to fine copies may be found between grades (d) and (G).

Another famous biography is *The Life of Sir Walter Scott,* by J. G. Lockhart (1794-1854). Published in 1837-8 in seven volumes, this work resembles the Scott Monument in Edinburgh—massive and doggedly romantic at the same time. As Lockhart was Scott's son-in-law, the tone is somewhat adulatory, but for all its defects, it is a work of real merit. A first edition, with the errata slip for volume one, could still be graded (g).

Earlier, Lockhart worked on a *Life of Robert Burns,* which was published in 1828 as the twenty-third volume of *Constable's Miscellany.* It is a far less distinguished biography and, though scarce in the first edition, is not highly valued. It is grade (i) for enthusiastic Burnsites. It is hopeful booksellers, rather than the pressures of demand, that account for its being offered occasionally in a much higher grade. Biographies of Burns can be numbered by the score, but the great poet has still to find the ideal biographer who will be neither sentimental nor denigrating in his view of a complex genius who wished to be democrat and gentleman, respectable husband and miscellaneous lover, untutored songster and sage litterateur all in one.

Even Burns has fared better than Shakespeare, of whom there is no authentic biography—but in his day nobody thought it worthwhile to detail the lives of such small deer as mere writers for the theatre. Nobody—not even the would-be tomb-openers can now make up for this sad lack. Had Shakespeare been of high birth he might have had his William Roper (1496-1578). Roper was the son-in-law of Sir Thomas More, martyr and author of *Utopia.* Though emphasising the saintly qualities of its subject, Roper's *The Mirrour of Vertue in Worldly Greatnes,* first published at Paris in 1626, presents a clear portrait of a great figure of Renaissance England. A complete copy of the first edition would be grade (G) or (F) according to condition.

As a Catholic, More is not included among *The Worthies of England,* 1662, by Thomas Fuller (1608-61). In this work, Fuller deals with Protestant heroes, in some cases giving useful details about the places where they lived and worked. For this reason, the book is valued by topographers as well as by historians. The first edition, in folio, is grade (I).

Fuller's contemporary, Isaak Walton (1593-1683), is always associated with his *The Compleat Angler,* yet, in its way, his *Lives* is a book of equal merit, and is written with a sympathy for the subjects such as would be expected of the author. It is worth reading even by those who are not deeply concerned with Donne, Wotton, Hoöker and Herbert. These were the four whom Walton included in the first collected edition, 1670, now grade (f), but he subsequently wrote a life of Bishop Sanderson (1587-1663), the writer of the preface to the Anglican *Book of Common Prayer.* Most modern editions of the *Lives* include the biography of Sanderson.

A younger contemporary of Fuller and Walton was a very different kind of biographer. This was John Aubrey (1626-97), who, combining many of the traits of Autolycus and Merlin, was described by his friend, Anthony A Wood, as 'a shiftless person, roving and magotie-headed'. Aubrey was uncommonly credulous and the only book of his certainly published in his lifetime was *Miscellanies, A Collection of Hermetic Philosophy, 1696,* probably grade (H) in the first edition. Throughout the latter part of his life he collected scraps of gossip and information about his contemporaries and immediate predecessors.

While some of these individual writings were widely known in the intervening two centuries, they were not published as a collection until 1898, when their editor, Andrew Clark, issued them as *Brief Lives* by John Aubrey, in two volumes. Hence the first edition of Aubrey's most important work, graded as (h), is the cheapest of his firsts. Even the person with no burning desire to study Aubrey's times can rummage through Clark's scholarly edition with delight. For the ordinary reader, however, the best edition is Anthony Powell's *Brief Lives and Other Selected Writings* by John Aubrey, 1949, originally priced at 8s 6d (42½p), but now catalogued at £1.50 ($.75) and more. Here it is possible to become as fascinated as Aubrey himself was with the curious characters of his day. There is, for instance, Judge Walter Rumsey: 'He was an ingeniose man,' writes Aubrey, 'and had a philosophicall head.'

He was much troubled with flegme, and ... he took a fine ten-der sprig, and tied a ragge at the end, and conceited he might putt it downe his throate, and fetch-up the flegme, and he did so. Afterwards he made this instrument of whale-bone. I have oftentimes seen him use it. I could never make it goe downe my throat, but for those that can 'tis a most incomparable engine... He wrote a little octavo booke, of this way of medicine, called *Organon Salutis.*

This book, *Organon Salutis. An Instrument to cleanse the Stomach* by W. R., 1657, is sometimes to be met with in the auction rooms. For a probable outlay of £200 or $520, it would be a worthy addition to the library of a wealthy collector of medical works. A sophisticated version of Rumsey's 'engine' is still occasionally used by the medical profession.

Aubrey knew and had a high regard for John Evelyn (1620-1706). No two men could have been less alike, except in their possession of inquiring minds. Evelyn was a precise and dignified gentleman, as can be gathered from his *Memoirs*, edited by William Bray, first published in 1818 and now universally known as Evelyn's *Diary*. Evelyn is nowhere so revealingly intimate as Samuel Pepys (1633-1703), the other great diarist of the time. Nevertheless, his literary self portrait of a wise and serious scholar is fascinating. The first edition in a really good binding is grade (d), but an acceptable reading copy might be (g). As Pepys's diaries are now being published in full for the first time, speculation in early editions would be unwise. This is shown by a slight fall in auction prices.

Gravity rather different from that of Evelyn pervades the *Journal* of John Woolman, first edition, 1774. John Woolman was a New Jersey Quaker, born in 1720, and an early campaigner against slavery. The *Journal* had a profound effect on Charles Lamb. It is quite rare in the first edition, though there are early editions to be had in grade (h).

The Rev James Woodforde (1758-1803) of Norfolk, England, was more worldly than John Woolman, so that his *Diary of a Country Parson*, in five volumes, edited by John Beresford, 1924-31, makes livelier reading. The original edition is grade (h), but there is an abridgement which should cost little more than £1 ($2.60). Parson Woodforde enjoyed his creature comforts far from the scenes of political intrigue, in which he showed little interest. Those who wish to gain insight into the backroom politics of the end of the eighteenth and the beginning of the nineteenth centuries should turn to *The Creevey Papers,* two volumes, 1903, edited by Sir Herbert Maxwell. The papers are selected from the diaries and correspondence of Thomas Creevey (1768-1838), a prominent Whig MP of his time. The book should be found in grade (h).

Later events notwithstanding, the closing decades of the eighteenth century, the first half of the nineteenth century and the period of the Civil War are of prime importance in the history of the USA. Fortunately, good biographies of the great men of those momentous years are not too hard to find. A sound first edition of Washington Irving's *Life of George Washington,* five volumes, New York, 1855-9, may be had of the right type of bookseller in grade (g). Much more difficult is the quaint *Life and Memorable Actions of George Washington,* written and published by Mason L. Weems about 1800. Weems combined the offices of parson and colporteur, peddling his books around Mount Vernon and over a wider area. The seeker of a first edition of Weem's *Washington* might find one in grade (a), but he may have to go to (H) for the fifth edition of 1808 for it is the one in which the story of young George Washington and the cherry tree was given to the world for the first time.

American life and politics in the first half of last century can fruitfully be studied in the twelve-volume *Memoirs* of John Quincy Adams, the sixth president. These were edited by C. F. Adams and published at Philadelphia between 1874 and 1877. Collectors interested in the Civil War period will naturally turn to books about Abraham Lincoln (1809-65).

The amount of Lincolniana available is so large that it is easy to build up a sizeable library quite quickly. A first of *Lincoln, the True Story of a Great Life by* William H. Herndon and Jesse W. Weik, Chicago, no date, but 1889, should present no difficulty for the purchaser willing to pay out in grade (g). A number of other items may be collected at reasonable cost. Lincoln's *Address delivered at the Cooper Institute*, New York, 1860, *The Political Debates between Lincoln and the Hon. Stephen A. Douglas*, Columbus, Ohio, 1860, and *The Trial of Abraham Lincoln, New* York, 1863, should still be in grade (i), the same grade as for Stanley Kimmel's *The Mad Booths of Maryland*, New York, 1940, a biographical study of the brilliant but unbalanced family of actors which included John Wilkes Booth, Lincoln's assassin.

Since Lincoln's time, many politicians and statesmen have written their own memoirs and biographies. It is to be regretted, therefore, that Sir Winston Churchill did not leave behind him anything like a complete autobiography, though he revealed a great deal about himself in several of his books, including *My Early Life*, 1930. Like almost all of Sir Winston's writings, this is now something of a collector's piece in grade (h). The prize Churchill item, however, is *Mr Brodrick's Army*, first edition, 1903, a copy of which, in cloth, with the original wrappers preserved, was sold at Sotheby's in 1969 for £1,500 ($3,750). By contrast, a good working set of his *The Second World War*, in first editions, 1948-54, may be had for little more than £6 ($15).

Sir Winston Churchill's various literary works demonstrate how difficult it can be to separate biography from history. In practice, few people confine themselves purely to the collection of biography; their interests are usually literary or historical as well. Yet a collector who restricted himself to this one subject would have a fascinating field in which to work. Simply by choosing the eminent men and women of a particular period, or, perhaps, famous sportsmen down the ages, or even the lives of great failures, he would give himself a lifetime's happy hunting.

Building a comprehensive biographical library of great engineers would keep a collector out of mischief for a long time, though he could make a flying start thanks to Samuel Smiles (1812-1904), the biographer first of George Stephenson (1781-1848), the locomotive designer, then of many other heroes of the Industrial Revolution. His *Life of George Stephenson* was published in 1857 and followed with *Lives of the Engineers,* three volumes, 1861-62, *Industrial Biography,* 1863, *Lives of Boulton and Watt,* 1865, and *Men of Invention and Industry,* 1884. His revised edition of *George Stephenson,* 1873, contained a memoir of Robert Stephenson, George's son and successor. In 1894, Smiles turned his attention to a great pottery manufacturer with *Josiah Wedgwood, His Personal History.* Firsts of these works are grade (i).

It is a simple step from biography to history proper. The real historian, including the serious amateur, will not be content with gathering together the standard books written by those who have gone before. They will tell him only what is already known; he wants to uncover new facts which may lie hidden in little-known books apparently unconnected with history, and in important private papers. The owners of these rarely do other than entrust their editing to someone with high academic qualifications, or sell or bequeath them to universities or institutional libraries.

The less favoured private student-collector, however, may have opportunities to gain useful source material if he can perform the feat of keeping his eyes about him and his ear to the ground. Old account books, deeds, wills and indentures are still liable to be discarded as waste paper by lawyers, old-established business firms and local government officials. A patient collector who is willing to wade through cartloads of scrap is sometimes rewarded with a real find.

Apart from such gleanings, the historian will also have to obtain certain up-to-date books, but these must be of his own choosing from publishers' lists, and he will also have to keep in touch with the past through the medium of certain more ancient authoritative works. The earliest of these for the English-speaking peoples is the *Anglo-Saxon Chronicle*. Perhaps the edition most often met with in salerooms and the catalogues of antiquarian booksellers is that of 1861, translated by Benjamin Thorpe, in two volumes. It is satisfactory to work from and should be grade (h).

Next must come the Venerable Bede's *Historia Ecclesiastica Gentis Anglorum*, written by Bede some time before AD735. There are modern translations available, but the affluent historian-collector might prefer to invest, at grade (G), in a copy of the first English edition, *History of the Church of Englande*, translated by Thomas Stapleton and published at Antwerp in 1565.

The next comparable landmark is William the Conqueror's *Domesday Book*, compiled in 1086. A curious edition appeared in two undated volumes in 1793. No place of publication was named and there were no title-pages. This issue was not complete and two further volumes were published in 1816, with title-pages supplied for the earlier volumes. Today, the value of the four together is difficult to assess—perhaps they should be placed in grade (I). But they are put up for sale only at rare intervals. *Domesday Studies*, edited by P. E. Dove, two volumes, 1881-91, would be of more use to the serious student and might be tracked down in grade (h).

The full text of *Magna Carta*, 1215, is not easily found. The last fine edition was published in 1938 and is grade (f). Earlier editions were published in 1514, 1527, 1531-2, 1542, 1587, 1618, and, sumptuously printed in gold letters and illuminated, in 1816. The ordinary version of this edition might be

(G), but one of two copies printed on vellum was sold in 1967 for £600 ($1,500).

Almost the earliest Scottish historian of importance was the Dundonian, Hector Boece (1465-1536), who wisely preferred to live in Aberdeen as the first principal of the city's older university, King's College. His *Scotorum Historiae a prima gentis origine* is in many places quite fabulous—in the real sense of the word. Non-Latinists who can cope with Middle Scots will appreciate this if they read *The History and Croniklis of Scotland,* Boece's work as translated by John Bellenden and published at Edinburgh in 1540. This edition is well in grade (D) and is seldom brought forward for sale. The edition of 1821, also an Edinburgh publication, is also rather scarce, but if obtainable should be (e).

Boece's unhistorical account of the life of Macbeth was cribbed by Raphael Holinshed (d 1580), and incorporated in his *Chronicles of England Scotlande and Irelande* ('England' written without a final 'e'), two volumes, 1577. The *Chronicles* supplied Shakespeare with the basis of his tragedy, *Macbeth,* which is no less a masterpiece for being wildly inaccurate. Imperfect copies of the first edition of Holinshed appear from time to time, but the two volumes together, in good condition, would be worth something like £1,600 ($4,160).

One of the most informative histories of the seventeenth century did not appear till 1702-4—*The History of the Late Rebellion,* in three volumes, by Edward Hyde, Earl of Clarendon, with a current value which would put it in the (d) grade. There were many historians in the eighteenth century, including David Hume and Oliver Goldsmith, but their books are long obsolete. They have a certain antiquarian value and are bought mainly by those who like their libraries to emanate an air of old-world scholarship. Edward Gibbon (1737-94) was the greatest historian of the period. He looked back on the civilisation of Rome with a fresh eye and what he wrote in

The Decline and Fall of the Roman Empire, six volumes, 1776-88, though it may require correcting and supplementing, can never be entirely superseded. Despite the decline and fall of classical studies, there is still sufficient demand for the work for it to be placed in grade (H) as a first edition.

Certain books are attractive to some collectors simply because they are hard to find and not because of intrinsic merit. As it was first issued in 1851, *The Fifteen Decisive Battles of the World* by Sir Edward Creasey (1812-78) is sadly out of date. Yet its reputation for scarcity in the two-volume first edition is such that its grading as (f) bears little relation to its value to the historian.

One of the earlier historians of America was a Scot, William Robertson, who produced his *History of America*, two volumes, in 1777, while the War of Independence was still raging. This is not a popular work today and the original edition should be obtainable well down in grade (h). Soon after the United States of America came into being, they began to produce able historians of their own. A consulter of T. L. Bradford's *Bibliographer's Manual of American History* edited by S. V. Henkels, and produced in five quarto volumes at Philadelphia between 1907 and 1910, will be surprised at the number of historical publications that came from the presses of America in the late eighteenth and early nineteenth centuries.

Before the second half of the century, W. H. Prescott (1796-1859) had produced his *History of the Conquest of Mexico*, three volumes, 1843, and *History of the Conquest of Peru*, two volumes, 1847. Both works as firsts would be grade (d). John L. Motley (1814-77), of Massachusetts, was another notable historian, though his interest was not centred on the Americas. His best-known work is *The Rise of the Dutch Republic*, three volumes, 1856, now grade (i) and not likely to rise in value very fast.

In Britain, comparable historians were Thomas Babington, Lord Macaulay (1800-59) and Thomas Carlyle (1795-1881). Neither writer is feverishly collected, though fine sets of their works sell quite well as library furniture. Macaulay's *Lays of Ancient Rome,* first edition, 1849, sometimes rises to grade (g) in the salerooms, yet there are booksellers who have had moderately-priced copies of this edition on their shelves for years. Carlyle's *French Revolution,* three volumes, 1837, may have a saleroom rating of (f) and his *Chartism,* 1840, of (i) but his other firsts are to be had at very ordinary prices, unless they are signed or association copies.

Although John R. Green's *A Short History of the English People,* 1874, was a pioneer work in many ways and is extremely elusive as a first, it is little collected and may be had for little more than one of the later illustrated editions which sell for about £6 ($15), or rather more if they are handsome sets in leather.

Few books by later historians have been raised to the dignity of collectors' items and sell either on their value to the student, or as impressive shelf-fillers. Collectors turn rather to broadsides and pamphlets of historical interest. In America, the biggest demand is for broadsides—single printed sheets—connected with the Revolution. As an example, a sheet with Bunker Hill connections, beginning 'This Town was alarmed on the 17th Instant at Break of day,' and dated 'Boston, 26 June 1775' sold recently for $300 (£120). Proclamations concerning the Jacobite struggles of 1715 and 1745 might fetch similar prices in Britain. No British broadside, however, could approach in value the premier American example. This is the first issue of the *Declaration of Independence,* published at Philadelphia in 1776, with no date shown. Its value would now be somewhere in the region of half a million dollars (£200,000).

A fascinating aspect of broadside collecting is concerned

with the reputed confessions and last dying words of notorious highwaymen and other criminals. Some of the confessions were genuine, many were not. They were also issued as broadsheets, which are broadsides printed on both sides, as chapbooks, which are small pamphlets, and occasionally as proper books, in duodecimo or octavo. Prices of these vary enormously, from grade (i) to grade (d) and above.

Probably the narratives of Charles Johnson, who published *A General History of the Pyrates* in 1724 and *A General History of Highwaymen* in 1734, are more authentic than those of the broadsides etc. Johnson's books are among those seldom found in good condition as firsts. Without imperfections they are grade (e), but are more often listed with details of defects and sold *w.a.f.* (with all faults—implying that the seller accepts no responsibility for condition) in grade (i).

Much of Johnson's inspiration for his work on pirates must have stemmed from John Esquemeling's *Bucaniers of America* which, as a book originally written in Dutch and first published in Holland, hardly comes within the purview of this guide. However, an English edition in four parts, usually bound either in one volume or in two volumes with part four as the second volume, was published at London in 1684 and is grade (H) if complete. The fourth part is the most highly esteemed and the first three parts together may be no more than (g).

William Dampier (1652-1715), was both pirate and legitimate explorer, so he may serve to bridge the gap between books of history and those of voyages and travels. His three volumes of *Voyages* were published between 1699 and 1703 and reveal that despite his reputation for coarseness and brutality, he was a skilled navigator and explorer—at least by his own account. The *Voyages*, which may be graded (b) for the three volumes, take us to the coasts of Australia and many strange places in the old and new worlds. For a sense of adventure, however, Dampier is outclassed by Sir Walter Raleigh in his *Discovery of Guiana.* The accepted first edition, published in 1595, was entitled *The discouerie of the large rich, and bewtiful empire of Guiana. Performed in the yeare 1595,* published in that same year. The second edition, also 1595, had the word 'empire' in the title altered to 'Empire' and there are slight internal variations. Still in 1595, there was a third edition, this time with 'Empire' replaced by 'Empyre'. These variations affect the price, so that the first would be grade (D) while the other editions might be (G). But all are rare and the next appearance of a copy of an early edition in a saleroom could show these estimates to be too low.

In the eighteenth century, George, Lord Anson (1697-1762), when a naval captain, circumnavigated the earth in the years 1740 to 1744. His account of the adventure, *A Voyage Round the World,* was published in 1748 and has thrilled readers ever since. The first edition is approaching (a).

Beyond journeying between London and Paris, Richard Hakluyt (1552-1616) was no voyager himself. His fame comes from the collection which he made: *Principall Navigations,* in three parts, 1589, which brought together as stirring a selection of adventures as can be found and which has been mined for material by other writers ever since. It would hardly be safe to estimate the price of the first edition. It has sold for as little as £250 ($650) and as much as £2,600 ($6,760). The earliest 'miner' of Hakluyt's collection was Samuel Purchas (1576-1626), another armchair traveller, who published *Purchas His Pilgrimage* in 1613, grade (e), and *Purchas His Pilgrimes,* four volumes, in 1625-6, grade (D). It is this latter work, combined with the effects of opium, which led Coleridge to write his dream poem, *Kubla Khan.*

Romance and realism are to be found in *The General Historie of Virginia,* 1624, by the resourceful Captain John Smith (1580-1631). It is as much a book of travel and exploration as

Page 149 *The American 'Phiz': this engraving from the 1875 New York edition of Fenimore Cooper's* The Pioneers *shows the affinity of US artist F. O. C. Darley (1822-88) with Hablot Browne ('Phiz'), the illustrator of many Dickens first editions. Darley, whose work this is, provided some of the most successful illustrations for the early American editions of Dickens*

Page 150 *A masterly illustration drawn and engraved by William Hogarth for an edition of* Don Quixote

Page 151 *A windmill for drainage and irrigation as illustrated in William Blith's* The English Improver Improved, *1649*

Page 152 *Modern bookbinding: an example of the work of a present-day Gloucestershire craftsman, T. B. Merrett, happily combining the new and the traditional*

of history. It was Captain Smith whose life was saved on two occasions by the Indian princess, Pocahontas. The first edition would be grade (a).

In the two centuries after John Smith, the frontier was pushed ever westwards and confrontations with the Indians took place much deeper in the American interior. The nobility and the savagery of the indigenous tribes were recorded by several observers, particularly George Catlin (1796-1872), who lived with the Indians, studying their customs and drawing them in the course of their everyday activities. Catlin's *North American Indian Portfolio,* with thirty-one hand-coloured lithographs, was published about 1845, though no date is given. This book is certainly grade (A) and is sure to rise. His other well-known work is *Manners of the North American Indians,* two volumes, 1841. Though a less important work, it is grade (I)—and even the Edinburgh reprint of 1926 is not to be had below grade (f).

Francis Parkman (1823-93) was another important historian of old America. He wrote many books, but the one most consistently collected is *California and the Oregon Trail,* as published in two parts in paper wrappers at New York in 1849. In this state it is a grade (E) item and is probably a good investment.

Throughout the nineteenth century, America was being opened up by idealists and adventurers. Few were of the stamp of William Penn, whose Quaker principles helped the peaceful establishment of Philadelphia in the late seventeenth century.

The story of the development of the West is often one of violence, though popular fiction and film and television drama have often put too much emphasis on this aspect. Collectors of the Americana of the period, by amassing books, pamphlets, waybills and other ephemera, are helping to piece together the jigsaw of the pioneering days and if a complete picture ever emerges it may be more creditable than is generally supposed. Some of the collectable material is recorded in Charles Evans's *American Bibliography*, in fourteen volumes, including two supplements and an index, Chicago and Worcester, 1903-34-55, but even that vast work does not list all that can be gathered, most of it at a great expense either of money or time. The opening up of the West was an epic adventure and there were plenty of minor Homers to tell of it, in prose rather than poetry. Here are some works which go towards presenting the epic, with their price grades: *Journal of the Sufferings of Captain Parker H. French's Overland Expedition to California*, Chambersburg, 1851 (A), *A Plea for the Indians* by John Beeson, New York, 1857 (a), *Hair-Breadth Escapes of 'Grizzly Adams'* by James C. Adams, no place or date of publication, but New York, 1860 (H), *Murder and Mob Law in Indiana* by James M. Hiatt, Indianapolis, 1872 (h), *Seventy Years on the Frontier* by Alexander Majors, edited by Colonel P. Ingrahan, Chicago, 1893 (h), *Reminiscences of Frontier Life* by Isaac B. Hammond, Portland, 1904, and *My Life and Experiences among Our Hostile Indians* by Oliver O. Howard, Hartford, no date, but 1907 (g).

While many Americans were venturing across the plains on prairie schooners, others were finding an outlet for their energies by taking to real schooners, and other vessels, and sailing the seas. It should be remembered that though the clipper ship reached its highest development in the British vessels, *Thermopylae* and *Cutty Sark*, the basic clipper design was American. Not entirely without justification, American enthusiasts might claim their *Flying Cloud* and *Dreadnought* as equals of the British ships in speed and beauty of line.

Richard Henry Dana (1815-82) had his non-fiction classic of the sea, *Two Years before the Mast*, published at New York in 1840. A really fine copy of this first in original cloth is likely to be grade (F), though acceptable copies should cost much less. Joshua Slocum (1844-1909?) was another famous American sailor. In *Sailing Alone around the World,* New York, 1900, he describes his great single-handed voyage on board the sloop *Spray*. He made a second voyage on which he disappeared, so the date of his death is unknown. As a first, his book is nothing like as valuable as that of Dana's. It may remain in grade (i) for a time, but will probably rise steadily in the years ahead. *The Cruise of the 'Cachalot' round the World,* is another great true story of the sea, written by the Englishman, Frank Bullen (1857-1915) from his experiences on an old whaler. The first edition has a present value much the same as Slocum's book and is as likely to increase in price within a few years.

The Yorkshireman, Captain James Cook (1728-79), is the most celebrated circumnavigator of all time, with the possible exception of Ferdinand Magellan (1480-1521) who was in fact killed before he could complete the journey. Cook was a remarkable man, justly praised in English maritime histories and long since accepted by Australians as one of themselves. He was of humble origin and rose to the top by sheer merit. Because he knew from his own experience what life on the lower deck could be like, he was always considerate of his crew and on his first voyage to the Antarctic there was only one death on board the two ships under his command, the *Resolution* and the *Adventure*. Having regard to the conditions prevailing at the time, this was as remarkable an achievement as boldly sailing his ships among the icebergs of the uncharted southern seas.

Cook was not only an outstanding sea captain, but a painstaking surveyor and geographer. Dampier had explored part of the Australian coast before him, but it is fitting that Cook's name should be more closely associated with the island continent and its little sister, New Zealand. Bibliophiles of varying interests converge when Cook's published works are offered for sale, thus making them hard to buy. His *Journal of a Voyage round the World in H.M.S. Endeavour*, 1771, would not be too dear in grade (H), and his *Voyage round the World in 1772-5*, two volumes, 1781, in grade (F). Most desirable of all is a set of Cook's first, second and third voyages in nine volumes, including the atlas, issued over the years 1773-77-84, probably in grade (C).

Well-known books, like *Two Expeditions into the Interior of South Australia*, two volumes, 1833, by Charles Sturt (1795-1869), now grade (c) and J. Maclehose's *Picture of Sydney*, published at Sydney in 1839, grade (H) or (G) are not for everybody. It should be remembered, however, that interesting titbits of information on the early days of Australia can be found in quite minor books, including works of fiction. A rather poor novel, such as J. R. H. Hawthorn's *The Pioneer of a Family*, London, 1881, can give reasonably accurate descriptions of the Australian way of life in the nineteenth century, though overlaid with evangelical zeal. For details of such books, the collector should consult E. M. Miller's *Australian Literature, A Bibliography to 1938*, Sydney, 1940, or, better, the revised edition, extended to 1950, edited by F. T. Macartney, published in 1956, also at Sydney. S. A. Spence's *Bibliography of Selected Early Books and Pamphlets Relating to Australia 1610-1880*, published 1952, and Sir Maurice Holmes's *Captain James Cook, R.N., F.R.S., A Bibliographical Excursion*, 1952, should also prove helpful. The patient bibliophile who is prepared to do his own hunting should be able to collect a wide range of useful Australian items at little more than $A3 (£1.40 or $3.50) a time.

The number of collectors of African travel books is growing every day. Books relating to this continent go back to quite early times, but probably the first sober and reliable account of exploration in the English language is to be met in *Travels in the Interior of Africa*, 1799, by Mungo Park (1771-1806).

The area which this Scottish surgeon-explorer made his own as a traveller was the Niger valley. As a first edition, the *Travels* would rank as (c). The collector who wants to spend less should look for *Niger: The Life of Mungo Park*, Edinburgh and London, 1934, by Lewis Grassic Gibbon (J. Leslie Mitchell), which should cost little more than £2.50 ($6.50).

Other early books of African travel will prove as dear and as difficult to find as that of Mungo Park. James Bruce (1730-94), was a Scottish wine merchant who was seized with wanderlust and travelled widely in Abyssinia. His failure to reach the ultimate source of the Nile in no way detracts from the interest of *Travels to Discover the Sources of the Nile*, his book which was published in five volumes at Edinburgh in 1790. It also is grade (c). John H. Speke (1827-64) was the man who did discover where the Nile began and recounted his adventures in *A Journey of the Discovery of the Source of the Nile*, 1863. A good copy would be grade (f).

The most distinguished explorer of Africa was David Livingstone (1813-73), whose *Missionary Travels in South Africa* first appeared in 1857. Livingstone was already famous when the book was published, so a large first edition was printed. The first issue of this edition is hardly distinguishable from the second and there is usually little difference in value, condition being equal. Both are grade (f) if they are in clean original cloth. The great popularity of the book can be gauged from a statement in a letter written in 1863 by Charles E. Mudie, owner of the celebrated circulating library, and quoted by P. H. Muir in *The Book Collector* in 1953. Mudie states that 'the exact number of copies of Livingstone's *Africa* at one time in circulation in the Library was 3,250'. Not all the Mudie copies would have been firsts, and in any case they would now be frowned upon because of their library labels. Even so, on this evidence there ought still to be a reasonable supply of the first edition available.

Everybody, one presumes, links the name of Livingstone with that of Sir Henry H. M. Stanley (1841-1904). His famous book is *How I Found Livingstone,* 1872. Though also grade (f) as a first, it is probably marginally more expensive than Livingstone's work, because of greater scarcity rather than intrinsic merit.

Livingstone and Stanley both had a single-minded devotion to Africa. Not so Sir Richard F. Burton (1821-90), who nevertheless spent several years travelling in that continent. His most important African books are *First Footsteps in East Africa,* 1856, grade (g), and *Abeokuta and the Camaroons Mountains,* two volumes, 1863, grade (e). His other travel books include *Personal Narrative of a Pilgrimage to El-Medinah and Meccah,* three volumes, 1869, grade (i), and *Etruscan Bologna,* 1876, low in grade (i). Some of the ground covered by Burton in his journey to Mecca was travelled over again by Charles M. Doughty (1843-1926), who described his wanderings in *Travels in Arabia Deserta,* two volumes, with a map in an end pocket, 1888. Doughty's is not an easy style of writing, but the book is ultimately rewarding to read. As a first it is grade (f).

Love of adventure as much as missionary zeal sent George Borrow (1803-81) to Spain in 1835 on behalf of the British and Foreign Bible Society. The result was that classic of travel, *The Bible in Spain,* three volumes, 1843, to be had in grade (i). Richard Ford (1796-1858) spent nearly four years in Spain just before Borrow went there, but his *Handbook for Travellers in Spain* was not published till 1845. The title is deceptive, for Ford's book is as different from an ordinary guidebook as chalk is from cheese and many a collector would be glad to have a copy of the 1845 edition even in grade (f) or (e).

Edward Lear is more widely known as a writer of nonsense verse than as a traveller, yet those who are familiar with them find his illustrated travel journals just as delightful as his verse. The most highly prized is *Illustrated Excursions in Italy,* two volumes with fifty-five lithographs, 1846. The landscapes are very fine and the volumes together are sold in grade (E). Among his other works are *Journal of a Landscape Painter in Albania,* 1851, grade (f), and *Journals of a Landscape Painter in South Calabria,* 1852, grade (c).

While Lear was travelling in the heat of Italy, Sir John Franklin (1786-1847) was sailing the Arctic seas in two famous ships of the Royal Navy, the *Erebus* and *Terror,* searching for the North-West Passage. He had already explored the waters of the far north and told his story in *A Journey to the Shores of the Polar Sea,* 1823, a book which now changes hands in grade (b). Franklin's two ships sailed from England in May, 1845, and were last seen by a whaler two months later. Thereafter, all was silence. Many expeditions were sent to find Franklin, but it was the *Fox,* fitted out by Lady Franklin and commanded by F. L. McClintock, which brought the discovery of the fate of Franklin and his men. Sir John had died in 1847 and the rest of his crews not long after—but they had found the North-West Passage. McClintock told his story in *The Voyage of the 'Fox' in the Arctic Seas,* 1859. The book was an immediate bestseller, so that fine copies of the first edition, with map in pocket, would be grade (h), but there should be inferior copies to be found at much less.

The tragedy of Franklin in the far north resembles that of Captain Robert Falcon Scott (1868-1912) in the Antarctic. Scott also reached his goal, but he, too, did not live to tell the tale. Today, the record of Scott's journey to the South Pole, *Scott's Last Expedition,* two volumes, 1913, edited by Leonard Huxley, and containing Scott's own journal, is a collected item. In satisfactory condition it would be grade (i). Even more highly valued—a fine copy would be grade (f)—is Apsley Cherry-Garrard's account of the expedition, *The Worst Journey in the World,* two volumes, 1922. Cherry-Garrard (1886-

1959) was himself a distinguished bibliophile.

Like Roald Amundsen, who reached the South Pole ahead of Scott and everybody else, the first man to arrive at the North Pole, Admiral Robert E. Peary (1856-1920), survived the homeward journey and wrote a book about his successful expedition: *The North Pole.* The edition favoured by collectors is the true first, known as the General Hubbard Edition, published at New York in 1910 and in grade (h).

It is but a step from polar exploration to mountaineering. This subject has now an extensive literature of its own, with a growing following. The classics include *Scrambles Amongst the Alps,* 1871, by Edward Whymper (1840-1911) and the same author's *Travels Amongst the Great Andes of the Equator,* two volumes, 1891-2; A. F. Mummery's (1855-95) *My Climbs in the Alps and Caucasus,* 1895; *Mountaineering in the Sierra Nevada,* 1872, by Clarence King (1842-1901), *The Epic of Mount Everest,* 1926, by Sir F. E. Younghusband (1863-1942); *The Kangchenjunga Adventure,* 1930, by F. S. Smythe (1900-49), and *The Conquest of the New Zealand Alps,* 1922, by Samuel Turner. To these should be added Sir John Hunt's *The Ascent of Everest,* 1953, (published in the United States as *The Conquest of Everest,* 1954) though copies of the first edition are too plentiful for it to be ranked as a collector's item. The first important English book on the Scandinavian mountains is *Norway and Its Glaciers,* 1853, by James Forbes (1809-68), which is partly a scientific study of glaciation. Most of these mountaineering books—and many others —are available quite cheaply in first editions. The two named Whymper books, the Clarence King and Forbes's *Norway* may be in grade (h), but most of the others should be low down in grade (i).

Those who like to do their climbing and travelling vicariously will find they are well catered for in cheap reprints, but they should also look out for volumes of the Hakluyt Society's publications which give accurate and carefully edited versions of many of the world's great books of travel. In long runs, they would average about £6 ($15) a volume, but odds might be had at about £2 ($5) each.

CHAPTER EIGHT

Topography

Portmanteau words have been well known ever since Lewis Carroll defined them through the mouth of Humpty Dumpty. But collectors and booksellers are more at home with what could be called umbrella words—those they employ to impose a kind of unity on assemblies of books on widely different subjects. In their usage, topography is probably the most widely stretched umbrella of all. Ostensibly meaning the description and study of place, this accommodating term shelters much material which is not at all closely related.

Enthusiasm for topographical books usually stems from local patriotism. The Warwickshire man who loves his native Alveston and becomes possessed by the spirit of collecting is seldom so narrow in his interests as to devote himself exclusively to books about his own little village. He will normally expand into neighbouring districts and outwards to embrace the whole of his county. He will gather as much material as he can find and afford on Warwickshire botany, ornithology, geology, archaeology, history, agriculture, industry and so forth. The literature of his county may so beguile him that his umbrella may ultimately extend over the plays of Shakespeare and the novels of George Eliot.

In much the same way, an Ayrshire man may become a collector of the works of Robert Burns and a native of Concord,

Massachusetts, may expand his topographical interests to include books by the many literary men associated with his small town—Thoreau, Hawthorne, Emerson and others. A man brought up in, say, Worsley, Lancashire, living within a stone's throw of the Duke of Bridgwater's Canal and surrounded by cotton mills and coal mines, may start as a local topographer then move outside the shelter of the umbrella into the field of industrial archaeology in general.

The collector who is not ensnared by literature or otherwise enticed from his regional interests should still have plenty of material on which to work. He will gain a fair idea of what can lie ahead of him by acquiring a modern large-scale map of his chosen area. Perhaps this map shows a mainly hilly part of England, with the land falling away quite steeply to the north and east. Just north of the hills, two Roman roads meet. In the middle of the territory there are the remains of a Roman villa. A railway line almost bisects the map from south-east to north-west, with evidences of branch lines which have recently been closed. Many of the towns and villages have names ending in -ington, with a sprinkling of -inghams; on the eastern edge there are a few place names ending in -by. Two towns on the Roman roads have names ending in -cester, while there is one name containing *pen* in the extreme south-west. The map also shows big stretches of cultivated land studded with orchards. The valleys are well wooded though the high ground appears to be rather bare. There are few indications of mines or canals.

A good deal more can be inferred from the map. The roads, the -cester towns and the villa speak of Roman occupation. The -inghams and -ingtons are unmistakably Anglo-Saxon, -ham being indicative of early and -ton of later settlements. The Danes, who once held a large part of northern and eastern England, seem not to have pushed far into the area, as their characteristic place-name ending in -by occurs only in the eastern part of the map. There being only one *pen* name, the Celts must have been driven out, or completely subjugated, quite soon after the arrival of the Saxons.

Since much of upland England was given over to sheep rearing during the Middle Ages, it would be safe to suppose that this area profited from the ancient trade in wool and still has relics of this past prosperity in fine medieval churches and houses. The prevalence of orchards hints that cider is a popular drink with the inhabitants; the distribution of place names would suggest that the local speech is of the west Midland or south-western variety, free from the faint Danish or Celtic echoes still to be heard in other parts of England. The lack of mines and canals indicates that the Industrial Revolution did not leave many scars on the area, so it may well have extensive tracts of relatively unspoilt land and, in consequence, a thriving tourist industry.

What in fact has been described is a map of the Costwold Hills and the immediately surrounding country. Though illustrative of the nature of the task awaiting the collector of Cotswold books, the description should serve as an example for those who wish to tackle the collection of works on other areas of a similar size.

The Cotswold topographer need not work too hard on Roman or Saxon Britain, though he should possess some relevant books. His resources should be husbanded for the buying of material on later periods, where there is so much to be garnered—information about the growth of the English wool trade, the development of ecclesiastical and domestic architecture and, perhaps, the manufacture of cider. As regional dialects are fast dying, books about the language of the area are important—for the light that local speech throws on social history if for nothing else.

Books dealing with the Cotswolds as a whole and the constituent towns, villages and parishes will form the major part of his collection. He should be prepared to track down every book which has Cotswold (or Cotteswold) in its title, at least for examination if not for purchase. The Cotswolds are mainly in Gloucestershire, with extensions into Oxfordshire, Worcestershire and Warwickshire, so books concerned with any of these counties should be looked at for possible material. There are specialised bibliographies of most British counties, not all of the highest standards. The Cotswold collector, however, is particularly fortunate, for he can avail himself of *The Bibliographer's Manual of Gloucestershire Literature*, by F. A. Hyett and W. Bazeley, published in three volumes between 1895 and 1897, with a supplement in two volumes, by Hyett and R. Austin, 1915-16. This work lists more than enough Cotswold material for a lifetime's collecting. If the collector has no access to a set of this work, he can try to obtain for consultation the *Catalogue of the Gloucestershire Collection* of Gloucester Public Library, compiled by R. Austin and issued in 1928. Within this single volume there are 15,333 entries of books, pamphlets, magazines, serial publications and individual articles relative to the county. Only the most manic of Gloucestershire bibliomanes would attempt to surpass this collection or to improve on its purely Cotswold section.

Most county bibliographies do not discuss the finer gradings of first and subsequent issues of books. Local topographical works have seldom been subjected to the kind of close scrutiny which has produced the fearsome number of real and bogus points which delight or intimidate collectors in other fields. At present, the connoisseur of topography worries little about matters of priority of issue and concentrates on condition and completeness. He is happy with the best edition of a book, whether it be the first or the fifteenth.

British topographical collectors soon learn that one of the most desirable books for them is *Britannia* by William Camden (1551-1623), with its fine maps and useful county surveys.

Though they do not despise the first edition of 1586, nor subsequent editions up to the sixth in 1607, the seventh edition of 1610 is the one they really covet, for this is the first English edition (translated by Philemon Holland), the others being in Latin Even a good classical scholar will find the 1610 edition easier to work from. For this reason and because of the quality of the maps, a good copy of this first English-language edition would be grade (E) in the Scale of Values (page 12), but those of the earlier dates could be well down in grade (H) and occasionally very much cheaper. Several editions with fine maps were produced later in the seventeenth century and during the earlier part of the eighteenth. They, too, are wanted for their maps and are not far below the 1610 edition in price. However, a new translation by Richard Gough first appeared in 1789 and was reprinted in 1806. The text is more readable than that of the previous editions, though the maps are less quaintly decorative. The topographer who wants a copy of this edition to work from might find one grade (a). Though most of the editions in English are entitled *Britain*, the work is almost always spoken of as Camden's *Britannia*. A reprint of the 1695 edition with maps after Robert Morden and an introduction by Stuart Piggott is published in Britain by David & Charles, and in the US by Johnson Reprint Corporation.

Collectors whose work centres on a small area may dream of owning a *Britannia* but prefer to spend their money on books which more directly concern them—old county histories, perhaps. Many British counties have monumental histories, such as *The History and Topographical Survey of the County of Kent* by Edward Hasted (1732-1812), four volumes, Canterbury, 1778-99, grade (H), and *The History and Antiquities of the County of Dorset* by John Hutchins (1698-1773), two volumes, 1774, grade (c). Here the price gradings must be taken with caution, as old books on local history are rapidly mounting in value and are especially highly prized in the areas to which they pertain, by many who are not collectors. This is equally true of the histories of certain particular towns and villages. The rise in value of these can be shown by turning again to the Cotswolds for an example. *The History and Antiquities of Chipping Campden*, was published by the author, Percy C. Rushen, in 1899. Though he did not expect to make a profit, Rushen hoped he would recover his costs from sales. Things did not go smoothly. This is what he wrote in a letter to one buyer, some months after the book was issued:

> The cost is 5/6 post free, which amount please forward to me as I am publishing the book myself. I have had to abandon the subscription list for lack of subscribers and am therefore offering copies to the general public @ the above price, hoping thereby to dispose of more copies.
>
> As there will be an actual out of pocket loss on the publication, I... shall therefore esteem it a favour if you will introduce the work to those of your friends &c. likely to be interested in the subject...

In the course of the next decade, a series of events, the chief of which was the establishment of the Guild in the village, brought Chipping Campden out of its decline and raised it to an eminence which it had not enjoyed for 300 years. Rushen was able eventually to sell all the copies and to bring out a second edition in 1911 (though undated), revised and enlarged, but poorly printed and bound. It also cost 5s (25p) a copy (5s 6d post free) and sold a little more readily than the first edition.

Today, the demand for Rushen's book, though limited, far exceeds the supply and some people would be willing to pay up to £10 ($26) for a good copy of the first edition and at least £6 ($15) for a second edition.

The position is much the same as regards other such books of narrow local interest, British or American. When Mark Doolittle wrote his *Historical Sketch of the Congregational*

Church in Belchertown, Massachusetts, and had it published at nearby Northampton in 1852, it cost only a few cents a copy and showed no appreciable rise in value in the following hundred years. Now, though its appeal is still strictly limited, the few who want it would gladly pay $20 (£8) or more for it.

Many local histories, such as Hutchins's *Dorset* already mentioned, were produced on a subscription basis. In America in particular, some of the writers or compilers sought to cover their expenses by undertaking to incorporate pictures of the persons or homes of the subscribers, giving these a degree of prominence consonant with the amount of the subscription. This tends to inflate the present prices of such books as they are sought by buyers who are not interested in local history but will pay highly for items containing portraits of their great-grandfathers or illustrations of their ancestral homes. In the paucity of fresh information contained, some of these pictorially-financed histories resemble certain modern so-called guide books issued by companies more interested in revenue from advertising than in real topography.

Among many good local histories and the like, not overrun with solicited illustrations, there may be mentioned: *The history and Antiquities of the City of Dublin* by Walter Harris, 1766; *The History and Antiquities of Shrewsbury* by Thomas Phillips, 1779; *A Description of Matlock Bath* by George Lipscomb, 1802; *The History and Antiquities of the Church and City of Lichfield* by Thomas Harwood, 1806; *Picturesque Memorials of Salisbury* by Peter Hall, 1834; *A Guide to Carlisle* by Samuel Jefferson, 1842; *Historical Memorials of Northampton* by C. H. Hartshorne, 1848; and *A Handbook to Newcastle-on-Tyne* by J. C. Bruce, 1863. Where obtainable, and none is plentiful, these should be priced between the (i) and (g) grades.

Equivalent American works often cover whole counties rather than individual towns and belong on the whole to a rather later period. The dearest of them are those concerned with areas in the West which were still being opened up when the books were produced. Here is a short but fairly representative selection: *Gazetteer of the State of Vermont* by Z. Thompson, Montpelier, 1824, (h); *Historical Reminiscences of Summit County* by General Lucius Bierce, Akron, 1854, (g); *Guide to Denver* by S. B. Woolworth, Omaha City, 1862, (G); *Upper Mississipi* by George Gale, Chicago and New York, 1867, (g); *History and Directory of Nevada County* by Edwin F. Bean, Nevada, 1867, (d); *Guide to Santa Barbara Town and County* by E. N. Wood, Santa Barbara, 1872 (c); *History of Westchester County* by J. T. Scharf, two volumes, Philadelphia, 1886, (g). American local history books published in the present century are creeping up in price and buyers would be lucky to find the following below the (g) grade: *North Platte and Its Associations* by Archibald R. Adamson, North Platte, Nebraska, no date, but 1910; *History of Custer County, Nebraska* by W. L. Gaston and A. R. Humphrey, Lincoln, 1919; *History of Natrona County* by Alfred J. Mokler, Chicago, 1923.

Australian topography published before the present century is scarce, keenly collected and highly priced, typical examples being David Collins's *Account of the English Colony in New South Wales*, two volumes, 1798-1802, (F); Andrew Bent's *Van Diemen's Land Pocket Almanack*, published at Hobart in 1824, (G); Charles J. Baker's *Sydney and Melbourne*, 1845, (f); William B. Withers's *History of Ballarat*, 1870, (d); Ernest Favenc's *Western Australia*, 1887, (h). One of the Australian topographical 'prizes' is *South Australia Illustrated* by George F. Angas. Published in 1847, it contains sixty hand-coloured lithographs of what was then almost virgin territory. Scarcity and desirability put it in grade (A). A facsimile, produced in 1967, is grade (d).

Ties of blood and language probably account for the interest taken in British topography by collectors in the other English-speaking nations. Thousands of books concerned with places in England, Wales and Scotland are shipped abroad every year and almost none of them returns to its native country. This is one reason why supplies of items which were once common are drying up at the sources. For as long as they remained inside Britain, they kept circulating. When a private library was sold on the death of its owner, the books came on the market to be reabsorbed into another British collection. Now this cycle has been broken. Another cause of scarcity of local material is the demand to 'make it new' so typical of our present century. Well-worn books which were revered by their earlier owners have been discarded as too drab or parochial by misguided heirs. Too many treasures have been destroyed by the Veneerings of our time who judge books by the impressiveness or glossiness of their exteriors.

The wise collector learns to look beyond outward appearances and develops a special kind of visual and mental acuity. For instance, the devotee of the history and topography of the Aberdeen region will be conditioned to seize on every book with 'Aberdeen' in its title, but his cultivated perceptiveness will take him further. There is virtually nothing about its theme and setting to be gleaned from the title of a forgotten novel of the nineties of last century—*The King of Andaman*, by James Maclaren Cobban. With its title suggestive only of a romance of the Indian Ocean, it would be ignored by any but the experienced Aberdeen bibliophile. He, however, would notice the unusual surname of the author and recall that an Aberdeen printer of the early nineteenth century bore the same name and would hope to find some connection in the book. Ordinary examination would show that the novel is set in a Scottish city called Inverdoon and colourfully depicts the lives of depressed weavers in a district named Ilkastane. Inverdoon is easily identifiable with Aberdeen and Ilkastane with Gilcolmston, an area of the city now largely cleared and rebuilt. Much information of value to the Aberdeen historian-topographer can be pieced together from the novel, which is well worth a place in his collection.

It has already been mentioned that imaginative literature is often allowed the shelter of the topographical umbrella, particularly in the case of books like *The King of Andaman.* The Aberdeen regional collector is not likely to become too involved with such literature as the area is not rich in outstanding poets and novelists. In this respect, the counties of Dorset and Wiltshire provide a marked contrast. Together they provide the settings for most of the novels of Thomas Hardy and several of Anthony Trollope. In Hardy, who re-created Wessex as a distinctive part of England, the spirit of place is powerfully felt. Every Wessex child born into a literate family learns at its mother's knee that Hardy's towns and villages have their easily-recognised equivalents. Tolchurch is really Tolpuddle, Casterbridge is Dorchester and Melchester is Salisbury—a city of three aliases, for its old name was Sarum and it is also the Barchester of Trollope.

Some collectors determinedly limit themselves to a very small area within which to work and, without positively cheating, acquire a fair quantity of material. The hypothetical hamlet of Mudcombe Parva is in a quiet backwater. It has little natural beauty, has played no part in national history, has produced no famous men and is recognised by the few outsiders who know it as the dullest place in Britain. Seemingly it has nothing to offer the collector, yet, if it exists, it must have been written about at one time or other. Its name should appear in official publications in connection with rating, census-taking and elections. If it has, or once had, a railway station, it should be listed in timetables. Even if the great county histories have left it out, it ought to appear in some county directory. If it stands anywhere, it must stand on earth, with rock beneath, and therefore the stuff of its foundations will be described in a geological survey. It will have vegetation and wild life, with certain plants, insects, birds and beasts predominating. Though these may be no more than dandelions, blackbeetles, sparrows and mice, they all have their individual descriptive literature which can be collected as having a special bearing on Mudcombe. The nucleus of a collection can be formed from such elements and in time, other particles will begin to gather round it.

Boldness is always the collector's friend, even if he is a mere Mudcombian. He should find out which universities have departments of local studies likely to be interested in Mudcombe and try to enlist their aid, perhaps on a *quid pro quo* basis. He should apply to his nearest public library for help and go through the files of the local newspaper which circulates in Mudcombe, snatching at every crumb of information which may lead to the finding of a book or pamphlet containing a reference to the place. Few priests or parsons are unwilling to co-operate, and will usually give access to church records. All available registers of births, marriages and deaths should be consulted in the furtherance of Mudcombe knowledge. If printed information is still sparse, the collector should compile his own handwritten or typewritten notes in the hope that they will pay a dividend sooner or later. It may be that the Mudcombe collector has paid little attention to the work of Egbert Smith, a promising young poet. One day, however, he reads one of Smith's poems which contains a line about 'a dull grey village behind God's back.' This is so evocative of Mudcombe that he works on the clue and on checking his notes finds that a certain Egbert Smith from London married a local girl in 1905. He then writes to the poet and finds he is the grandson of this couple and that he visited Mudcombe several times during his boyhood. At last he has found a writer with local connections and collects his books as part of the Mudcombe heritage. In actual fact, few places are as barren as Mudcombe. Almost every parish has had something written about its history, probably printed in an obscure little book or pamphlet.

Some of the most attractive local items are such pamphlets. Rarely they go back to the seventeenth century, some belong to the eighteenth and large numbers to the nineteenth. Many are the work of clergymen, particularly those of an ecclesiological or archaeological nature, as: *A Description of the Norman Font in St Chad's Church, Mudcombe* by the Revd Thos Brown, Curate in Charge, Marlchester, 1849. But they can be on almost any subject. Such small fry are called *ephemera* (Greek: *ephemeros*—lasting for a day). They were not intended as works for posterity so they were merely stitched or stapled in paper outer wrappers. Because of their obviously high mortality rate, they are hard to find. Inexperienced collectors misguidedly reject some scarce piece of ephemera because of the high price which may be asked for it. They consider it is blatant profiteering for a bookseller to demand £5 ($13) for a thin, paper-covered booklet like *Michaelmarsh and Its Antiquities* by A. W. (A. Wilkinson), published in 1867, a real example, of Hampshire interest. After all, it is possible to buy a large, handsomely bound book of the same period for half that amount. This is a mistaken attitude. Well-bound books are equipped to survive—flimsy pamphlets are not, and seldom do.

Many localities—cities, counties or wider areas—have their own historical, antiquarian, archaeological and natural history societies, or societies which combine all or some of these studies. Most of them publish their transactions yearly or at longer intervals and some additionally produce new scholarly books on aspects of their chosen subjects. Ever-mounting costs have reduced their activities, but several still flourish. Few have been established for less than a hundred years so their publications, despite forbidding outward appearances and often ponderous language, are great repositories of information. Long runs of transactions, in uniformly bound volumes or original paper-covered parts, come on the market from time to time, to be bought mainly by university and institutional libraries. The private buyer turns away from them regretfully, thinking of the large amount of shelf space they would occupy. If they are within his means he should nevertheless buy them and find room for them with as little ruth as Palissy the potter showed when he burned the family furniture to achieve his ends. If he truly cannot accommodate them he should find out where they can be consulted to note those parts or volumes which contain the most useful articles for his purposes. These few can then be bought as odds.

A complete run of *The Proceedings of the Somersetshire Archaeological and Natural History Society*, from 1850 to the present, would cost at least £160 ($416), but broken runs would be cheaper in proportion. Single volumes and parts, however, can be quite dear at upwards of £2 ($5) a volume. Individual articles from the transactions were sometimes reprinted as separate pamphlets. They, too, can be dear considering their small bulk, but the buyer pays for the convenience of having only the article he wants without its contiguous irrelevancies. What is true of the Somerset society will hold good for the transactions of other similar societies. It should be remembered, however, that the surviving societies are always glad to welcome new members and can sometimes supply out-of-print volumes and offprints at prices below those of the general market.

Another important source of information is the series of Victoria County Histories, published by the Oxford University Press. The series is by no means complete, though volumes have been issued from time to time during the past seventy years. One of the first sets to be finished was the *Victoria*

History of Hampshire and the Isle of Wight, edited by H. A. Doubleday and others, and issued in six folio volumes between 1900 and 1914. This work, like all the other volumes in the series, is excellently illustrated and supplied with numerous maps. It has been out of print for some time and is a grade (H) item. Other Victoria Histories are still in a rather confusing state of preparation and availability. Some, like Hampshire, are complete, but out of print and only occasionally offered for sale others, such as Oxfordshire, have odd volumes still in preparation, while little progress seems to have been made with London since the first volume was published in 1909. The position is further complicated in that some of the early issues are being reprinted in a different sequence. These fine reprints have an average price which lies in grade (h) and will undoubtedly increase in value as they, too, go out of print. The high cost will prevent most people from building up a complete set of the whole series, even if they live long enough to see the publication of the final volume, but every collector of topography should try to obtain every available volume pertaining to his own county.

At the time when the Oxford University Press was embarking on this mighty series, its sister, the Cambridge University Press, was preparing a far more modest issue of topographical works—the Cambridge County Geographies. Almost every British county was covered and the authors were carefully chosen as men with a good knowledge of the areas about which they wrote. Every book in the series was of a standard worthy of the Cambridge University Press, yet none has enjoyed the high reputation it deserves. Good, clean copies may still be had for little more than 25p ($0.65) each.

In a similar class, though always more popular, are the Little Guides, published originally by Methuen & Co Ltd. The series was started at the end of last century and was extended bit by bit to cover most of England and Wales, with the inclusion of some foreign places as well. The books were slim and pocket size, bound in green cloth in the early days, but latterly in red. They were well illustrated with line drawings (many by E. H. New) and photographs. After World War II, they were produced jointly by Methuen and B. T. Batsford & Co Ltd. A few titles may still be found as new books. In the earlier period of their publication they sold for 3s 6d (17½p) and secondhand copies should not cost more than 40p ($1) today.

Until recently, volumes in Macmillan's *Highways & Byways* series could be had almost as cheaply as copies of the Little Guides. Now they seem to be moving into the class of collectors' pieces. The series was rather more ambitious than the previous two and artists of the calibre of F. L. Griggs and Hugh Thomson were employed as illustrators. Publication began in 1897 and continued until 1948, when Seton Gordon's *Highways & Byways in the Central Highlands* was published, with illustrations by Sir D. Y. Cameron. The authors were wisely chosen and included Andrew Lang (*The Borders*), Sir Frederick Treves (*Dorset*), E. V. Lucas (*Essex*) and Clement Shorter (*Buckinghamshire*). *Thomas Hardy's Wessex*, by Hermann Lea, is different in style from the others, but is one of the best. Reprints and revised editions were produced, but anyone wishing to collect the complete series would be well advised to do so on a first edition basis. All the volumes are dated and it is stated on the verso pages of the titles if they are reprints or revised editions. The later volumes were issued in near-white dust-jackets, most of which have gone. Fine copies of firsts should not cost more than £1.50 ($3.90) each on average, though prices have gone higher than this at sales where there has been keen competition.

Bibliophiles in every field like to supplement their collections of printed books with manuscript items and other apposite material. This is very true of topographers. They delight in documents, wills, indentures, old account books, notes of past lectures by antiquarians and village worthies, photographs, maps and prints. The last two raise an ethical problem. Every day, old atlases and volumes of steel and copper engravings are pulled apart by dealers who sell the maps and prints singly. This they justify by maintaining that they are performing a service. The man who wants only the Kent map from an early *Britannia* should be able to buy it, they argue, without having to pay the prohibitive price of the whole book. In the same way, the collector of prints of Northumberland does not want a large book of steel engravings which contains a hundred or more illustrations of places in which he has no interest. He wants only the one Northumbrian print. Some dealers feel a little uneasy about breaking good books, but with a shrug of the shoulders they ask why they should appoint themselves conservationists when those who buy the books from them are quite liable to do the breaking themselves. There is no simple answer to this. Everybody must make up his own mind on the issue. Breaking is a long-established practice and will probably be with us for as long as there are any books left worth breaking.

Since they were never issued in books, old Ordnance Survey maps can always be bought with a clear conscience. They are worth collecting in the first and also the revised editions because of the indications they give of Britain's changing towns and countryside. Original copies of the first survey are scarce and need be pursued only by those who value the feel of ancient authenticity. The publishing firm of David & Charles has now completed a reprint of the ninety-seven sheets of the original survey of England and Wales at one inch to the mile. With these available the collector may have the reprinted sheets for everyday use and originals to gloat over as only fanatical collectors can.

The same publishers are among the firms which are reprinting many important old books on topography and local history. These new issues are a godsend to the collector of average means with little time for intensive bookhunting. Most booksellers will be happy to supply information about available reprints.

Old books are essential, but it is important to find places for new books in a topographical library. They may never acquire a particular eminence as first editions, but in case they do, it is just as well to buy them as soon as they are issued.

The scope of an ideal topographical library is now becoming clear. The collector who takes a wide view and has no financial worries will have a fine array of the classics of his subject. The pride of his British section will probably be a 1610 edition of *Britannia* which may be paired with a copy of the 1789 edition. His two sets of the first Ordnance Survey maps—originals and reprints—will be set alongside those sheets of later editions which are most in key with the rest of his collection. They will be supplemented by a copy of Charles and John Greenwood's *Atlas of the Counties of England and Wales*, 1834, with its key map on the title-page and its forty-six coloured maps of counties, an item which is now grade (H). This may rest beside Samuel Lewis's *Topographical Dictionary of England, Wales, Scotland and Ireland*, 1831-46, in twelve volumes, including two atlases, and now valued (f). There will be room on his shelves for books of topographical engravings of the type dealt with in chapter seven, and for representative runs of the transactions of at least one local antiquarian society. Books on his home area will abound and he will have some on other places which are of interest to him. His ephemera, including recent maps and guide books, and possibly postcards dating from Victorian times to the present, will be kept in box files; his individual old maps and prints, if not framed and hung on the walls, will be contained in portfolios which he may have made for himself from sheets of cardboard covered with buckram. Deeds and other manuscripts will probably be stowed in drawers, safe from dust and worm.

The present chapter has already given some idea of the sort of American and Australian topographical works likely to be owned by the connoisseur, but as these are newer countries a clear line cannot be drawn between topography and travel or exploration and his library would also contain many of the books discussed in chapter seven. Perhaps he would also have some of the following: Arthur Dobb's *An Account of the Countries Adjoining to Hudson's Bay... intended to shew the great Probability of a North West Passage*, 1744, in grade (F); *The American Gazetteer*, three volumes, 12mo, London, for Millar & Tonson, 1762, grade (G); *A Map Exhibiting all the New Discoveries in the Interior Parts of North America* by Aaron Arrowsmith, 1802, grade (G); *American Scenery* by N. P. Willis and W. H. Bartlett, two volumes, 4to, 1840, grade (a); W. H. Bartlett's *Canadian Scenery*, two volumes, 4to, 1840, grade (H); D. Appleton's *Northern and Eastern Traveller's Guide*, 12mo, New York, 1854, grade (h), and *Pictorial Illustrations of New Zealand*, 1847, by J. C. Brees, grade (H); *Handbook to Australasia*, 1859, by William Fairfax, grade (g); John Davis's *Tracks of McKinlay and Party across Australia*, 1863, grade (e); S. T. Gill's *Australian Sketch Book*, undated, but 1865, grade (G), and Andrew Garran's *Picturesque Atlas of Australasia*, undated, but 1886, grade (h). There are few old American and Australian books specifically concerned with regional dialects, so the state of Virginia is fortunate in having Bennett W. Green's *Word-Book of Virginia Folk-Speech*, Richmond, Va, 1899, grade (h).

It would require an average yearly expenditure of at least £500 ($1,300) for twelve years to build up an international library to this standard, but a satisfactory topographical collection could be achieved in ten years by spending no more in that time than a keen amateur photographer would pay for equipment and materials over the same period. On this lower level of expenditure the collector would temper the catholicity of his tastes and work in a narrower field—though he need not go to Mudcombian extremes of straitness unless he wanted to. A topographical library founded on well-known collectors' pieces and tastefully developed by careful buying will be a fairly safe investment, but even a modest gathering together of humble, but unusual items should increase in value over the years. It must be borne in mind, however, that a book like *The King of Andaman* may be worth its weight in gold to the Aberdeen enthusiast but is only fit for the bargain shelves of booksellers in England and America, and Rushen's *History of Chipping Campden* is of little value save to the Cotswold collector.

CHAPTER NINE

Natural History

Those who would become collectors of natural history books should take their cautionary text from St Matthew: 'Wide is the gate, and broad is the way, that leadeth to destruction, and many there be which go in thereat'. In this branch of bibliophily it is only too easy for the collector to find himself faced with financial ruin almost as soon as he has started on his journey. They are the sirens of the book world, those great natural history folios, full of magnificent plates drawn, engraved and coloured by master hands. A victim of their allure could part with £20,000, or $52,000 in acquiring the mere beginning of a collection. Unless he has almost unlimited resources, the votary must seek the strait gate and keep to the narrow path. However, he would be wise to learn of the temptations he is likely to meet, so this chapter will make mention of some of them.

Botany began as a utilitarian study. Though the word comes from the Greek *botane*, meaning grass or fodder, the early botanists were concerned mainly with the identification of medicinal herbs and, in books called herbals, sought to teach how and where they could be discovered. The earliest printed book of this nature was the *Liber de Proprietatibus Rerum*, by Bartholomaeus Anglicus, initially published, probably at Cologne, about 1472, and first printed in England in

1495. This book, like the next known herbal, *Das Puch der Natur*, Augsburg, 1475, by Cunrat von Megenberg (usually known as Konrad, with no further identification), dealt with other matters as well as the properties of plants. *Das Puch der Natur* was not directly translated into English, but material from it was incorporated in several later English herbals. It was the first printed book with botanical illustrations cut in wood, predating by fifty-one years the first English illustrated herbal, *The Great Herball* of 1526, printed by Peter Treveris, who, without much foundation, has been suggested as the author as well as printer, the work being anonymous.

Before the appearance of this illustrated book, another purely English herbal had been published, with a long explanatory title: *Here begynneth a new mater, the which sheweth and treateth of ye vertues and proprytes of herbes, the whiche is called an Herball*, printed in 1525 by Rycharde Banckes, London, and thought to have been written by Walter Cary. None of these books is for the collector on the narrow path. Each is liable to cost more than £5,000 ($13,000) if complete, and a mere dozen consecutive leaves could sell at £50 ($130).

The best-known English herbal of Elizabethan times is that of John Gerard (sometimes given as Gerarde, but not in the first edition), published as *The Herbal or Generall Historie of Plantes*, in 1597. The first printing must have been quite large, for the book is not among the rarest of the period. It turns up relatively frequently in imperfect condition, but even a good copy should be in grade (G) of our Scale of Values (page 12). The enlarged edition, edited by Thomas Johnson and printed in 1633, is a more scholarly work and may cost at least as much as the first. This Johnson was the earliest English plant hunter, but he did not live to complete his projected English flora.

Nicholas Culpeper (1616-54) was the author of the most popular English herbal of all time. Since 1653, when it was first published as *The English Physitian Enlarged, or the Herbal,* his book has run into many editions and has been the mainstay of many a practitioner of cottage medicine. Culpeper was a physician who had individual methods of applying astrology to medicine. His book has little value as a guide to the properties of plants and the first edition is not all that highly regarded by collectors. It should be procurable in grade (g).

Copies of early herbals sometimes have the illustrations coloured by hand. Unless this has been done with rare distinction, these copies have no extra value as the colouring was probably done much later than the time of issue. Botanical works with coloured plates contemporary with publication hardly begin before the eighteenth century, as far as England is concerned. John Martyn (1699-1768) is credited with producing the first English book with colour-printed plates other than the primitive woodcuts of early days. Because it is a landmark, his *Historia Plantarum Rariorum,* issued in parts from 1728 to 1736, is collected by others besides natural history fans. The colouring is feeble and the plates have historical rather than aesthetic or botanic appeal. Perhaps non-botanists should be left to pay the £1,000 ($2,600) or more that is often asked for a set.

During the seventeenth and eighteenth centuries—and indeed till much later—botany was still regarded as a branch of medicine, as in the first English monograph on mistletoe, by Sir John Colbatch, issued in 1720. The title reads: *A Dissertation Concerning Mistletoe: A most Wonderful Specifick Remedy for the Cure of Convulsive Distempers.* This is one of several treatises on plants belonging to the same period. Though the modest collector has to forgo the pleasures of the coloured-plate books, he can enjoy rounding up a selection of such items at much lower cost. They should not rise above grade (h) in the foreseeable future and give a fascinating insight to the medical ideas of the time.

The interest in trees which emerged in the seventeenth century was also utilitarian. Some of it was medical (William Cole, in *Adam in Eden*, 1657, wrote: 'Wall-nuts have the perfect Signature of the Head: The outer husk or green Covering, represent the *Pericranium*, or outward skin of the skull, whereon the hair groweth, and therefore salt made of those husks or barks, are exceeding good for wounds in the head'), but for the most part the concern was with the uses of timber. John Evelyn, the diarist, wrote of trees as both useful and beautiful things in his *Silva; or, a Discourse of Forest Trees and the Propagation of Timber in His Majesty's Dominions*, issued in two parts in 1664 and now usually bound in one volume. The first edition of this splendid early study of arboriculture may be available in grade (b), but there can also be found in grade (h) a fine edition published at York in 1776, with thirty-eight beautiful copper-engraved plates, well worth a place in any library.

By far and away the most important English botanist contemporary with Evelyn was John Ray (1627-1705). He is regarded as the father of systematic botany, for he took the first steps towards establishing a natural method of classifying plants according to families. If the beauty of his books equalled their scholarship they would be beyond price. As it is, his *Flora*, 1665, and *Catalogus Plantarum Angliae*, 1670, are each grade (a) and his greatest work, the *Historia Plantarum*, three volumes, 1686-8 and 1704, is grade (F).

Robert John Thornton (1768-1837) could be regarded as a John Ray in reverse. His scholarship is deficient, but his great book is renowned for the beauty of its plates. Thornton was a physician who became obsessed with the idea of producing a book which would be a lasting monument to the genius of Linnaeus, the Swedish natural historian. He engaged some of the most highly-qualified artists of his day to paint the original pictures for the plates, with a team of twelve experienced engravers to interpret the paintings. Every plate, done in mezzotint or aquatint, colour-printed, and finished by hand in water-colour, is a masterpiece of its kind.

Thornton, who himself did the illustration of roses, was not content with straightforward delineations of the chosen subjects. He insisted that the flowers should be tastefully placed against appropriate backgrounds. There are, or should be, twenty-eight flower-pieces in the book, besides a portrait of Linnaeus in Lapp costume and several other engravings. The title of the whole work is *The New Sexual System of Linnaeus*, but the section with the illustrations in colour is *The Temple of Flora*, which was also published separately. The entire undertaking appeared serially between 1799 and 1807, but the priority of the various issues is still in some doubt. The most authoritative information on this aspect of the book is to be found in *Flower and Fruit Prints of the Eighteenth and Early Nineteenth Centuries*, by G. Dunthorne, published in a limited edition in 1938. A complete early issue of *The New Sexual System of Linnaeus* might be had for under £2,000 ($5,200), but investors might like to know that it has more than doubled its price in ten years, providing the equivalent of a dividend of 10 per cent per annum. The price is sure to keep on rising, but possibly not at this high rate. In their author's own lifetime, the parts cost only a guinea, or later 25s (£1.25) each, but did not find a ready sale. Thornton tried to sell some by lottery, but even that effort was unsuccessful. He lost a great deal of money on his life's work and died in poverty.

A more successful illustrated botanical work was begun twelve years before *The New Sexual System*. It was conceived by William Curtis (1746-99), but even he could hardly have imagined that his work would be continued to the present day. In February, 1787, the first volume of the *Botanical Magazine* appeared. It was an instant success and brought some much-needed money to Curtis, its originator, writer and editor. In the course of the previous ten years he had produced the two fat folio volumes of the *Flora Londinensis,* 1777 and 1787, which gave illustrations and descriptions of the wild plants growing in and around London. He had given up his work as demonstrator and keeper of the garden of the Society of Apothecaries to prepare this *Flora* and was deeply disappointed when it failed to pay its way. In the *Botanical Magazine* he courted popular support by featuring showy exotic plants instead of the humble natives of the *Flora.*

The *Botanical Magazine* was in a flourishing condition when Curtis died, so it was willingly taken over by John Sims (1749-1831) and later by Sir William J. Hooker (1785-1865). Sir William was succeeded as editor by his son, Sir Joseph D. Hooker (1817-1911). When Sir Joseph resigned at the age of 87, other editors were found and publication continued until the end of 1920, but by then it was running at a loss. With the last part of volume 146, it looked like the end of the road. However, H. J. Elwes, a keen naturalist, and some friends bought the copyright and made it over to the Royal Horticultural Society, which capable body has been responsible for publication ever since. It has not appeared with the regularity that it did in Curtis's day, but it has been kept alive, a proud and beautiful monument to the botanists and horticulturalists of England.

The owner of a complete set of the *Botanical Magazine* from 1787 to date would be a man to be envied. Long runs do become available from time to time, but the set would be costly to acquire as the usual price for single volumes varies between £15 and £30 ($39 and $78) according to age and condition.

There was great botanical activity throughout the nineteenth century. Anybody combing the shelves of the decreasing number of provincial secondhand bookshops could acquire dozens of small books with pleasing coloured illustrations of flowers native and exotic, some with the colouring done by hand, some printed by the Baxter or other process. The individual cost of these books should be small, though some non-specialist booksellers who are moderate in their charges for other books are inclined to overprice some quite insignificant botanical books, especially those with coloured plates.

In the 1850s and sixties, the London publishers, Routledge, Warne & Routledge, produced *Reeve's Popular Natural History,* a series of twenty-four square 16mo books in green, blue, or brown bead-grained cloth, intended to be read by young people. Every book contained twenty coloured plates of variable quality. Ten of the twenty-four dealt with botanical subjects. It should still be possible to build up a complete set for little more than £24 ($60). This is only one example of what the modest collector could achieve in the field of natural history.

The influence of the Sowerby family on nineteenth-century popular natural history is quite important. James Sowerby (1757-1822) published the thirty-six volumes of his *English Botany* between 1790 and 1813, after giving up his share in the work of illustrating the *Botanical Magazine*. He did over 2,500 drawings for *English Botany* as well as writing the text. A set of this work would be in grade (H). The second edition is considered inferior and is worth considerably less. The third edition, edited by J. T. B. Syme, or J. T. Boswell as he later called himself, and published between 1863 and 1892 in thirteen volumes, sometimes sells at auctions in grade (e). James' grandson, John E. Sowerby, published his *British Wild Flowers,* with ninety coloured plates, in 1890 and this book is (h). James's son, George B. Sowerby, was a careful portrayer of shells.

The work of Evelyn was continued last century by P. W.

Watson with *Dendrologia Britannica,* two volumes, 1825, and by John C. Loudon (1783-1843) with *Arboretum et Fruticetum Britannicum,* eight volumes, 1838. Both books are grade (I), with the Watson as the slightly dearer. Though there are 172 coloured plates in *Dendrologia* and 412 in *Arboretum,* those in the latter work are inferior in finish. On the other hand, Loudon's book is the more informative and those who want the work purely for study would do well to seek out the second edition, with uncoloured plates, published in 1844 and probably in grade (h) or (g).

One of the most attractive books on fruit trees produced last century is the three-volume *Pomologia Britannica* of John Lindley (1799-1865), with 152 hand-coloured plates, published in 1841. Lindley was a distinguished botanist and horticulturist whose name is commemorated in the fine Lindley Library of the Royal Horticultural Society. If a present-day admirer of Lindley would like a representative first edition of one of Lindley's works and cannot afford the *Pomologia* in grade (G), he might find a first of the author's *Ladies' Botany,* 1834, in grade (i).

As botany freed itself of its medical ties and became a subject of scientific study in its own right, the desire to find out more about exotic floras became even stronger. The era of the plant-hunters had begun. While Joseph D. Hooker was sailing the southern seas with HMS *Erebus* and *Terror* (later commanded by Franklin, as mentioned in a previous chapter), collecting material for his *Flora Antarctica,* 1844-7, Robert Fortune (1813-80) was preparing his expedition to China, which ended shortly before the publication of his *Three Years' Wanderings in Northern China,* 1847. Fortune was sent to the Far East by the Botanical Society of London and returned with a wealth of information and specimens. His literary style is a little rugged, but his book is well worth a place in a natural history collection if found in grade (i).

J. D. Hooker forsook Antarctica for the Himalayas on behalf of Kew Gardens and the first fruits of his expedition was *Rhododendrons of Sikkim-Himalaya,* edited by his father, Sir W. J. Hooker, and published in parts between 1849 and 1851, with thirty hand-coloured plates. The complete book should be within grade (H). J. D. Hooker's *Himalayan Journals* in two volumes, with coloured lithographs, followed in 1854 and is now grade (f), but the best was to come in the following year, with the beautiful *Illustrations of Himalayan Plants.* This contains twenty-four splendid coloured plates prepared by W. H. Fitch from Hooker's original sketches. About £220 ($570) would be a fair price for the book if the plates are in fine condition. Hooker's other important plant-hunting book is the *Flora of Australia,* 1859, grade (b).

Many other plant-hunters have been active since the expeditions of Fortune and Hooker; some of these will be dealt with in the next chapter, but the attractive work of J. E. Brown should be noted now: *The Forest Flora of South Australia,* the nine parts of which, in folio size, were published at Adelaide between 1882 and 1890. A good set should be grade (H).

The earliest printed books on birds were concerned with the hunters and the hunted—the hawks and falcons on one side and the gamebirds and waterfowl on the other, though the hunted of those days also included a miscellaneous selection of passerines and other small birds. Even when ornithology was put on a scientific basis, the favourite instrument of the field naturalist was the gun. This was responsible for the temporary extinction of the osprey in Britain and probably hastened the total extinction of other birds in several parts of the world. Salvation came with the high-speed camera which made possible the close observation of birds without the need for killing.

Scientific ornithology can be considered as beginning in

1676 with the posthumous publication of *Ornithologiae Libri Tres* by Francis Willughby, the whole work 'recognovit, digessit, supplevit J. Raius.' Rightly honoured by collectors, this book is now at least grade (a), but preference is given to the first English edition, published two years later as *The Ornithology of F. Willughby*. Besides being editor, as of the first edition, John Ray also translated this edition and was the probable author of the 'three considerable discourses' which were added: *Of the Art of Fowling, Of the Ordering of Singing Birds* and *Of Falconry*. This is a grade (H) book.

No other book of such importance to ornithologists was published for more than a hundred years afterwards, but there is plenty of material for the collector in the interim period. John Moore, a doctor who specialised in treating people for parasitic worms, had his *The Columbarium, or the Pigeon House* published in 1735. This natural history of tame pigeons is scarce and, although a small book without much appeal to the eye, is grade (g). A new edition, sometimes found in cloth, sometimes in paper covers, was edited by W. G. Tegetmeier and published in 1879. Even it is elusive, but it might be found somewhere, priced about £2.50 ($6.50). There are various twelvemos of the eighteenth century on bird-fancying for which the collector should keep his eyes open. One example is *The New and Complete Bird-Fancyer*, an anonymous work, undated, but published in 1784. It and similar books should cost no more than £4 ($10).

Though of some ornithological importance in its time, *A Portrait of Rare Birds, from the Menagery of Osterly Park*, published in two volumes in 1794 and 1799 (the second volume is undated), is now valued for the hundred hand-coloured plates it contains rather than the information it gives. It was the work of Willam Hayes, who went to Osterley Park in the former county of Middlesex to collect his material. At that time the house, designed by Robert Adam, was still relatively new and the menagerie was at its most flourishing. The book in its two volumes is grade (F). In the same period, John W. Lewin was preparing his *Birds of Great Britain* in eight volumes issued between 1796 and 1801. Although this book has 336 hand-coloured plates of birds and their eggs and is the first important avian fauna of Britain to be illustrated in colour, its market value is only about half that of Hayes's book. Lewin followed his work in Britain with a *Natural History of Birds of New South Wales*, a large folio with twenty-six coloured plates, published in 1822. This is much more highly prized than his British bird book, being grade (C). Lewin was also an entomologist and produced one volume of a projected *Insects of Great Britain*, with 46 coloured plates, in 1795. He completed his single volume *Natural History of Lepidopterous Insects of New South Wales* for publication in 1822. The British insect book may be grade (a), but the Australian one sells well up in grade (F).

The most celebrated bird artists of all time were John James Audubon (1780-1851) and John Gould (1804-81). As an American of French origin, Audubon specialised in the birds of his home continent. A copy of the first edition of his *Birds of America*, 1827-38, fetched £90,000 ($225,000) at auction in 1969, so the price would presumably be higher today. Other early editions of Audubon are less expensive, but still beyond the ordinary man's reach. A facsimile, with introduction and descriptive text by William Vogt, was published in 1937 and contained 500 coloured reproductions of the original plates, including sixty-five from editions later than the first. This edition might be found in grade (h) and a later two-volume facsimile, produced in America and Britain in 1966, may be in grade (g).

The Englishman, John Gould, began his long career as a bird artist with *The Birds of Europe*, five volumes, issued between 1832 and 1837. Containing 448 coloured plates, its present value is in the region of £2,000 ($5,200) as is his ***Birds of Great Britain,*** with 367 coloured plates, issued in twenty-five parts between 1862-73. His ***Birds of Asia,*** seven volumes, edited by R. B. Sharpe, 1850-83, with 530 coloured plates, is even less accessible to the ordinary collector at £7,500 ($19,500), and his ***Birds of Australia,*** 8 volumes including supplement, 1840-60, is in much the same class at $A13,400 (£6,030-$15,678). The humble buyer may gain a rough idea of the glories of Gould from a book published by Methuen, London, in 1967 and titled ***Birds of Australia: 160 colour-plates from the lithographs of John Gould,*** text by A. Rutgers. This was remaindered in 1970, but already seems to have gone underground. Even so, an unearthed copy should not cost more than £2 ($5).

Among books on the birds of Britain there is sometimes confusion between ***British Birds*** in six volumes, 1851-7, with many later editions, by the Rev F. O. Morris, and ***British Game Birds and Wildfowl,*** one volume, 1855, by Beverley R. Morris. The authors are quite distinct, as are the books. The Rev F. O. Morris' work has 358 hand-coloured plates and Beverley Morris' has only sixty. However, the Beverley Morris is grade (b) while the six volumes of F. O. Morris are (f) or below. Three volumes of ***Nests and Eggs,*** by the same author and uniformly bound, are sometimes added to the F. O. Morris bird volumes, but the extra three are unsatisfactory. The plates, reproduced by lithography, make many of the nests look as if they had been built of seaweed.

This is not the whole story of ornithological books. The collector can find further help in ***A Bibliography of British Ornithology from the Earliest Time to the End of 1912*** by W. M. Mullens and H. K. Swann, published in 1917, with a supplement in 1923, and in the same authors' ***A Geographical Bibliography of British Ornithology to the End of 1918,*** published in 1920. In the latter work the authors had the help of M.

Jourdain and others.

Entomologists are not so well served with books of the Audubon and Gould class. At least this makes things slightly easier for the bibliophile who does not possess a licence to print money. Reference has already been made to Lewin's two insect books. John Henry Leech's *Butterflies from China, Japan and Corea*, three volumes, 1892-4, deserves to be mentioned with them and is in grade (e). William Kirby's *European Butterflies and Moths*, 61 coloured plates, 1882, has a reputation high enough to put it in grade (h), but the illustrations are rather disappointing. The same may be said of such books as W. G. Wright's *The Butterflies of the West Coast of the U.S.A.*, 1906, which may be grade (h), and *The Butterflies of Australia*, Sydney, 1914, by G. A. Waterhouse and G. Lyell, which is (f), or even (e). A. A. Lisney's *A Bibliography of British Lepidoptera 1608-1799* was privately printed at the Chiswick Press in 1960 and, though without coloured plates, is as lovely as it is informative. It is scarce and well worth its place in grade (h). This book gives information about *The Aurelian*, 1766, by Moses Harris (1731-85), a most desirable insect book with forty-one quaint yet accurate coloured plates—grade (E)—but there is, of course, no place in it for such important early American works as the three volumes of Thomas Say's *American Entomology*, with fifty-four coloured plates, issued from Philadelphia between 1824 and 1828 (H). Say (1787-1834), a Quaker, has been called the father of American entomology.

The two important natural history works of Thomas Bewick, already mentioned in Chapter 5, should not be overlooked. *The General History of Quadrupeds* was first published at Newcastle-upon-Tyne in 1790 and *The History of British Birds* at the same place, in two volumes, 1797 and 1804. The *Quadrupeds* is grade (e), but *British Birds* is likely to be (H). Other early editions of these works will cost very little less if the engravings are clean and well printed. An unknown author took his cue from Bewick and produced a *Natural History of Quadrupeds* in 1796. Though it has forty-four hand-coloured plates it is not so eagerly pursued and is grade (h). One of the most desirable nineteenth-century books with plates of wild animals is William C. Harris's *Portraits of the Game and Wild Animals of Southern Africa*, 1840. This is folio size and contains thirty hand-coloured lithographs fine enough to earn the book a place in grade (A). On the whole, animals are not well served as regards illustrated books until modern times, and marine animals fare worst of all. There is, however, at least one worthy work which caters for them—*Marine Mammals of the North-western Coast of North America* by Charles M. Scammon, San Francisco, 1874, with excellent lithographs. It is in grade (d).

God banished mankind from the Garden of Eden and Darwin banished the Garden of Eden from mankind. In November 1859, Charles Darwin (1809-82) published *The Origin of Species by means of Natural Selection*, thereby striking orthodox religion a blow from which it has not yet wholly recovered. Darwin was a clear thinker and a scientist of genius, but the theory which he propounded in his book did not spring Athene-like from his head, nor was he its 'onlie begetter'. He assembled facts which were already known, put them in logical order and drew the conclusions towards which some of his contemporaries were reaching and from which others were shrinking. For 200 years, geological and biological studies had been moving inexorably towards natural selection as an explanation of the diversity of living forms, and the pace had considerably accelerated in the nineteenth century. In 1843 and 1846, the remarkable Scottish polymath, Robert Chambers, published anonymously his two volumes of *Vestiges of the Natural History of Creation, and the Explanation.*

Though working with insufficient evidence, Chambers anticipated Darwin in several particulars. In the chapter which explains his hypothesis of 'the progress of organic creation', Chambers declares: 'If it has pleased Providence to arrange that one species should give birth to another, until the second highest gave birth to man, who is the very highest; be it so, it is our part to admire and to submit.' These were brave words for 1843, even if the author did not put his name to them.

Working in the remote Malay Archipelago, Alfred Russel Wallace reached the same conclusions as Darwin at the same time, but withheld publication of his findings so that Darwin should have the credit which Wallace considered was Darwin's due.

Samuel Wilberforce (1805-73), Bishop of Oxford, became one of Darwin's most trenchant opponents, though many of the clergy and laity of all denominations were equally incensed by the Darwinian theory which seemed to strike at the roots of Christianity. If the story of the Creation and the Fall was not literally true, the sacrifice of Christ on the Cross and the redemption He offered became meaningless—or so they thought. Most churchmen are now reconciled to Darwinism and are prepared to share Chambers' attitude, but some still find difficulties.

There is no evidence that the depression which caused Hugh Miller (1802-56) to shoot himself was connected with a conflict between his fundamentalist religion and his geological researches, but in his books, *Footprints of the Creator*, 1850, and *The Testimony of the Rocks*, published posthumously in 1857, he sometimes seems to be fighting a rearguard action against the real testimony of the rocks. Perhaps his intellect pushed him on an evolutionary path which his religion would not allow him to tread.

The object of this digression is to suggest a field of activity for the natural history collector who cannot afford the high prices of colour-plate books. A collection which records the rise of Darwinism and the concomitant wrangles and attempted refutations should not be too costly to acquire. Even if the most important books in this field are too dear, there is still plenty of interesting material to be had at low prices.

The centrepiece of such a collection would be a first edition of Darwin's *Origin of Species.* The date on the title-page, 1859, should be sufficient evidence of a first edition, but it would be as well to check that there is a folding diagram at page 117 and thirty-two pages of advertisements at the end. The desirable condition is in original cloth, with half-title. At a price high in grade (F), this would be the dearest item in the collection. *The Descent of Man,* 1871, Darwin's other great book, was published in two volumes in 1871. Two issues of the first edition are recognised. The first issue has a list of errata on the verso of the title-page to volume two; the second issue has no errata, but lists the author's other works on the versos of both title-pages. The first issue should be grade (a) and the second, grade (c). The rest of Darwin's works should be more cheaply acquired in first editions, mainly in grade (g). These include his first book, which has a long title, usually abbreviated to *Journal of Researches* or *The Voyage of the 'Beagle',* 1839, *Variation of Animals and Plants under Domestication,* 1868, and the *Expression of the Emotions in Man and Animals,* 1872.

Thomas Henry Huxley (1825-95) was Darwin's great champion and the inventor of the term 'agnostic'. His books may be had for relatively little outlay. The dearest would probably be *The Evidence as to Man's Place in Nature,* 1868, at £12. In first editions, most of his others should cost about £4 ($10) or less. Some of the material in *The Principles of Geology,* three volumes, 1830-3, by Sir Charles Lyell (1797-1875) helped to point the way for Darwin, and Lyell's *Geological Evidences of the Antiquity of Man,* 1863, gave sound support to the theory of natural selection. Both books are grade (f). Chambers's *Vestiges of the Natural History of Creation* and Miller's *Footprints* and *Testimony* might be found for as little as £2 ($5) each.

The discoveries and controversies of the mid-nineteenth century gave a stimulus to scientific studies, reflected in the increased output of books on geology, zoology and allied subjects. The London publishers, Kegan Paul, Trench, Trübner & Co Ltd, went some way to meet the demand with their Internationl Scientific Series, begun in 1871 and continued until World War I. The series is distinguished by a uniform binding of fine sand-grained red cloth with bold gilt titling on the spine. Several important works on aspects of biology and other sciences were published for the first time in this series, which could be brought together at a cost of between 80p ($2) and £2.50 ($6.50) a volume. The series began with *Forms of Water* by John Tyndall (1820-93), who was a mountaineer as well as a railway engineer and physicist. At least thirty volumes in the International Scientific Series could be considered as pertaining to natural history.

Earlier, Sir William Jardine (1800-74) completed his Naturalist's Library, a series of forty volumes by different authors, concerned with animal life. Several were written by Jardine himself. The small volumes were bound in uniform purplish-brown grained cloth and contained hand-coloured plates, some of indifferent quality, but others, especially those in the two volumes on parrots (by Edward Lear) and the two humming-bird volumes, are beautifully done. The series was first published between the years 1833 and 1843 and a full set may now be well into grade (H), though only a few years ago it would have been (f). If the volumes were to be collected one by one, a few of the least attractive should be available at £1.25 ($3) and the others would rise according to desirability until the humming-bird volumes were reached, probably in grade (g) for the two. A few ill-informed dealers ask much more because they confuse the ordinary volumes with a special large-paper edition of the humming-birds which is justifiably grade (e).

One of the most rewarding of present-day series to collect is Collins' New Naturalist, begun in 1945 and still continuing. Some of the most distinguished naturalists of our time have contributed to the series, every volume of which is well produced, with good colour plates in nearly every case. The green cloth of the covers has a tendency to fade, even under the fine dust-wrappers, so the books should be shelved away from strong light. Among the best of the series—and therefore the most difficult to find—are No 9, *A Country Parish* by A. W. Boyd; No 27, *Dartmoor* by Harvey and St-Ledger-Gordon and No 29, *The Folklore of Birds* by A. Armstrong. Apart from the general series, several special monographs have been produced, the most sought-after of all being James Fisher's *The Fulmar*, No 6 in the monograph series. Collectors of natural history books should have a special regard for *The Art of Botanical Illustration* by Wilfrid Blunt, No 14 in the general series. Beautifully illustrated in colour, with the facts clearly stated and documented, it is a model for all books of its kind.

Many of the volumes have been reprinted or issued in revised editions, but all are worthy of being collected in first editions, preferably in the dust-wrappers, which are among the best in modern commercial book production. Prices will vary greatly, from £6 ($15) for a fine copy of Fisher's *The Fulmar* to £1 ($2.60) for the least popular titles. Although the series is primarily concerned with Britain, many long runs of the New Naturalist have found places on the shelves of American collectors.

Some bibliophiles specialise in collecting books on the natural history of selected small areas. The most celebrated work of this kind is *The Natural History of Selborne*, by Gilbert White (1720-93). The first edition, with nine engravings, appeared in 1789, but since then there has been a profusion of others, abridged, enlarged, adapted, edited, annotated, illustrated in colour, with steel engravings, woodcuts, lithographs, photographs and line drawings. The gathering together of all these has already been suggested as a pleasant task for the admirer of Gilbert White. The vademecum here is Edward A. Martin's *A Bibliography of Gilbert White*, preferably in the revised edition of 1934.

John Aubrey wrote the natural histories of two English counties. His *Natural History of Surrey* was published in five volumes in 1719 and is now grade (H). His *Natural History of Wiltshire* was edited for the Wiltshire Archaeological Society by J. E. Jackson and published in 1862, but a recent reprint of this edition, published by David & Charles, is now available. In *The Old English Farming Books*, 1947, G. E. Fussell mentions an earlier edition of this Wiltshire natural history, produced in 1685, during Aubrey's lifetime, under the title of *Memoirs of Naturall Remarques in the County of Wilts.*, but no copies of this are known to exist.

A pattern for all county ornithologies was provided by J. A. Walpole-Bond when he produced his *A History of the Sussex Birds*, three volumes, 1938, well illustrated with fifty-three colour plates. It should be grade (h). The model county flora is *The Flora of Gloucestershire*, 1948, edited by the Rev H. J. Riddelsdell, G. W. Hedley and W. R. Price, and published by the Cotteswold Naturalists' Field Club. It is grade (h) too. Some other counties and regions are almost as well served, but there are many which lack worthy ornithologies and floras. The first steps towards providing these might be taken by collecting such relevant printed material as is presently available.

CHAPTER TEN

Farming, Gardening, Country Life

> Fortunatus et ille, deos qui novit agrestes,
> Panaque Silvanumque senem nymphasque sorores.
> *Georgics*, Bk II: lines 493-4

Virgil tells us that the man is lucky who has known the gods of the countryside: Pan and gnarled Silvanus and the sister nymphs. We cannot all be thus fortunate, but we can always strike up a vicarious acquaintance with the rustic deities by way of books—and in the end the fireside farmer may be less careworn than his practical counterpart. Certainly the collecting of books on farming, gardening and country life is one of the pleasantest aspects of bibliophily.

The oldest farming book printed in English is *The Boke of Husbandry,* printed about 1510 and believed to have been translated by Walter of Henley from a thirteenth-century tract ascribed to Robert Grosseteste. It is a robber's rather than a collector's piece as the only known copy is in Cambridge University Library. However, it is available in facsimile in *The Manor Farm,* 1931, by F. H. Cripps-Day, along with a facsimile of *The Boke of Thrift, 1589*. Cripps-Day's book is probably grade (h).

The first undeniably English book on farming is Sir John Fitzherbert's *Boke of Husbandry,* 1523. This is still sometimes catalogued as being by Sir Anthony Fitzherbert, Sir John's brother, and G. E. Fussell (*The Old English Farming Books*, 1947) is an Anthony-ite. But the *Short Title Catalogue* gives Sir John, and most bibliographers follow this ruling. The first edition is so rare that it is unlikely ever to come on the market, but the book was popular for many years and there are a few later editions to be had, probably in grade (H) or above.

In so far as he gave his agricultural advice in verse, Thomas Tusser (1527-80) is entitled to be called the English Virgil. His doggerel hardly matches up to the Latin poet's hexameters, though there is some good sense in its quaintness. Tusser's *A hundreth good pointes of husbandrie* was published in 1557 and must have had some success, for the author followed it sixteen years later with *Five hundreth good Pointes of Husbandry, united to as many of good Huswifery*. Both Tussers are rare and best collected in late editions. A reprint of the *Five Hundreth Pointes*, edited by William Mavor, was published in 1812 and is grade (h) today. E. V. Lucas edited another edition in 1931, bound in leather, and now grade (g). In the same year there appeared *Thomas Tusser, His Good Points of Husbandry*, collated and edited by Dorothy Hartley. This contains a facsimile of *A Hundreth Good Points* from the British Museum copy and the text of the *Five Hundreth Points*, as well as a life of Tusser with his family tree and notes on various editions of the books. There is no reason why this book should cost more than £4 ($10) and it should be available for less.

Gervase Markham (1568-1637) is the next agriculturist of importance. He was a prolific writer and a great borrower of other people's material. Presumably he wanted his memorial to be *Markham's Maister-Peece: contayning all knowledge belonging to a Smith, Farrier or Horse-Leech*, 1610. It is certainly a favourite in the salerooms, where it is a familiar grade (D) item. The *Maister-Peece* was reprinted at intervals well into the eighteenth century and some of these later editions are not liable to rise out of grade (f) for some considerable time.

As might be expected of one who had served as a captain in Cromwell's army, William Blith's contributions to the literature of farming are soundly practical. He wrote two books, the second being an extended version of the first. *The English Improver* was published in 1649 and *The English Improver Improved* in 1652. In this case the later book, though sometimes regarded as a second edition, is preferable to the other, covering, as it does, a much wider area of farming. Many of Blith's ideas were ahead of their time and had to wait a hundred years before being fully put into practice. There are still doubts as to the acceptable collation of the 1652 edition. Some copies have three engraved plates, and one such was sold at Sotheby's in 1968, but most copies have only two. The copy from the Britwell Court Library was stated to have the three plates when originally sold, but when put up for sale again in 1966 it was found to contain only two, like most of the others. Was the third plate bound in special copies for a favoured few, or are all those which lack it to be considered defective? Nobody has yet given a definite ruling, so that two-plate and three-plate copies are almost equally desirable and are grade (d).

John Forster's book is another milestone in farming history: *England's Happiness increased: or a sure and easie remedie against all succeeding dear Years; by a plantation of the roots called Potatoes*. Issued in 1664, it is the first important English work on the cultivation of the potato. Andrew Yarranton (1616-84) wrote *England's Improvement by Sea and Land* and had it published in two parts in 1677-81. It was a wide-ranging book, but ultimately less important than *The Great Improvement of Lands by Clover*, his earlier work, published in 1663. Its importance lies in its advocacy of the cropping of clover as is done today, but the idea was allowed to lie fallow for a hundred years. Fussell (*op cit*) seems to doubt the existence of a book actually titled *The Great Improvement of Lands by Clover* as he was unable to trace a copy. The earliest edition of which he knew was published at Worcester in 1663 as *The Improvement Improved, by a second edition of the great improvement of lands by clover*. This latter work, as well as *England's Improvement*, is grade (a), but there are no price records of the edition untraced by Fussell.

Before the end of the seventeenth century, the first agricultural journal had been attempted, under the editorship of John Houghton (d 1705). It was called *A Collection of Letters for the Improvement of Husbandry and Trade*. The first series ran from 1681 to 1683 and the second from 1692 until 1702. A complete set would probably be graded as (H).

Mentioned rather slightingly by Fussell, the writings of Richard Bradley (d 1732) nevertheless give a fair picture of the farming practice of his day. Bradley was not a man of great scholarly attainments and is notorious for having pushed himself into the chair of botany at Cambridge University. He wrote voluminously and his *General Treatise of Husbandry*, 1721-2, grade (g), adequately sums up his ideas on agriculture.

Jethro Tull (1674-1741) is a far more important writer. A barrister turned practical farmer, he was not content to accept the traditional methods of cultivation. As a result of his experiments, he invented a successful seed drill, first used for sowing pulse crops and later applied to turnips and wheat. His method of sowing allowed regular cultivation of the land by means of a horse hoe, which, he maintained, increased the fertility of the soil and largely dispensed with the need for manure. He was wrong on this point, yet his methods of tilling the soil were a great advance. He placed them before the farming public in *The New Horse-Houghing Husbandry, or an Essay on the Principles of Tillage and Vegetation*, printed for the author, 1731. Collectors take this to be a single-edition book, quite separate from *The Horse-Hoing Husbandry*, folio, 1733, but Fussell (*More Old English Farming Books*, 1950) regards this latter as a reprint of the earlier work. Both have much the same price on their heads, well in grade (H).

As the eighteenth century advanced, farming books came thicker and faster from the presses. The agrarian revolution was under way throughout England, keeping pace more or less with the Industrial Revolution. Scottish farming lagged pathetically behind. One of the pioneers of land improvement in that country was Sir Archibald Grant of Monymusk who is credited with having written *The Practical Farmer's Pocket Companion*, published at Aberdeen in 1756. The rapid advance in Scottish farming after that date was to affect the agricultural writing of the next century.

New needs were met in the larger output of farming books. Robert Smith filled a gap in 1768 with his *Universal Directory for Taking Alive and Destroying Rats* (and all other kinds of four-footed and winged vermin). Other days have brought other methods, but this book, in grade (g) is perhaps the only classic in its field.

Before the end of the century, two outstanding farming writers had emerged—Arthur Young (1741-1820) and William Marshall (1745-1818). By all accounts, Marshall was the better farmer, but his literary efforts have not achieved the renown of those of Young. The persistent prompting of Marshall helped to establish the Board of Agriculture in 1793, but it was Young who was appointed its first secretary, much to Marshall's chagrin.

Marshall methodically examined the state of agriculture in various parts of England then wrote a series of books on his findings. The first was *The Rural Economy of Norfolk*, 1787. Like its successors in the series, it was in two volumes. The *Rural Economy of Yorkshire* was published in the following year, then came *The Rural Economy of Gloucestershire* (with a section on Wiltshire), 1789, *Midland Counties*, 1790, *West of England*, 1796, and *Southern Counties*, 1798. One would hope to find these priced within the (h) grade, with variations according to condition.

Marshall was prolific and wrote many other books, but for sheer volume of output he cannot compare with Arthur Young, who is credited with 250 books and pamphlets. Some of his earlier works were the products of tours of inspection which he made in various parts of the country, the first being *A Six Weeks Tour through the Southern Counties of England and Wales*, 1768. The next was *A Six Months Tour through the North of England*, 1770, but best of all was *Travels, during the Years 1787, 1788 and 1789. Undertaken . . . with a view of ascertaining the Cultivation etc. of the Kingdom of France*, which was published in 1792. As such books go, this is not uncommon and should be in grade (c). The others named are (f).

Once appointed secretary of the Board of Agriculture, Young supervised the production of a series of general views of the agriculture of British counties and wrote six of them himself: *General View of the Agriculture of the County of Suffolk*, 1794, *Lincoln*, 1799, *Hertford*, 1804, *Norfolk*, 1804, *Essex* (two volumes), 1807, and *Oxford*, 1809. All were soon reprinted, but all first and early editions are grade (h). Reprints of editions of the Suffolk, Lincoln, Norfolk and Oxford volumes are now published by David & Charles, along with others in the series, including *Sussex*, 1813, by the Rev Arthur Young, son of the great Arthur Young.

Young's works carry agriculture into the nineteenth century, where we meet another travelling agriculturist, the famous William Cobbett (1762-1835). For a time he served as a sergeant-major in the army and brought some of the characteristics of his rank back with him into civilian life. Politically he began as a Tory and ended as a Radical. The work most often linked with his name is *Rural Rides*, first published in book form in 1830, reprinted from his *Weekly Political Register* which ran from 1802 until his death. Cobbett held decided views about most things and did not care whom he offended. In *Rural Rides*, within a few pages, he manages to insult Scotsmen and the Cotswolds, but in a sergeant-majorly sort of way, and, as the bark of warrant officers is generally worse than their bite, a Scot who happened to be a Cotswold man by adoption would surely forgive him.

Though classed here as agricultural, *Rural Rides* is also topographical, political and a great deal else besides, well deserving its place as an English classic. Grade (d) is a fair placing for a good first edition, and the fine three-volume edition of 1930, edited by G. D. H. and M. Cole, should be grade (e). There are many other editions and abridgements to be had quite cheaply.

Cobbett was not a modest man, as can be seen from the title of one of his books: *A Treatise on Cobbett's Corn*, 1828. Having seen in America how useful maize could be as a fodder plant, he conceived the idea of popularising it in England under the name of Cobbett's corn. Climate as much as conservatism thwarted his efforts, but the book is still collected and is grade (g). He was a genuine friend of the poor and in *Cottage Economy*, 1822, he tried to show how cottagers could make the most of the little plots of land at their disposal. It should be grade (i). There are many other books by Cobbett worth collecting and looking for at low prices.

Anybody seeking a painstaking survey of world agriculture up to 1825 should find what he wants in John C. Loudon's *Encyclopaedia of Agriculture*, published in that year. Within its 1,226 pages, Loudon packs a staggering amount of information covering agricultural botany, zoology and chemistry, the cultivation of food and forage crops, and the breeding and training of farm animals (including the esculent frog!). Besides giving general surveys of farming in Europe, Asia, Africa and the Americas, the book fits in studies of ancient agricultural methods and provides detailed reviews of the state of farming in most of the British and Irish counties. It concludes with helpful bibliographies of agricultural books in English, French, German and Italian. Loudon was one of Scotland's gifts to England in return for the vital help in land improvement received during the eighteenth century. A copy of the *Encyclopaedia of Agriculture* should not cost more than £16 ($42) today.

In all probability the best agricultural library in Britain is that of the Rothamsted Experimental Station, Harpenden. Its *Library Catalogue of Printed Books and Pamphlets on Agriculture published between 1471 and 1840*, compiled by Mary S. Aslin, was first published in 1926, but appeared in a second, much enlarged edition in 1940, and a supplement was issued in 1949. Few collectors could hope to approach this library in completeness, but many take it as a guide in the formation of their own collections.

After 1840, the number of books on farming published year by year makes it almost impossible to give the collector a lead. For those who combine an interest in Victoriana with farming there is *Breeds of Domestic Animals of the British Islands*, two volumes, folio, 1842, by David Low (1786-1859). Though their manner of execution makes them period pieces, the fifty-six coloured plates in the volumes are fine things of their kind. The book is grade (H) for the two volumes. Somebody who would rather have an imposing set of books than Loudon's closely-printed one-volume encyclopaedia might like to acquire *The Rural Encyclopaedia*, in four large quarto volumes, edited by the Rev J. M. Wilson and first published in 1847. It is prized by industrial/agrarian archaeologists for its illustrations of Victorian farm machinery, and is grade (i).

There is so much of interest to the collector among the plethora of later farming books that he must be highly selective. The period since 1840 has seen the development of mechanical farming and artificial fertilisers. Both were of paramount help in feeding the rapidly-growing populations of the last hundred years, but the fertilisers and to some extent the machinery are now being blamed for having contributed to our present-day problems of pollution and erosion. The acquisition of certain key books, such as *Organic Chemistry in its Application to Agriculture and Physiology*, 1840, by Justus Liebig (1803-73), and J. C. Nesbit's *On Agricultural Chemistry and the Nature and Properties of Peruvian Guano*, 1854, could provide the basis for an unusual collection on fertilisers. Neither would be high in grade (i).

Gardening is not always easy to separate from farming and many of the early books on agriculture could well be placed in horticultural collections. One of the first English books exclusively devoted to gardening is *Paradisi in Sole Paradisus Terrestris*, 1629, by John Parkinson (1567-1650). Parkinson seems to have been a cheerful, one might almost say a sunny man, for the title of his book translates as 'Park-in-sun's earthly paradise'—*paradisus* meaning both park and paradise. Although he was an apothecary he was not particularly concerned with the medicinal uses of plants in this book. Its contents may best be summarised by quoting from the title-page:

> A Garden of all sorts of pleasant flowers which our English ayre will permitt to be noursed up: with a Kitchen garden of all manner of herbes, ravies, and fruites for meate or sause used with us, and an Orchard of all sorts of fruit-bearing trees and shrubbs fit for our Land, together with the right orderinge, planting, and presarving of them, and their uses and vertues.

The book is full of practical advice, a little of which still holds good. The ravies referred to are radishes. Grade (G) is not too high for the first or second (1635) editions, but a facsimile, published in 1904, should cost a good deal less—grade (h).

John Reid produced in 1683 at Edinburgh his *Scots Gardner* which provided for Scotland a book such as Parkinson had given to England. Though the first edition is the dearest, in grade (H), the most interesting is the expanded one of 1766 which contains a 'Gardener's Kalendar', a florist's vade-mecum, a practical bee-master, the Shepherd of Banbury's rules on the weather and the Earl of Haddington's treatise on forest trees. This edition may be found in grade (b) or below.

When John Evelyn, who did much for arboriculture, brought out a translation of J. de la Quintinye's *The Compleat Gard'ner* in 1693, it had long-lasting effects, though English gardeners soon modified the ideas of Quintinye, chief director of the gardens of Louis XIV of France, to suit their own requirements. A copy of this edition should be found in the (d) range. Fussell mentions another translation of this work, brought out by George London and Henry Wise in 1699, probably grade (e), but is silent on the Evelyn edition.

The craze for chinoiserie in the second half of the eighteenth century extended to landscape gardening. The architect, Sir William Chambers (1726-96), used his alleged knowledge of Chinese gardens in drawing up his *Plans of Gardens and Buildings at Kew*, 1763, a folio which is now grade (H). His later *Dissertation on Oriental Gardening*, 1772, has often been ridiculed and has only about a quarter of the value of *Plans of Gardens*, yet it was partly responsible for the willow-pattern look of several gardens of the period. It is a pity that neither Lancelot (Capability) Brown (1715-83) nor William Kent (1684-1748) left behind any substantial works on the landscaping at which they excelled.

John Abercrombie approached gardening from a severely practical angle in *Every Man His Own Gardener*, 1767. The first edition was stated to be 'by Mr. Mawe and other gardeners', but was wholly Abercrombie's work. He was shy about putting his name to the book and paid Thomas Mawe, as a better-known authority, £20 for the use of his name. *Every Man His Own Gardener* was one of the most successful gardening books of all time, running into nearly thirty editions. By 1800 the sixteenth edition had been reached; in 1824 a new edition appeared, edited by R. Forsyth; in 1845 it was revised by W. Gowans. Another new edition was issued in the 1860s, with an added treatise on drawing-room gardening by George Glenny. The final edition was published in 1879. Even then the story was not ended. Several cheap gardening guides of later dates have distinct Abercrombie features and it is still possible to buy new gardening books in which ghostly shadows of the once flourishing perennial can be discerned. A collector who does not mind a certain sameness in his reading matter might specialise in the various editions of *Every Man His Own Gardener*. Some would be rooted out with difficulty, but on average they would cost no more than £5 ($13) each.

During the nineteenth century the range of fruits, flowers, trees, shrubs and vegetables was greatly increased and practical books on their cultivation were popular. Some such were considered as suitable reading on railway journeys and were produced as yellowbacks. European plants were taken by emigrants to other parts of the world. Nostalgic gardeners from England who wanted to grow their national flower in Australia were at length catered for by Thomas Johnson's *The Culture of the Rose*, Melbourne, 1866, now worth about $A36 (£16.20—$42) and in 1871, E. B. Heyne supplied *The Flower, Fruit and Vegetable Garden*, published at Adelaide, for gardeners not solely concerned with roses. It is a grade (h) book. One of the most important early American gardening magazines was *The Horticulturalist and Journal of Rural Art*, begun in 1846 and published variously from Albany,

Rochester and New York. Though individual volumes might be picked up for under $10 (£4), the cost of a fair-sized run would probably average out at $15 (£6).

Along with the international and intercontinental circulation of known plants, new plants were being discovered in remote places and brought to the gardens of Europe, America and Australia. Robert Fortune and J. D. Hooker provided exotics from China and the Himalayas, as has already been noticed. American plant-hunters of the past include Humphry Marshall, whose *Arbustum Americanum*, 1785, is grade (b), and Henry Barham, whose *Hortus Americanus*, Kingston, Jamaica, 1794, deals with South American and West Indian plants and is of much the same value as the book previously named. Thomas Nuttall published the *North-American Sylva* at Philadelphia between 1842 and 1854, in three volumes. Recorded prices for this book show big variations, but it could now be placed in grade (e) with some safety.

The plant-hunters of more recent times operated mainly in Asia, and have added many extraordinarily beautiful flowers to our alpine gardens. The two most important hunters at the beginning of the present century were George Forrest (1873-1932) and Ernest Henry Wilson (1876-1930). Forrest has left behind him plenty for the gardener, but next to nothing for the bibliophile. *The Journeys and Plant Introductions of George Forrest*, edited by J. M. Cowan, 1952, gives an account of his seven expeditions to China, with extracts from his writings.

Wilson was much more articulate. He was a Gloucestershire man, born in the Cotswolds, and his early explorations in Asia were undertaken for a British nursery firm. Later he was employed by the Arnold Arboretum of Harvard University. His most important book is *A Naturalist in Western China*, 1913. The American edition appeared in 1929 under the name of *China, Mother of Gardens*. Either copy would be grade (h).

Reginald Farrer (1880-1920) was next on the scene. He was both a practical gardener and an explorer with a love amounting to obsession of alpine plants. Rock gardeners who are also book collectors will give a proud position on their shelves to Farrer's *The English Rock Garden*, two volumes, 1919, which is not far up grade (h). More general collectors will want his *The Rainbow Bridge* and *The Eaves of the World*, both published in 1921, after Farrer's death.

Frank Kingdon-Ward (1885-1958) was a geographer as well as a plant-hunter and made twenty-two expeditions to China, Assam, Tibet, Burma and Indo-China, between the years 1911-57. His scarcest book is *The Land of the Blue Poppy*, 1913, which must now be graded (g). Of his others, the best are *The Riddle of the Tsangpo Gorges*, 1926, *A Plant Hunter in Tibet*, 1934, and *Burma's Icy Mountains*, 1949. These should be available at under £6 ($15) a copy.

Unaccountably, the books of the later plant-hunters almost never appear at important auctions and this causes book-buyers to believe that they are extremely scarce. They appear quite often, however, in lists issued by dealers specialising in gardening and natural history books.

The supplies of exotics which became generally available as a result of plant-hunting helped to break down the formalism of European and American gardens, as rhododendrons, azaleas and alpine flowers call out for a wild setting. Nineteenth-century exuberance also became the enemy of floral regimentation, as can be seen in an extraordinary book published at Rochester, NY, about 1880, but undated. It was written by Jack Vick and is called *Vick's Flower and Vegetable Garden*. It should be collected by those who are interested in luxuriant Victorian typography—if Victorian is an allowable adjective for an American book. There is no reason why it should cost more than $5 (£2) if it can be found.

The apostle of planned informality was William Robinson.

His *English Flower Garden,* first published in 1886, had fourteen editions, the last in 1926. None of the editions should cost more than £4 ($10), so perhaps the collector should try to obtain the first and the last to illustrate the development of Robinson's ideas and his steadfast faith in woodcut illustrations. He refused to have anything to do with photographic blocks, insisting to the end that they were inadequate for plant illustration. Besides writing other books, Robinson edited *The Vegetable Garden,* translated from the French of Vilmorin-Andrieux and first published in 1885. The first edition is much the best as it deals with a remarkable range of usual and unusual vegetables, including caterpillars and snails—not the creatures, but plants which closely resemble them. These are absent from the later editions. This work should cost no more than the *Flower Garden.*

In her quietly impressive writings, Gertrude Jekyll carried Robinson's ideas much further. Her books are now eagerly collected, have greatly increased in price in the last few years and are fairly sure to keep rising. Buyers have not yet begun seriously to discriminate between the different editions and are prepared to pay as much for a fifth as a first. Miss Jekyll's titles include *Wood and Garden, Home and Garden, Children and Gardens, Wall and Water Gardens* and, with Sir L. Weaver, *Gardens for Small Country Houses.* A fine copy of the last named is climbing to the top of grade (i), but the others may still be around £2.50 ($6.50). The same author's *Old English Household Life* and *Old West Surrey* are not gardening books, but studies of bygone cottage furniture, utensils and smallware.

There is a group of writers who are hard to classify. Though they write about nature, they are not naturalists in the strict sense, nor are they agricultural writers or plant-hunters. Their line of descent can be traced back ultimately to Jean-Jacques Rousseau. The outstanding figure in the group is Henry

David Thoreau (1817-62). After an unsettled career, he was befriended by Emerson, but subsequently took to the wilderness and lived almost as a hermit. This experience led to his writing ***Walden, or Life in the Woods***, published at Boston, Mass, in 1854. A fine first edition of this book would be reasonable if in grade (f) as, indeed, would be firsts of his other works, including the posthumous books, ***The Maine Woods***, Boston, 1864, and ***A Yankee in Canada***, Boston, 1866.

The English Thoreau is Richard Jefferies (1848-87), a Wiltshire journalist who became a champion of the depressed agricultural workers then went on to write some carefully observed books on the English countryside and a few novels which are not entirely satisfactory. His first 'hit' was ***The Gamekeeper at Home***, 1878, followed by ***Wild Life in a Southern County***, 1879, ***The Amateur Poacher***, 1880, ***The Life of the Fields***, 1884, ***The Open Air***, 1885, and others. He also wrote two books for children, ***Wood Magic***, two volumes, 1881, and ***Bevis***, three volumes, 1882. ***Bevis*** is indisputably the better, but both would be grade (h), like most Jefferies firsts.

W. H. Hudson (1841-1922), was a true naturalist as well as an open-air writer and novelist. His novels, ***Green Mansions***, 1904, and ***The Purple Land That England Lost***, 1885, are not negligible, nor is his ***A Naturalist in La Plata***, 1892, but his more general writings are the most rewarding. Because of scarcity, the novels are grade (f), but ***A Shepherd's Life***, 1916, should be (g) and is the best Hudson of all.

When Edward Thomas, already mentioned in this book as a poet, wrote his ***Life of Richard Jefferies***, published in 1908, he dedicated it to Hudson, thus establishing a link between the three. Thomas was forced to do hack work for a large part of his career, but even at their most mechanical, his books are touched with a sincere love of nature. ***The South Country***, 1909, contains some of his best prose. When Thomas was killed in World War I, comparatively few people fully appreciated his work. His widow, Helen Thomas, wrote in two parts a moving and intimate biography of her husband, thinly disguising him as 'David'. The two parts were published in one volume in 1931: *As It Was ... World Without End.* This undoubtedly brought a wider public to Thomas's works, which are now scarce in first editions, though not highly priced as yet—most are well down in grade (i).

The works of John Burroughs (1837-1921) could be collected for an outlay comparable with that on those of Edward Thomas. Burroughs wrote a number of nature and country sketches from his fruit farm in the state of New York and has been described as a lightweight Thoreau. With the gradual urbanisation of the area about which he wrote, his works are enjoying a revival of interest. They include *Wake Robin,* 1871, *Birds and Poets,* 1878, and *Field and Study,* 1919.

Beekeeping is a pursuit associated with farming, gardening and life in the country. It has a considerable literature of its own, dating, in English, from 1574, when Thomas Hyll's *A Profitable Instruction of the perfite ordering of bees* was published. It is too scarce and expensive—grade (D)—to be pursued by the ordinary collector. If he is able to buy in grade (b), however, he may consider the acquisition of an early edition of *The Feminine Monarchy or a Treatise concerning Bees and the Due Ordering of them,* by Charles Butler (d 1647). This book is particularly important in that it was the first to show that the hive is ruled by a queen, not a king as had been previously supposed. The first edition was published in 1609, but the edition of 1634 is more interesting. It is entitled *The Feminin' Monarchie, or the Histori of Be's* because at the time of its publication the author had become an enthusiast for reformed spelling.

Joseph Warder made use of material from Butler in *The True Amazons: Or, the Monarchy of Bees,* with further contributions from his own observations. He has a delightful way of bursting into verse every now and again, as when, in describing the division of labour in the hive, he writes:

> The Burying of the Dead here some contrive,
> Some nurse the future Nation of the Hive:
> Some feed their Young, whilst others cleanse the Cell,
> And some prepare for Winter Hydromel.

His pretensions as an apian palingenesist are impressive until it is realised that bees which are apparently dead may only be comatose. He claims 'I have many hundred Times rais'd dead Bees to Life, tho' not such as have been drowned'. First he describes methods using the heat of his hands, or the warmth from a fire, then he continues:

> At other Times, I have taken four or five *Dutch* thin Boxes, and with a Nail (or Bodkin) making Holes in the Covers to give them Air, have gone and fill'd these Boxes with dead Bees, and put them in my Breeches Pockets (that of the Coat or Waistcoat is not warm enough) and so let them remain half an Hour or more; and then opening the Boxes in the Garden, they have all gone Home as before.

This work first appeared in 1726 and is now grade (h). It ran through at least eight editions.

Other important bee books are: *The Ordering of Bees* by John Levett, Gent, 1634, *A New Discovery of an Excellent Method of Bee-houses* by John Gedde, 1675, *The Honeybee its Natural History, Physiology and Management* by Edwin Bevan, 1827, and Thomas Nutt's *Humanity to Honeybees,* 1832. More recent developments in beekeeping have largely stemmed from America and for many beekeepers their Bible is still *The ABC and XYZ of Bee Culture* by A. I. Root and others, published at Medina, Ohio. This publication first appeared in 1877 as *The ABC of Bee Culture*, with A. I. Root as sole author. After running through many editions, it became *The ABC and XYZ of Bee Culture* in 1910, with articles by other contributors. Since then it has been regularly brought up to date. A collection of selected editions would give a useful history of the development of apiculture in the course of about a hundred years.

Hustlers down the centuries have turned to bees for their inspiration; contemplative men have preferred to cast their minds—and other more tangible objects—in the direction of fish. The best-loved dissertation on fishing is Izaak Walton's *The Compleat Angler, or the Contemplative Man's Recreation.* Few books have been so universally popular among the English-speaking peoples. It exists in at least 150 different editions.

The first edition was published in 1653, the second in 1655, the third in 1661 and the fourth in 1668. A complication arises with the fifth edition, 1676. It is normally found as three books in one: Walton's *Compleat Angler,* the second part of the *Compleat Angler,* by Charles Cotton, and *The Experienc'd Angler,* by Colonel Robert Venables. Though this is the fifth edition of Walton's book, it is the first of Cotton's and the fourth of Venables's, which is really quite extraneous. Subsequent editions of the *Compleat Angler* usually contain Cotton's work, but omit the Venables, which, incidentally, was first published in 1662.

A sound first of Walton's book would certainly be grade (C). A set of the first five editions, the last volume being bound up with the Cotton and Venables as usual, sold in 1968 for £4,600 ($11,500). Some quite early editions have been offered in (e), but in this grade have had defects.

The best of the later editions are identified by the names of their editors, as—Moses Browne, 1750; Hawkins, 1760; Bagster, 1808; Major, 1823; Nicholas (two volumes), 1836; Marston (two volumes), 1888; Lowell (two volumes), 1889; Le Gallienne (thirteen parts), 1896-7, and so on. There are also the Tercentenary edition in two volumes, 1896, a beautifully printed Nonesuch edition of 1929, and an edition with coloured plates by Arthur Rackham, 1931. The selling prices of all these, as firsts of their own particular editions, range through grades (g) to (I), but there are other quite acceptable editions to be had more cheaply. The Bohn edition of 1856, for example, should be obtainable in original cloth for under £4 ($10). On the other hand, there are special copies which rise above the price normally asked for their editions. The Arthur Mitchell copy of the first Sir H. Nicholas edition sold for £250 ($625) in 1965 and should now be worth double. This copy is in four volumes instead of two, has extra illustrations in colour and is bound in levant morocco with silk-lined endpapers. The bindings are uniformly decorated in appropriate designs in gold. It is a real treasure.

The Compleat Angler was by no means the first English book on the sport of fishing. That honour goes to *The Treatyse of fysshynge wyth an angle* which first appears as an addition to the second edition of *The book of Hawking, hunting and blasing of arms*, 1496 (see Chapter 5). Though this is too rare for any normal collector to hope to possess, there is a facsimile reproduction available, published by Elliot Stock in 1880. With patience it might eventually be hooked, grade (i).

The Experienc'd Angler by Venables, already mentioned, would be grade (H) for a first, but a fine large-paper reprint was issued in 1827 and might be procurable in grade (f).

Though not confined to fishing, *The Gentleman's Recreation*, 1674, by Nicholas Cox, deserves a place in the angler's library, if he can afford it. Its four parts deal with hunting, hawking, fowling and fishing. A first edition would be grade (H), but later editions, to 1721, should scale down to (e).

The eighteenth century produced a few interesting books on angling, including Robert Howlett's *The Angler's Sure Guide*, 1706, published under Howlett's initials, and Thomas Shirley's *Angler's Museum*, undated, but 1784. However, the great century of fine books for fishermen was the nineteenth, beginning with Charles Smart's *Practical Observations on Angling in the River Trent,* 1801—grade (d)—then moving into the period when some of the best angling books were issued with actual fishermen's flies contained in them. Examples of these are W. Blacker's *Art of Angling and Complete System of Fly Making,* 1842, and *A Quaint Treatise on 'Flees and the Art of Artyfichall Flee Making',* 1876, which provides fly-making materials as well as flies. Both books are roughly equal in value. If the flies and materials are intact, they should be grade (d). With all books which contain flies and materials, these accessories should be examined to make sure they are the originals and not modern substitutes.

Modern angling books deal with so many aspects looked at from so many different points of view that it must be left to the individual collector to decide what he will buy. He might, however, turn his eye to the beautiful angling books produced in limited editions by the Derrydale Press, New York, in the twenties and thirties of the present century and now mostly grade (e). They include Eugene V. Connett's *American Big Game Fishing,* 1935, and Henry Van Dyke's *Travel Diary of an Angler,* 1929. Both are delightful books in their different ways.

CHAPTER ELEVEN

From Religion to Railways

Book collectors of bygone ages generally gave pride of place in their libraries to books on religion, philosophy, Greek and Latin classics and ancient history. Few of today's collectors are so high-minded. Yet it is only in the past hundred years or less that these subjects have fallen from favour. Sir William Robertson Nicoll, who deserted the pulpit to make a solid fortune and an evanescent reputation as a literary man in the early part of this century, detailed his father's book-buying for a year in a sanctimonious biography, *My Father, An Aberdeenshire Minister*, 1908. In it he reveals that during 1862, out of a miserable stipend, his father bought over 500 books and pamphlets. Of these, about 260 were religious or philosophical works, sixty were classical and almost all the rest were 'improving' in one way or another. The only light relief was provided by Dodd's *Beauties of Shakespere* and Shelley's *Poems*. This one year's haul was typical of the library of 17,000 volumes eventually housed in Nicoll senior's small Scottish manse.

As a Free Kirk minister, Robertson Nicoll's father had austere tastes, but no more so than those of thousands of other nineteenth-century bibliophiles, clerical and lay. Even those bookmen whose real inclinations were more cheerful took care to give their libraries an appearance of sobriety by including in them a representative section on religion and philosophy.

The modern book collector feels no obligation to give shelf space to such books and, in relative terms, most of the once-favoured moral works have dropped in value. The genuine collector in this area can buy most of what he wants quite cheaply—some booksellers will let him have stacks of meaty nineteenth-century sermons almost for the taking away. However, some religious and philosophical items are still highly prized by parvenu book hunters who are prepared to give a great deal for them as collectors' pieces which they will never read.

The most important religious work in the western world is of course the Bible. While it is true that there are some very rare and valuable English-language Bibles, the possessors of old, or reputedly old, copies seldom own a valuable property. Impressive family Bibles, which may be over a hundred years old, are virtually without a market value. Apart from a few celebrated editions, English Bibles which pre date the first Authorised Version of 1611 (the King James Bible) average no more than £26 ($68) a copy in the salerooms. The actual first edition of the Authorised Version could be worth up to £2,000 ($5,200), but thereafter, with one or two exceptions, prices drop markedly. Certain Bibles, though not valuable as to content in the worldly sense, sell at high prices because of their exquisite bindings.

For an outlay of between £600 and £700 ($1,500-$1,800), spread over many years of searching, it should be possible to gather together a representative collection of the quaintly named Bibles, such as the *Printers' Bible*, 1702, where 'printers have persecuted me without a cause' occurs in Psalm 119—'printers' being an error for 'princes'—and the *Wicked Bible*, 1632, where the seventh commandment reads: 'Thou shalt commit adultery'. An extensive list of these Bibles is given in Brewer's *Dictionary of Phrase and Fable*.

Testaments, psalters and breviaries are in much the same class as Bibles. The many can be had quite cheaply, but a few are very expensive—indeed, one particular psalter, the *Bay Psalm Book,* may be the dearest printed book in the world. As far as is known, this is the first book to have been printed in the erstwhile Anglo-American colonies. It was produced at Cambridge, Mass, by Stephen Daye in 1640 under the title of *The Whole Booke of Psalms Faithfully Translated into English Metre.* Only eleven copies are known, all but two being defective. The last public sale was at the Parke-Bernet Galleries in New York on 28 January 1947. The item was described as 'a beautiful and perfect copy with the leaf of Errata [L14], "Faults escaped in printing"... Tiny portions of eight leaves skilfully repaired, with the addition of a few letters or numerals.' It sold for the then record price of $151,000, the equivalent of £37,750 at that time. This copy is unlikely ever to appear at a sale again, for it is in Yale University Library. From the names of its various owners, it is known as the Crownishield-Stevens-Brinley-Vanderbilt-Whitney-Yale copy. If it were to be sold, its price could well be more than three times the 1947 figure.

From the first period of printing to the present day, the output of religious, philosophical and moral works has been prodigious. It may be a poor reflection on the twentieth century that the majority of them are among the least desirable of books, but when it is remembered that so many of them are Protestant denunciations of Catholics, Catholic denunciations of Protestants, Calvinist denunciations of Arminians, Arminian denunciations of Unitarians and holier-than-thou Quaker scorn for all the warring factions, perhaps their neglect is not so shameful.

The devoted seeker after religious works will probably look for guidance from a higher Authority than this book, but it may help him to know something of approximate prices of well-known items. Richard Hooker (1554-1600) played an important part in shaping the constitution of the Church of England and the other Episcopal churches by writing *Of the Lawes of Ecclesiasticall Politie*. The first two volumes were published in 1594 and 1597, but the complete work was not available until 1662. The first two volumes alone are grade (F) in our Scale of Values, and it would overtop grade (A) to build up a set of all eight volumes in firsts.

Tolerant in theory rather than practice, Jeremy Taylor (1613-67) wrote *The Rule and Exercises of Holy Living*, 1650, and *The Rule and Exercises of Holy Dying*, 1651. They were for long enjoyed by the devout of many persuasions and the two first editions together are now grade (a). Taylor's contemporary, Richard Baxter (1615-91) was a Puritan whose *The Saints Everlasting Rest*, 1650, was formerly much esteemed, but is now at the bottom of grade (h).

While various divines were wrangling about the outward forms of religion, George Fox (1624-90) was suggesting that people should look to the light within themselves. Fox, founder of the Society of Friends, was a strange man, not altogether sane, perhaps, but with a great fund of piety and love of humanity. Though he wrote and published much while he was alive, his life's work is well summed up in his posthumous *Journal*, edited by his friend, William Penn, and published in 1694. A first edition would be grade (a).

William Penn (1644-1718) was one of Fox's early converts to Quakerism and was the founder of Philadelphia and the state of Pennsylvania. He, too, wrote on religion, at a more cerebral level than Fox. His *No Cross, No Crown*, 1669, is grade (g), but his less bulky writings are much more valuable. In 1968, a two-leaved pamphlet of his, in a silk folder and case, sold at Sotheby's for £1,500 ($3,750). It was *Information and Direction to Such Persons as are Inclined to America*, with no date or place of publication, though it is believed to have been issued about 1684. Robert Barclay (1648-90), an eccentric but highly intellectual Scot rationalised Fox's beliefs in *An Apology for the True Christian Divinity*, 1679, now grade (f).

John Wesley (1703) was surely the most energetic evangelist the world has even known. Besides travelling to other parts of the world, he journeyed the length and breadth of Britain on foot and on horseback and is said to have covered 250,000 miles and preached 40,000 sermons. In addition, he found time to write a great number of books and pamphlets on all sorts of subjects from ancient history to medicine, as well as his famous hymns. His three-volume *Collection of Moral and Sacred Hymns*, published at Bristol in 1744, and his *Means of Grace*, 1755, are grade (d). His scarce *Calm Address to Our American Colonies*, undated, but probably 1775, is of particular interest to American collectors and, if found, would be (H) or higher.

The saintly John Henry, Cardinal Newman (1801-90), was as great a figure in his way as Wesley, though quite different in belief and temperament. His most notable work is *Apologia pro Vita Sua*, 1864, which, in grade (h), has a value of about the same as the other Newman firsts.

Though they are often considered together, the only real similarity between *Religio Medici* and *The Anatomy of Melancholy* is the difficulty in classifying them. They are not medical, religious or philosophical, but a mixture of all three, with other elements besides. *Religio Medici* was written by Sir Thomas Browne (1605-82) and officially published in 1643, though it had been preceded by two unauthorised editions in 1642. A fine copy of the true first could rise above grade (A) and either of the unauthorised versions is liable to be grade (E). Robert Burton (1577-1639), had *The Anatomy of Melancholy* published in 1621. A fine first sold for £1,900 ($4,750) in 1969, but a slightly defective copy, put up for auction at the same time, fetched only £42 ($105), so this is a difficult book to value.

The first great English philosopher was Francis Bacon, Lord Verulam and Viscount St Albans (1561-1626). By forsaking the well-trodden paths of deductive reasoning and developing an inductive system, he helped to lay the foundations of scientific thought and investigation. He was also an authority on law and, on the flimsiest of evidence, a few zealots credit him with having written a number of plays under the name of a well-known man of the theatre. Prices for Bacon first editions range between grade (b) for *The Advancement of Learning*, 1605, to (A) for *Instauratio Magna*, 1620.

Thomas Hobbes (1588-1679) took a glum view of life, regarding war and insecurity as the only fruits of man's unguided existence and looking to authority for the provision of peace and order. His *Leviathan*, 1651, is grade (H) in a verified first issue of the first edition. Points of the first issue include vertical marks on the sword depicted on the engraved title page and the fact that 'Civil' is spelt with a single 'l' in the long form of the title, which therefore reads: 'Leviathan or The Matter, Forme and Power of A Commonwealth Ecclesiasticall and Civil'.

Perhaps John Locke (1632-1704) did not search his soul so deeply as did Hobbes, but he was more optimistic. His forward-looking *Some Thoughts Concerning Education*, 1693, might be found at a price comparable with that of *Leviathan*, but his *Essay Concerning Humane Understanding*, is more likely to be grade (F). George, Bishop Berkeley (1685-1753) follows on from Hobbes in *A Treatise Concerning the Principles of Human Knowledge*, first collected edition, 1734. This might now be (a).

David Hume (1711-76) was a clear and original thinker, but his scepticism precluded his forming a coherent system of philosophy—he was rather an upsetter of apple carts. As such, his effect on the course of European thought was profound and his *Treatise of Nature,* three volumes, 1739-40 is still a valued work in grade (E) as a first. Dugald Stewart (1653-1818) was influenced by Hume and he in turn, through Lord Brougham and other pupils, helped to shape Whig political philosophy in the early nineteenth century. Stewart's *Philosophical Essays,* 1810, falls within grade (g).

By way of Carlyle, if not directly, a little of Stewart's philosophy can be perceived in the writings of Ralph Waldo Emerson (1803-82). Emerson is not so highly regarded as he once was. A first of his *The Conduct of Life,* 1860, should be grade (i) and the first issue of the first edition of his *Essays,* 1841, grade (h).

Following on from Hume, philosophers in the first decades of the nineteenth century took political economy in their stride, though Adam Smith (1623-90) must be regarded as the real father of economics. In 1776 he produced the two volumes of his *Inquiry into the Nature of the Wealth of Nations,* a work which is now grade (D) in a first edition.

The developing interest in economics, with the added ferment of the Industrial Revolution, brought fresh problems to the attention of many thinking men. Thomas Malthus (1766-1834) brought out his *Essay of the Principle of Population* in 1798, a book which was a bitter pill to swallow in those days and has again come to the fore in recent years. It can be placed in grade (G) as a first and may even rise to (F). A little earlier than the publication of the Malthusian hypothesis, Thomas Paine (1737-1809) had frightened the English establishment with *The Rights of Man,* published at New York in 1792, with the date misprinted as 1742. Even the American revolutionaries thought Paine had gone too far in this book currently in grade (d)—though they had applauded his earlier *Common Sense: Addressed to the Inhabitants of America,* Philadelphia, 1776. This little volume, arguing for complete independence, is now worth about $15,000 (£5,750).

In every way, Robert Owen (1771-1858), the Welsh reformer, was a gentler person than Paine, but he was just as firm in his convictions. He wrote against established religion, but nevertheless won the support of some radical churchmen in his early attempts to alleviate the conditions of factory workers. His book, *A New View of Society*, 1813, is scarce and in grade (I). It sets forth some of the utopian ideas of community living he later tried to put into practice at New Harmony, Indiana.

Owen was a noble human product of the Industrial Revolution which was itself the product of many years of investigation, experimentation and theoretical writing. The beginnings, as far as the printed word is involved, go back at least as far as the seventeenth century, when there were published such books as Cressy Dymock's *A Letter to Mr. Samuel Hartlib Concerning an Invention of Engines of Motion*, 1652. In good condition, this item is liable to be grade (G).

Students of the Industrial Revolution and of industrial archaeology look mainly to a later period for their books. Some favoured items belong to the eighteenth century, but it is the nineteenth which provides the ordinary collector with material he can afford. As an example, there is *An Essay on Wheels, Comprehending the Principles and Their Application in Practice to Mill-work*, 1808, by Robertson Buchanan and Peter Nicholson. With luck and patience a copy might be found in grade (h).

It should be less difficult, though still hard enough, to unearth some volumes of *The Mechanics' Magazine*, which commenced in 1823. Odd volumes might cost no more than £3 ($7.50) apiece, though longish runs might average about £4 ($10) a copy. It is an unhappy thought that many runs of magazines of this nature have been thrown out in the past as so much rubbish. There may still be runs awaiting a similar fate and the collector can only pray that he may be standing in the way at the time of the chucking-out.

One of the best reviews of the industrial progress of the first half of the nineteenth century is given in the five volumes of the *Official Catalogue* of the Great Exhibition of 1851, a grade (g) item. A similar transatlantic review, though of a later period, is to be found in J. S. Ingram's *The Centennial Exposition,* undated, but published at Philadelphia in 1876 and presently grade (h).

Many important links in the chain of industrial expansion are described in a scarce and unusual book produced early this century—*Old Time Invention in the Four Shires* by Percy C. Rushen. No date or place of publication is given, but the double columns of each page help to identify it as a reprint in book form from a series of articles written by Rushen for the *Evesham Journal and Four Shires Advertiser.* There are no signatures, but the book collates as a small oblong quarto, cased in green cloth.

The four shires of the title are Gloucestershire, Worcestershire, Warwickshire and Oxfordshire, so that the details of inventions given include those of the ironfounders, the Darbys of Coalbrookdale, and of James Watt, during his long association with Birmingham. When dealing with inventions concerning the cotton industry, the author steps beyond the bounds of the four shires to deal with devices evolved in other parts of the country. The descriptions given are taken from the details supplied when the patents were granted. The first invention recorded in the book dates from 1693 and the last from 1810.

Probably the book was not published in the ordinary way; it is certainly uncommon. As it has never been offered at any important book sale and has rarely been listed in booksellers' catalogues, it is difficult to estimate its price. A keen collector who is offered a copy must look it over carefully and decide what it is worth to him The paper and printing are poor, the style is dry; the information is invaluable. Perhaps £5 ($13) would be fair.

The nineteenth century was the great era of railway development, so essential to the Industrial Revolution. Certain early railway items have sold quite cheaply in the past, but now everybody is only too well aware of their value. There is a quite recent record of only $15 (£6) having been paid for Thomas Hill's *Treatise upon the Utility of a Rail-way from Leeds to Selby and Hull,* Leeds, 1827. Although this is an essay of only thirty-two pages, its present value would be much more.

There are well-known items which have always been expensive and are maintaining their value. Thomas Talbot Bury's *Views on the Liverpool and Manchester Railway,* in two paper-covered volumes, is likely to advance steadily from the £1,000 ($2,600) it had reached in 1971. At grade (F), D. O. Hill's and George Buchanan's *Views of the Opening of the Glasgow and Garnkirk Railway,* 1832, can hardly catch up with the previous work in price, but it should enjoy a comparable advance.

Collecting early editions of *Bradshaw's Railway Guides* and other timetables can be fun for the hardworking, but they must be paid for—the first issue of the first *Bradshaw,* dated 19 October 1839, is likely to be in grade (d) if complete and in good order. Fortunately, reprints of some of the significant editions are available at more reasonable prices. There is also a current reprint of John C. Bourne's *History of the Great Western Railway,* 1846, at £12.60 ($32.50). This may be quite a lot of money, but the first edition is in grade (F).

T. G. Cumming's *Descriptions of Iron Bridges of Suspension,* 1824, appeared before railway development began, but as bridge-building is so closely bound up with railways, a collector in the railway field who could afford to buy it in grade

(g) would hardly be disposed to neglect it, nor, having the money, would he ignore Edwin Clark's *The Britannia and Conway Tubular Bridges,* 1850, in an octavo volume of text and a folio volume of plates, in grade (c) as a pair. Perhaps he might also hope to acquire John Roebling's *Long and Short Span Railway Bridges,* New York, 1869. It is a single folio with thirteen folding or double-page plates and would doubtless be grade (f). More in the railway collector's direct line is R. Armstrong's *An Essay on the Boilers of Steam Engines,* 1839, which should not be above grade (h).

Zerah Colburn helped in the development of the locomotives of two continents. In collaboration with A. L. Holley, he published at New York in 1858 *The Permanent Way and Coalburning Locomotive Boilers of European Railways,* and in collaboration with D. R. Clark, at Glasgow in 1860, *Recent Practice in the Locomotive Engine.* Both are grade (f) items.

Though they make their appearance rather later than the British books, there are many works illustrative of the growth of railroads in the American continent. A. C. Morton's *Report on the St. Lawrence and Atlantic Rail-road,* is quite early, being published at Montreal in 1849, and is now hard to locate even in grade (g). C. Exera Brown's *Gazetteer of the Chicago Northwestern Railway,* Chicago, 1869, is for the collector who can make the (H) grade, but a more modest item, the *Business Directory of the Northern Central Railway,* Syracuse, 1874, by Andrew Boyd, should be only (h) and is typical of several similar items worth searching for, including Eugene V. Smalley's short *History of the Northern Pacific Railroad,* New York, 1883, which might still be found in grade (i).

The collecting of Australian railway material is of recent development and few titles have come into prominence as yet. One of the best known is George Phillips's *Pioneer Railways for Queensland,* Brisbane, 1892, which should be grade (h).

Some railway enthusiasts specialise in the collection of old showcards, posters, leaflets, guide books and miscellaneous railway publications. There is enormous scope for the collector here and though supplies of material are not so plentiful as they once were, a good 'nose' should still lead to some useful finds. Roger Wilson's book, *Go Great Western*, 1970, illustrates what can be done in this direction.

If the railways provide an exceptionally colourful range of ephemera, they are equalled, if not beaten, by the theatre. Plays in book form have little of the magic of the theatre about them. It is the ephemera that capture the glamour of the stage and the imagination of collectors. There was a time when only really old playbills, programmes and posters were acceptable, but now the tendency is to gather together material right up to the present. Some collectors include old cinema posters and stills with their theatrical material, others like to keep them apart.

Undeniably, the really old theatrical playbills take the palm for romance, quaintness and conscious or unconscious humour. At one time the playbill served the double purpose of programme and poster, so it was crowded with information and printed in a wild assortment of eye-catching types. The metropolitan bills carry impressive names and record historic productions, but their provincial counterparts can be just as interesting.

Take the town of Warrington, in Lancashire. In the public library there a unique collection of local playbills is preserved. They date from the 1760s onwards. Elizabeth Kemble, sister of the great tragedians, John Kemble and Mrs Sarah Siddons, emigrated to America and became famous, first as an actress and later as a social worker under her married name of Mrs Whitlock. She was born at Warrington in 1761 and, sure enough, in the Warrington collection there is a play bill of that period listing two of the leading players as Mr and Mrs Kemble. From the evidence of the bill they could be no other than the Roger Kembles, parents of Elizabeth.

Some other great names appear on the Warrington bills, but as with most from the smaller centres, the interest often lies with the obscure players. What, for instance, happened to Henry Smith, the 'Infant Kean' who, at the age of nine, came to Warrington and played some of the major Shakespearean roles?

Then there is the poignant story of a Mr and Mrs Carr, as revealed by the bills. Salaries were low in the old provincial theatres, so the actors were given in turn a benefit night on which they were responsible for the arrangements and took all the profits. Mr and Mrs Carr's benefit at Warrington fell on 7 March 1821, and Mr Carr prepared a playbill to advertise the event. He chose to present 'A new drama in three acts, written by Mr Carr and performed at the Theatres Royal, Hull, and Sheffield, with unbounded applause, called *Omreah —Or, Fatal Revenge!*' Mr Carr then added to his bill some verse which ran:

Pray, critics, drive not with remorseless rage
My first production from a British stage;
But to my efforts this night be a friend,
And proof of approbation pray extend...
Beam kindly then and keep in mind the night
'That either makes me or undoes me quite.'

Mr Carr's tragedy was duly presented, but must have flopped badly. A bill dated 21 March appears, advertising another benefit for Mr and Mrs Carr. On it, Mr Carr explains:

The night appointed for my benefit was most unfavourable; the wetness of the evening, and the unfortunate accident which happened to a respected individual caused, I doubt not, the badness of the night, thereby making me a considerable loser...

An actor labouring under misfortune, has no resource but to throw himself upon the well-known candour and generosity of a British public, who are every ready to step forward and encourage the deserving. 'Tis not because success refused to shine upon my benefit is my only misfortune, 'tis because the loss I then sustained prevents me leaving the town in that honourable manner I have ever been accustomed to depart from others. Under these distressing circumstances, I throw myself upon the generosity of the patrons.

After 21 March 1821, there is no further mention of Mr and Mrs Carr on the Warrington playbills, but it is hoped that the second benefit, for which a different play by a different author was chosen, enabled them to leave the town in the style to which they were accustomed.

This illustrates the particular fascination of collecting old playbills. Among all the ballyhoo about Grand Indian Spectacles, Sagacious Dog Actors, and Awful Appearances of Bleeding Nuns, there can suddenly appear the stuff of genuine human drama—and off-stage at that.

However hard they work, few collectors will be lucky enough to acquire as splendid a sequence of playbills as those at Warrington Public Library, but there must still be plenty of good material to be brought to light. Bills bought through the normal channels could cost from £2 ($5) to £50 ($125) or more, according to age and content. Until the collector has made himself an expert on the subject, he should buy only from the most reputable of dealers. There are many fakes and forgeries in circulation and they are not always easy to detect. However, bills may be looked for in other places. There may still be some stowed away in odd corners of the storerooms of old-established shops which at one time exhibited the bills in return for free tickets.

The collecting of old plays has already been mentioned, but, Wilde and Shaw excepted, little information has been given on modern dramatists. The fact is that only a handful is presently collected, so here is virgin territory for the theatrically-minded bibliophile.

Among the many Irish dramatists of the present century, John M. Synge and Sean O'Casey are the most likely to endure. Synge's *The Well of the Saints,* Dublin, 1905, is definitely grade (g), if not above, but it is doubly collected as it was edited by W. B. Yeats. The best of Synge's plays is *The Playboy of the Western World,* Dublin, 1907, and although it also may be grade (g) it should be somewhat cheaper. His other plays are probably grade (h). Most of O'Casey's plays, *The Plough and the Stars,* 1926, and *The Silver Tassie,* 1928, fall into grade (i). His *Two Plays,* 1925, containing *Juno and the Paycock* and *The Shadow of a Gunman,* is grade (h).

Samuel Beckett is Irish by birth and a disciple of James Joyce, but he has written most of his plays in French, then translated them into English. Typical of Beckett values is the first English edition of *Endgame,* 1958, in grade (i).

Among the uncollected English dramatists are Somerset Maugham (though high prices are paid for signed copies of his plays as well as for his novels) and Sir Noel Coward. Coward is no earthshaker, but his comedies mirror, with justifiable satiric distortion, the manners of the English upper middle classes between the wars. In the future they will be valued as social documents if not as masterpieces of drama and should be collected now, while they are cheap. Good Coward firsts should be obtainable below the £2 ($5) mark.

Eugene O'Neill, Arthur Miller and Tennessee Williams are the obvious representative American dramatists of the twentieth century. O'Neill will be the most expensive and already his *The Hairy Ape,* undated, but New York, 1922, and *'Anna Christie',* New York, 1932, are in grade (g), though O'Neills in signed limited editions are considerably higher. A first of Tennessee Williams' *The Glass Menagerie,* New York, no date, but 1945, would be grade (h) and a first of Arthur Miller's *Death of a Salesman,* New York, 1949, would be (i).

The theatre in English-speaking countries was confused in the 1960s and is in a turmoil in the seventies. It is not yet time to buy the plays of our younger dramatists at fancy prices, but there is no harm in investing in their first editions on publication. Their work is often obscure, but seldom dull, so nothing is lost if the books lose all their value in a few years. They will at least have entertained the intelligent reader.

CHAPTER TWELVE

Hunting and Caring for Books

A helot unlucky enough to have had his head turned by a glimpse of Helen of Troy as the bride of Menelaus might have spent a wretched few weeks bewailing the hopelessness of his love, but doubtless he would have recovered in the end and settled for some nubile lady helot. So with the bibliophile who becomes infatuated with the rare and wonderful only to be brought down to earth when he fumbles with the very small change in his pocket. He suffers agonies of frustration for a time, then turns with Spartan resignation to such books as are within his means—and lives happily with them ever after.

In reviewing various aspects of book collecting, the previous chapters have named more Helens than helots, largely because the great majority of books are not valuable enough to be individually price-recorded and so given the dignity of collectors' pieces. Nevertheless, there are plenty of humble books which are worthy of notice. For example, it should be possible to find at least one copy of the first edition of John Masefield's *Sard Harker*, 1924, in the course of a day's tour of English bookshops, priced at under 80p ($2). Though sometimes collected as a poet, Masefield is ignored as a novelist, hence the low cost of *Sard Harker* and others of his prose works. Yet his novels are more readable than those of many a writer who is collected by the slaves of current trends—and he is a poor sort of bookman who allows fashion completely to override his own tastes and inclinations. It may be that at some future date Masefield's novels will be much sought after and those who have bought them cheap purely for enjoyment will have made a financial gain. But even if they never rise in value, the buyer will have lost nothing by acquiring some pleasant novels at low prices.

He who would make a tour of English bookshops, searching for cheap Masefields, or pursuing bigger game, may have difficulty in finding the premises. Ask an inhabitant of any town how to get to the nearest butcher, baker or boutique (whatever that may be) and he will usually be able to give clear instructions. But inquire of him where the nearest antiquarian bookseller is to be found and he will look either puzzled or shocked—as if he had been asked for directions to a *balneator* or a brothel.

Help can come from one or other of the guides to antiquarian booksellers: *A Directory of Dealers in Secondhand and Antiquarian Books in the British Isles,* Sheppard Press, London, and the *Annual Directory of Booksellers in the British Isles specialising in Antiquarian and Out-of-Print Books,* published by The Clique Ltd, London. Both give essential information about almost all British antiquarian booksellers—if and when their premises are open to the public, the subjects in which they specialise, and whether they issue lists and catalogues. The Sheppard Press produces similar guides to book dealers in North America and in the continent of Europe. Besides providing the information which makes productive tours of shops a possibility, these guides are just as useful to stay-at-homes, for they enable collectors to make contact and do business with the large number of dealers who conduct a postal trade. Most of these booksellers issue their catalogues free, but will soon stop sending them to unresponsive clients. Those booksellers who make a small charge will continue to send for as long as catalogues are paid for.

Though they may present other difficulties, the more elaborate catalogues will be almost free from abbreviations; other lists may contain many. A person of ordinary intelligence should have little difficulty in translating most of these contractions, but some are given in a glossary at the end of this book. Here is a catalogue entry showing some typical abbreviations:

DICKENS (Chas.). *A Christmas Carol,* trial iss. of 1st edn., t.p. and hf.t. in red and green; cold. plts. and wdcts. by Leech; 12mo, orig. brown cl., a.e.g., yellow e.p.s., mco.-bkd. c.; Lond., Chapman & Hall, 1844; top of sp. nicked, front cvr. sltly. rubbed, mild foxing on fp., o/w v.g. copy of excessively rare item £500

This translates as:

DICKENS (Charles). *A Christmas Carol,* trial issue of first edition, title-page and half-title in red and green, coloured plates and woodcuts by Leech; duodecimo; original brown cloth, all edges gilt, yellow end-papers; morocco-backed case; London, Chapman & Hall, 1844; top of spine nicked, front cover slightly rubbed, mild foxing on frontispiece, otherwise a very good copy of an excessively rare item £500

The contractions used by booksellers have never been completely standardised. Title-page, written in this entry as t.p., often appears as title-p. and is sometimes shortened to title, while hf.-title is often used for half-title. An alternative to mco.-bkd. is mor.-bkd. and c. is more often used for *circa* (about) than for case. Frontispiece can appear as front. and frontis. The subject of the entry is described as excessively rare and, with some qualification, as a very good copy. 'Excessively rare' is a phrase seldom met with outside booksellers' catalogues. In this case it truly means that very few copies of the item exist, but it can be used with more enthusiasm than veracity and potential buyers should regard it with some scepticism. 'Very good' usually means what it says, but there are booksellers who use a wide range of descriptions of condition, with 'very good' some way down from the top, as: 'mint' (or 'as new'), 'very fine', 'fine', 'near fine', 'exceptionally good', 'extremely good', 'very good', 'really good', 'good', 'quite good', 'goodish', 'fairly good', 'fair', 'rather worn', 'worn', 'very worn' and 'poor'. The collector ordering by post need not spend sleepless nights worrying over such descriptions. He should accept them for what he thinks they are worth and if the books he buys do not come up to his expectations, he should send them back with a request for the return of any money paid. If he acts promptly, no decent bookseller will demur.

If a dealer is found consistently unsatisfactory, the collector will drop him, and *vice versa* if the collector is continually niggling.

An elaborate catalogue may contain an entry (imaginary) like this:

CALDBORNE (Geffray or Geoffrey). *Here begynneth the boke of the merie gest of Pope Jehanne*, 4to; J. Rastell, 1524: sole edition; blind-tooled seventeenth-century panelled calf with raised bands; signatures A-L^4 (unnumbered); A_1 and L_4v blank, text A_2-L_3; colophon L_4r; wormhole from A_1 to D_3 scarcely affecting text; K_2-L_4 heavily damp-marked. Not in S.T.C. £4,000

Most of the terms used have already been explained, so the main difficulty here is in interpreting the symbols. L^4 signifies a four-leaf gathering signed L, while L_4 denotes the fourth leaf of such a gathering. The recto (upper page of a leaf) is denoted by 'r' and the verso (second or lower page) by 'v'. The meaning of 'signatures A-L^4' is that there are gatherings in fours signed consecutively from A to L, making eleven gatherings in all with the normal omission of J. 'A_1 and L_4v blank' means that nothing is printed on the first leaf of the book nor on the second side of the last leaf. The text runs continuously from the second leaf (A_2) to the penultimate leaf (L_5). The colophon, a note giving such details about the book as its author, printer and place and date of printing, is on the first side of the final leaf. The pages are unnumbered, so the extent of the wormhole is explained in signatures, but it runs from the first leaf of the book through to the fifteenth. Similarly, the damp-marking affects the last seven leaves. Obviously the book has no title-page and no proper title. This is quite usual in books printed before about 1530. No place of publication is given, but Rastell is known to have been a London printer.

The collector who buys mostly through catalogues should not neglect bookshops, but visit them whenever the opportunity arises. None of his wants may be on the shelves of the shops he visits, but he can learn a lot simply by looking through what is displayed. Most booksellers are happy to let customers inspect their stocks at leisure and while they are not likely to take umbrage if the browser buys nothing, they will think more highly of him if he makes a token purchase, be it no more than a tired paperback.

As the wise woman maketh a friend of her physician, so does the bibliophile make an ally of the bibliopole. This is the advice John Carter has to give (*Taste & Technique in Book-Collecting*, Cambridge University Press, 1948):

> No bookseller resents a reasoned scepticism in bibliographical matters, nor an honest difference of opinion as to the value of a book. Indeed, a good bookseller respects, appreciates and is glad to profit by both, when they are backed by knowledge and experience. What he does resent is a collector who regularly assumes that he is about to be deceived and automatically regards a marked price as something to be reduced. He will sell to such a one reluctantly and with a sour heart. For though booksellers are destined always to be parting from books, they have a liking for them and a pride in their own stock. The grocer who sells a pound of butter cares nothing who eats it. But the bookseller who has a

> fine thing to dispose of would rather sell it to someone who will appreciate it... A sale is a sale, even if it is made with a sigh. But the customer who prides himself on being 'tough' would be surprised if he knew how often a book which he wants, and is known to want, has been kept in a drawer during his visit, to be sold, sometimes for a smaller profit, to another in whose collection the bookseller has been encouraged to take a personal interest.

Collectors should put in an appearance wherever there are books to be had—jumble sales, junk shops and charity gift shops. Some have allowed enthusiasm to overcome dignity to the extent of inspecting dustbins and trashcans for possible finds.

Attendance at important book auctions in the leading salerooms should be a part of every collector's education. Before attempting to bid more than small amounts he should make himself thoroughly familiar with what goes on, over several visits, remembering that some of the most successful collectors find it wiser to commission an expert to bid for them than personally to enter the arena. Completely to avoid book sales, however, is to miss one of the great thrills of the game.

There was a time when auctioneers handling unimportant house sales regarded books as a nuisance, bundled them up in large miscellaneous lots and knocked them down quickly to anybody who was rash enough to make an offer. This happens less often now. If they appear to be of any possible value, the books are prominently listed in the auctioneers' catalogues, which are then sent to a wide circle of dealers.

Sometimes good buys can be made at small sales if the private collector is sensible. He can occasionally go one bid higher than the dealer who has to think of reselling at a profit. It is wrong to assume, however, that the dealer can always be safely outbid. He may bear a commission from some client prepared to pay any amount for an item particularly desired, or he may set out deliberately to break any private opposition. In such a circumstance he purposely forces up the prices of the early lots and buys them with a dissembled air of satisfaction at having bagged them cheaply. If this does not shake off a persistent rival, he will continue to force the pace, but, by using his skill and experience in bidding, drop the lots on others at the inflated prices. Unless they are wildly reckless, his rivals will realise he is making them pay too much and will leave a clear field for the dealer.

Though it is illegal in Britain, and members of the Antiquarian Booksellers' Association are pledged not to participate, a dealers' 'ring' may still operate in some places. To allay suspicion, two or three of the participating dealers will make the bids on behalf of the ring, using a breaking technique on the opposition. As a general rule, the ring will acquire most of the best lots. When the sale is over, the members of the group will bid for the pooled purchases at a second auction, referred to as the 'knock-out'. Here the bidding on most lots will be higher than at the real sale and the extra money made will be shared out as a dividend among the participants at the end of the second sale. Sometimes the workings of the ring are even more complicated.

It is popularly believed that these illegal arrangements depress prices at sales. This is not always true. There have been occasions when booksellers in the ring have wittingly pushed up prices at sales where there have been good books available, but few takers. They realise that it is bad for their business if they allow the prices of certain items to fall below a respectable level.

In America, where the laws governing auctions vary in the different states, rings scarcely exist. The university buyer, the individual collector and the bookseller bidding on commission tend to dominate the sales, leaving little room for a dealers' combine to operate.

Everybody who attends sales regularly is sure to obtain a

good bargain sooner or later and is entitled to tell the world about it. It is just as legitimate to take pride in non-bargains of the right kind. For a collector to have desired a book so strongly that he has been prepared to pay a record price for it is something of a feather in his cap. What he usually keeps quiet about is a mistake, like paying up to the hilt for what he took to be a scarce first edition but which in fact proved to be a second impression.

Building a collection takes time and patience. He may scour the bookshops, attend all the best sales, scan the catalogues of dozens of dealers, yet the collector may still find that the items he wants continue to elude him. Perseverance and friendly relations with booksellers are needed, but further help is available.

Booksellers can advertise their customers' needs in *The Clique,* a trade publication issued weekly from London and given over almost entirely to such advertisements. As it has a wide circulation in the book trade, it often produces results. Its complementary magazine is *The Book Market,* published weekly by the same firm. In it, booksellers advertise lists of books which they have for sale, thus giving their colleagues opportunities to notice and buy items specially wanted by their customers.

The *Antiquarian Bookman* is issued weekly from Newark, New Jersey, USA. Besides listing advertisements of books wanted and for sale, this journal gives regular news of books of all kinds—old, new, specialist and out-of-print. *A Bookman's Yearbook* is issued yearly by the same company.

The Clique, The Book Market and the *Antiquarian Bookman* circulate on both sides of the Atlantic, as do two important annuals: *Book Auction Records* and *American Book-Prices Current. Book Auction Records,* often abbreviated tc BAR, is described as a 'priced and annotated record of London, New York, Montreal, Melbourne, Edinburgh and Glasgow book-auctions'. It must be used with caution as the entries are of necessity short and cannot give detailed descriptions. The apparent sudden drop in one year of a certain book as recorded in BAR may be due to a copy's poor condition and not to any falling off in demand. Slavish adherence to BAR prices would also drive every antiquarian bookseller in Britain and America out of existence. Sellers are liable to approach a dealer with a book and quote the price as £50 according to the last BAR figure. If he buys it at that price he then must face the customer who will argue that the selling price must be £50 as that was the last recorded price at an important sale. Some subscribers wish that BAR would give more information, but that would increase the price of what is already an expensive publication. *American Book-Prices Current* is better on description, but is not so wide-ranging as BAR.

The Book Collector, a London quarterly, deservedly enjoys an international circulation. The articles, many written by distinguished bibliophiles and bibliographers, are of the highest standard and can throw light on puzzles and problems which beset the beginner. *The American Book Collector*, issued ten times a year from Chicago, is slightly less rarefied than the English publication, but may be of even greater help to the beginner whose interest is mainly in American books, though it is by no means a one-nation publication. *The Private Library*, the quarterly journal of the Private Libraries Association, issued from London, starting from modest beginnings, is now a most useful magazine.

Besides seeking external help, the collector should develop a kind of awareness which springs from knowledge and familiarity, but seems to work independently of the two. Quite recently, a collector of T. S. Eliot firsts was hopefully scanning the cheaper shelves of a small bookshop. He saw no Eliots, but a book in an attractive Victorian cloth binding caught his eye. It was titled *Poetic Souvenir* on the spine. Rather than leave empty-handed, he bought the book for 25p and went off without troubling to inspect the book properly. When he got home, he found that between the covers were the two volumes of John Clare's *The Village Minstrel and Other Poems,* bound in one. He checked and found both volumes were complete first editions, dated 1821. The publishers, Taylor & Hessey, London, must have been left with some unbound copies on their hands and, at a later date, had had them cased in red cloth, under a non-commital title. Within a few months, the Eliot collector exchanged this item for a copy of Eliot's *Homage to John Dryden,* 1924, a book for which he would normally have had to pay at least £20. His developed eye picked out from the shelves what was perhaps the only book worth more than 25p—though even he did not immediately realise quite how valuable it was.

Some bookmen give the impression of being clairvoyant in the way they can tell without opening a book whether or not it is 'right'. The first general edition of T. E. Lawrence's *Seven Pillars of Wisdom* was published in July 1935. The second and third impressions were issued in August of the same year. All have apparently exactly similar bindings in brown buckram, yet there are some dealers who are so familiar with the book that they can often pick out a first impression from the others without looking inside. They would not score 100 per cent in a prolonged test, but would do much better than the 33.33 per cent that chance could earn them.

The importance of collecting books in the best possible condition has already been emphasised. But what should a collector do if a sub-standard copy is all that he can find, or afford? Throughout the English-speaking world, bibliophiles are agreed that he should try to leave it as it is, giving it the best protection possible. This is done by putting it in a case, cardboard or leather, specially made for it. The case should not be too tight-fitting, for if the book has to be pulled out with force it will wear more quickly than if placed naked upon a shelf. The most impressive type of case, made to look like a book, is called a soleander, but a careful amateur can make his own adequate, if less elaborate case.

If the original binding of a book is in a really desperate state, it may be wise to have it rebound. If it is an important book, this should be done as finely as the owner can afford. To case-bind some rare seventeenth-century book in serviceable grey cloth is little short of criminal. It should be given the full treatment in leather, or left to disintegrate rather than be subjected to such a humiliation. It is a matter of personal taste whether an old book should be bound in modern style or after the fashion of its own time. Some bookbinders can design so that the finished product does not look like a fake antique, yet harmonises with an old text.

Where the spine of a leatherbound book has gone, but the sides have survived, the book can be rebacked, that is, given a new spine. This is a difficult job which should be left to an expert who will probably charge almost as much as for a complete rebind.

As regards minor repairs and restorations, it is difficult to state where the border lies between the acceptable and the unacceptable. Soap and water can be used to wash the grime from some types of old cloth covers, but the result is seldom satisfactory. There are, however, several liquid 'book restorers' available. They remove grime and certain stains quite effectively. When their distinctive odour has gone, there is nothing left to show that they have ever been used—if they have been applied judiciously. Where there is a tiny fray at the corner of a cover, little harm is done by touching it with a spot of latex gum. If the titling-pieces of leather books have come loose, they should be restuck with ordinary starch paste, not with patent glues or gums. Centuries of experience have shown that starch has no deleterious effect on leather, but as yet there is no way of knowing what effect modern adhesives may have after a hundred years or so—an important consideration when it is realised that nobody is ever the absolute owner of a good book: he is merely its guardian during his lifetime or until he transfers the responsibility by sale or gift.

Leather books are often polished with shoe cream and those who do so may say that the cream 'feeds the leather'. As leather has no digestive system, it cannot be fed. What is meant is that the surface of the leather can be clogged up with heaven knows what sort of stuff which may do as much damage as good in the long run. Unreadable books in conventional nineteenth-century calf or morocco bindings may be doctored in this way, but really valuable old bindings should never be so abused. Frequent handling with clean hands and an occasional rub with a silken cloth ought to keep them in good order, but if the leather is at all brittle, it should be given a dose of castor oil.

A soft rag should be lightly smeared with the oil and rubbed gently over the leather, which is then wiped with a dry rag. That is enough for one day. The same should be done on successive days until the oil has been absorbed below the surface without the leather's becoming saturated. If the book has unavoidably to face harsh conditions, some paraffin wax should be added to the castor oil. This is done by shredding a little wax into the oil then heating till the wax melts. In *Bookbinding and the Care of Books*, 1901 and subsequent reprints, Douglas Cockerell suggests that the wax should be a quantity weighing about half as much as the castor oil, but this is a little too much. Beeswax can be substituted for paraffin wax, but it costs more and is no better for the purpose.

Bookworms, which can do a great deal of damage, are just as liable to attack new books as old. They are the larvae of several species of beetle belonging to the genus *Anobium*, the commonest being *Anobium domesticum*. They are identical with woodworms, though it appears that certain races are better adapted to a diet of paper than others. Some bookworms are the grubs of *Xestobium tessellatum*, the notorious death-watch beetle, but this is rare.

Worming of books often begins at a corner of the spine, where the eggs are laid. When the grub hatches, he eats out a tunnel through the leaves and finally escapes as a mature beetle, having spent an intermediate period as a fat pupa, cosily wrapped in a little cocoon. The perfect insect has wings and can fly quite a distance to cause infestation elsewhere. Books are also wormed by grubs who start life in the wood of shelves and continue their tunnelling from the wood to the books.

Treatment is lengthy, but fairly simple. An infested book should be examined and all living grubs removed. It should then be put in a sort of gas chamber consisting of an airtight box in which there have been placed some pieces of cotton wool soaked with ether. The soaked cotton should not be allowed to touch the book. Twenty-four hours in the closed box will kill off any grubs or developed insects, but not the eggs and possibly not the pupae. The book should be left for a week or more for the eggs to hatch, then the treatment should be repeated. If this is done twice more, the book will be free from pests.

The procedure is also effective against the booklouse, *Atropos divinatoria*, a tiny insect which can be seen scuttling merrily among old books and documents, often in large numbers. It has a great appetite for glue and paste and in course of time can seriously weaken bindings.

Library hygiene is essential if infestations of such pests are to be avoided. Books and shelves should be dusted and examined regularly. If the wood shows signs of recent worming it should be given appropriate treatment and pieces of camphor or naphthalene should be placed in suitable corners of the shelves to discourage further attacks. At one time potassium cyanide was employed as a fumigant, but it is a deadly poison and despite the fact that it is mentioned in some old manuals on the preservation of books it should never be used—it is no more effective than ether.

Sunlight is another enemy to be guarded against. Bookcases and shelves should never be placed where direct sunlight can fall on them. If this is not possible, they should be provided with curtains to keep the devastating rays off the books and prevent their becoming faded. Dustwrappers are not sufficient protection. Under continued exposure to sunlight, the design of the wrapper can be photographed on the cloth cover of a book.

Human beings are among the worst despoilers of books, so the bibliophile is careful not to let any Tom, Dick or Harry handle his treasures. Tom may drag a book from the shelf by placing a finger at the top of the spine and pulling hard; Dick, on finding that a tightly-bound book does not easily open, may seize the covers and double them back till they meet, thus cracking the binding; Harry may be an inveterate finger-licking fumbler with a genius for rucking up leaves.

The collector with the easiest mind is he who does all his own dusting. He brushes the outsides of his books lightly and goes through the leaves to make sure that no dust has lodged between them. If it has, he flicks it away with a feather duster, trying to use it as a fan instead of letting it touch the paper and cause smearing. Few things horrify the bibliophile more than the sight of books being dusted roughly—perhaps by the cruel method of taking a volume in either hand and bashing them together as if they were a pair of cymbals.

Human ill-treatment of books does not end with handling and cleaning. The amateur repairer can inflict serious wounds on books. It sometimes happens that one of the covers, usually the front, of an old leather-bound volume becomes detached.

The would-be book cobbler re-affixes it by means of several strips of transparent cellulose tape, or sometimes a glue-soaked strip of cloth. If the book is ever to be reinstated the tape or cloth has to be removed and a proper repair executed—and the removal can cause serious damage. There is no harm in using cellulose tape, inside or out, on the worn tenth or later impression of a modern paperback, but it should not be applied to any book which is likely to be of value. Repairs should be entrusted to a qualified person, or the collector should take a course in bookbinding and become proficient in the work himself.

One of the worst crimes committed against books is the removal or mutilation of endpapers. Fear of black magic seems still to linger in the minds of many apparently civilised people. When they come to sell books on which their names have been written, they are so terrified lest the names fall into the hands of sorcerers who will work evil against them that they tear out the endpapers which bear the names. The result is not only unsightly—it makes the book incomplete and weakens it. Sometimes only the part of the endpaper bearing the name is cut out, or an ink solvent is applied. These mutilations are equally deplorable. There is no dishonour in selling a book with its original owner's name on it. Rather is it a privilege to have one's name discreetly written in a book destined to form part of some cherished private, or even public, collection.

Conversely, many collectors are prejudiced against books which carry a former owner's name as evidence of perfectly legitimate defloration. This preoccupation with the maidenly state does no honour to an old book. If it is still *virgo intacta* after fifty or a hundred years, the obvious implication is that it has never been read—surely a poor commendation for a book deemed worthy of collecting. Bibliophily would be a more warmly human activity if there was general agreement that every owner of a book should write his name in it, the first making a start at the top left corner of the front free endpaper and the others following in order. In time, the book would be something more than just any old copy.

A really well-designed book-plate, neatly affixed to the front paste-down endpaper, should also be looked on as an enhancement. It is possible to buy mass-produced book-plates which incorporate some more or less appropriate design and read '*Ex libris*...', or, 'From the library of...', and the owner is expected to write his name on the dotted line. These should be avoided as lacking in individuality. The collector should have his own personal book-plate or equivalent. Not everybody can afford to commission an artist of standing to design his plate, but rather than settle for an inferior design, the collector should seek out a really good printer to supply him with a personal book-label, distinguished by its typographical excellence. In time, the front paste-down endpaper of a book can become a sort of palimpsest as one owner's plate is pasted over the one before.

Book-plates are legitimately stuck into books—nothing else is. It is known for a collector to cut out the listed details of a book from a dealer's catalogue and paste this on an endpaper. The proper place for such a cutting is in a dated scrapbook. Other compulsive cutters-out stick photographs, extracts from newspapers, or fragments of information from dustwrappers into books. These, too, are more at home in a scrapbook, though if they are not of sufficient bulk to put a strain on the covers, they may be loosely inserted, as may other relevant material—authors' letters and the like.

What should be done about dustwrappers? Certain authorities maintain that since the dustwrapper is not an integral part of a book it may be discarded, but it is difficult to accept this when a printed note inside the book declares 'wrapper designed by J. Smith', or when a photograph printed on the wrapper is included in the list of illustrations. Yet wrappers are fragile things and however well cared for will in time become frayed and worn. The collector must either resign himself to this, or, as is sometimes done, he can remove the wrapper and file it away, substituting a loose brown-paper jacket of his own making, or leaving the book unclothed on his shelves.

A somewhat similar problem arises with certain books published in the early part of this century. They were bound in cloth or boards, but instead of their being titled directly on the spine, paper titling-pieces were used. Realising that the paper labels would wear or discolour, the publishers issued duplicate labels with the books, lightly stuck on one or other of the back endpapers. Is a book of this type complete if the original label has been discarded in favour of the duplicate? The question has only recently loomed large in bibliographical circles and no final answer has been given.

There is no need for the collector to fash himself with thermometers and hygrometers in his library. Books should be maintained at an even temperature and should not be allowed to become too dry or too damp. A room temperature which is comfortable, if coolish, for a human being, in an atmosphere with a pleasant sense of its being neither too moist nor too dry, is ideal for books. They enjoy a bit of a breeze now and then. This can be supplied by reversing the action of a vacuum cleaner. The stream of air blows away the dust and is alleged to prevent paper from becoming brittle.

Books must be kept in an upright position on the shelves. They should neither be packed too tightly nor allowed to flop at an acute angle. It is dangerously easy to shelve books reasonably tightly yet slightly keeled over. Once books have acquired the obliquity which this position imposes it becomes almost impossible to straighten them out again. Where a shelf has to be left unfilled, verticality can be maintained by the use of a metal book-rest.

Older works on bibliography recommend to collectors various elaborate methods of cataloguing which daunt the beginner. These may profitably be ignored. A man who is sufficiently intelligent to become a book collectors should have wit enough to devise his own author and title card-index system. Even if it is an ill-favoured thing, it will be his own and he will know how to use it. If he puts reference numbers on the cards, he will also write the numbers on the front endpapers of the books to which they pertain, but lightly, in pencil, so that they can easily be erased if necessary. If he tries to place the books in a strictly logical order he will often find he has to partner fat folios with slim duodecimos and his library will look like a frozen Hal Roach comedy, with incongruous Laurels and Hardys gazing down from every shelf. Logicality must sometimes give way to common sense. In any case, if he is a true booklover he will seldom have to consult his catalogue. He will know exactly where in his library to find his friends even if they ultimately be numbered by the thousand.

Besides keeping a card index, the collector will also have an accessions book into which he will enter every acquisition as it is made, giving details of how and where it was obtained and the price paid. More should be given than bare statements of fact. The accessions book will be much more interesting in later years if it is written up in anecdotal style. As has already been mentioned, a scrapbook is also worth keeping. It will contain informative cuttings from many sources about books and bookmanship, and anything else the compiler deems worthy of inclusion.

The most important thing of all is for the collector to enjoy and use his library. Some bibliomanes become so absorbed with points, priorities and variants that they cease to look on a book as something to be read. They have the snaffle and the bit all right, but forget about the bloody horse. They buy good books which have long remained unopened in the technical sense and refuse to take the paperknife to them. They invest in first editions so fine that they never dare lay a finger upon them except to dust them. A few fanatics maintain two libraries—one in which the books are regarded as inviolable and the other in which they may grudgingly be consulted and read. Eccentricities of this sort must never be allowed to develop, nor will they if the book collector exercises his common sense at all times and adds to it the closely allied senses of proportion and humour.

A glossary of terms used in book collecting

This list gives only a few of the words that the book collector is liable to meet. For the most complete list of such words ever compiled he should consult John Carter's delightful *ABC for Book Collector.*

ana, written and printed material about a particular author or subject, often added to the name of the author or subject to make a new word. In combination it usually takes the form of *iana* or *eana*, as Sussexiana, Whitmaniana, Coleridgeana etc.

antiquarian books, a loose term, but when a dealer states that he sells 'antiquarian, secondhand and out-of-print books', 'antiquarian' can be taken to mean 'old and desirable', 'secondhand' to mean 'old and not very desirable' and 'out-of-print' to mean 'recent, but no longer available from publishers' stocks'. However, an antiquarian bookseller may specialise in first editions of the present century, which, desirable though they may be, are not old.

association copy, a copy of a book having special links with the author, with somebody else associated with the book, or with some other important person. Henry Irving's copy of *Dracula*, for example, would be an Irving association item.

backstrip, an alternative name for the spine of a book, used particularly, though not exclusively, of a cloth or paper spine.

bibli-, a prefix denoting 'book' or 'books' when compounded with other words derived from Greek. The statement in the text that there is no such word as 'bibliology' may not be strictly true, but it is almost never used and has not the precise meaning suggested in Chapter I.

bibliomane, bibliomaniac, while the two words are really synonymous, bibliomane is more often used of a book collector who is wildly enthusiastic and bibliomaniac of one who is an abandoned fanatic.

bibliopegist, a bookbinder or a collector of fine bindings.

bibliophily, the love of books. Used as a synonym for book collecting, as bibliophile is used for book collector.

bibliopole, a bookseller in his Sunday best.

binder's cloth, a single copy of a book which has been specially bound in cloth is in binder's cloth as distinct from the original cloth used for the rest of the edition. The term 'binder's leather' is never used.

black letter, this is a term commonly used for English **Gothic** types, though it correctly pertains only to a special style of Gothic.

blind-tooled, decorated with impressions from bookbinders' tools, but not gilded. Where the impressions have been made from blocks, a bookcover is said to be blind-stamped.

boards, the outermost parts of a book. The boards may be paper-covered or overlaid with leather or cloth. When no covering other than paper is used, the book is described as being in boards, otherwise it is stated as being in leather or in cloth.

bookplate, a label bearing an engraved device, specially printed to show the ownership of a book and normally pasted on the front inner cover. Where there is no engraving, the equivalent is a book label.

bookworm, a devourer of books, human or insect. Slight worming in old books is to be expected and hardly counts as a defect provided the holes do not seriously affect the text or illustrations. A surprising number of worms are obliging enough to make meals only of the margins.

breaker, a biblioclastic bookseller who breaks books to sell the plates for framing. A book considered suitable for his purpose is also called a breaker or a breaking copy.

broadsheet, an unfolded sheet of paper with printed matter on both sides. The term is applied mainly to sheets of ballads and street songs as sold by pedlars until quite recently, but it is also used of proclamations, news items etc similarly produced on single sheets. It is sometimes applied to a broadside (qv).

broadside, an unfolded sheet of paper with printed matter on one side only, otherwise agreeing in every respect with the broadsheet. While theatrical playbills are technically broadsides, they are usually considered and collected separately. See *The Broadside Ballad* by Leslie Shepard, 1962.

calf, a smooth, hardwearing leather tanned from calfskin, employed for leather bindings from early days to the present. Natural calf is a pale fawnish colour, but it is usually dyed in some shade of brown or in other colours. Tree calf is highly polished and bears a design which is supposed to resemble a tree but is more like the graining of walnut veneer. Sprinkled and mottled calf leathers have little flecks of different colours on them and diced calf has an allover design of small lozenges pressed on it. A book described as bound in antique calf will probably be a modern rebind in ancient style.

called for, a booksellers' term meaning that such-and-such is necessary for the completeness of the book, according to some good authority.

cancel, a substitute leaf introduced after the sheets of a book have been printed and folded (*folium cancellans*).

cancelland, an unacceptable leaf which has to be removed (*folium cancellandum*).

cap, the headcap and tailcap are the shaped tops and bottoms of the spines belonging to books bound in leather in the traditional way.

casing, a method of fitting covers to a book without lacing the cords to the boards. Most books in cloth are cased.

chapbook, single sheets as for broadsheets could be folded to make small booklets, often 8vos and 16mos, but also in other formats. Like broadsides and broadsheets, they could contain ballads, but the subjects ranged widely, from folk tales by way of reports of murders to accounts of the lives of famous and notorious people. 'Omnibus volumes' exist, made up from several chapbooks sewn together and bound in boards. Chapbooks, hawked in the streets and from door to door by chapmen, flourished from the seventeenth to the nineteenth centuries. A chap, meaning a fellow, is a shortening of chapman.

colophon, a paragraph giving details of printer, author, date and place of printing etc, placed separately at the end of a book. Early books were printed without title-pages and bore colophons instead, though some books have both. Many printers put their trade marks with the colophons and when the marks came to be placed on title-pages they were sometimes called colophons.

cropped, a book which is shaved (qv) may suffer only slight damage to the text, but when it is described as cropped or cut into, it can be assumed that the damage is serious.

cut, a book with cut edges which has had the roughness of the edges of the paper smoothed down and the leaves separated.

disbound, short but integrated pieces of printing which have been broken from a parent volume to be sold separately are so described.

dustwrapper, the paper jacket put round most modern books for additional protection—also called a dust jacket.

editio princeps, the first printed edition of a work already in existence as a manuscript book before the introduction of printing. The term is most commonly applied to the first printed editions of Greek and Latin classics, but is equally applicable to books in other languages. It is sometimes used grandiloquently for any important first edition.

endpapers, blank leaves at the front and back of a book. The paste-down endpaper is stuck down the inside of the cover and its next neighbour is the free endpaper. Blank leaves at the fronts or backs of books other than these are called flyleaves.

ephemera, pamphlets, broadsides, handbills and the like produced without thought of their being preserved for posterity.

ex-library, a book which has identifiably been at one time an item in a lending library is so described.

extra-illustrated—see grangerised.

fore-edge painting, the fore-edge (sometimes pronounced 'forridge') of a book is the edge opposite the spine. A fore-edge can be slightly and evenly opened out and held fast while a painting is applied to it. When the book is firmly closed and the whole edge gilded, the painting cannot be seen, but when the edge is opened out again, the picture is revealed. In this way a dull book can be converted to a sophisticated and expensive toy, esteemed by collectors who are not fond of reading. The technique was popular in the late eighteenth and early nineteenth centuries—Moore's *Lalla Rookh* seems to have been a favourite subject—but the art is still practised, mainly on old books.

format, refers to the number of times each whole sheet has been folded to provide the leaves of a single gathering for a book. The names of the different formats are given in Chapter 1.

foxing, marked with brown spots and blotches, often caused by the action of dust on certain chemicals in paper.

gathering, the unit for sewing a book together, formed when the printed sheet has been folded the number of times required by the format. As a gathering normally carries a signature it is sometimes referred to as such.

grangerised, a book which has had a number of extra illustrations bound or tipped in is said to be grangerised, after James Granger, an eighteenth-century publisher who issued a history of England with blank leaves on which the owners could paste illustrations of their own choice. Where a large number of extra leaves has been tipped in—that is, gummed along their inside edges and forced into position between two of the original pages of a book—considerable strain is put on the binding which breaks up fairly soon. Grangerised books should be professionally rebound after the insertion of the extra leaves. An alternative term is extra-illustrated.

gutta-percha binding, an unfortunate substitute for a sewn binding, invented about 1840 by Thomas Hancock. A caoutchouc binding is virtually the same thing.

half binding, a binding where the leather covers little more than the spine of a book, but triangular pieces of leather are also supplied at the outer corners. A leather half binding is often described as being in half leather. Half bindings in cloth are occasionally met with. Half bindings with a generous allowance of leather are often called three-quarter bindings.

half-title, the leaf in front of the title-page, carrying the title of the book and little or nothing else. It is sometimes called a 'bastard title', but this is not because its absence or presence in some cases can cause difficulties for bibliographers.

headband, a protective band sewn inside the top of a spine. The equivalent at the base is a tailband, but both may be spoken of as headbands. Many modern headbands are stuck on instead of being sewn in.

high spot, an author's high spot is the book widely accepted as his best. Some collectors devote their energies exclusively to acquiring the first-edition high-spots of a select number of authors. A slightly different use of the word is seen in 'Audubon's *Birds of America* is one of the ornithological high spots', meaning that it is one of the finest bird books ever produced.

hornbook, a leaf of paper or vellum bearing some rudimentary educational memoranda (the alphabet, the numbers 1 to 10 and the Lord's Prayer, perhaps) and slipped between a thin layer of clear horn and a wooden backing fitted with a handle so that it looks like a small square hand-mirror. Genuine examples from the sixteenth, seventeenth and eighteenth centuries are rare, but 'manufactured' specimens are not unusual. Andrew W. Tuer's *History of the Horn-Book*, 1896, should contain two replicas of hornbooks in packets at the end of the book.

impression, an impression is the complete number of books of an edition printed at one time. The first edition of the collector is normally the first impression.

incunabula, books from the earliest period of printing, up to 1500. Incunable is widely used as the singular, with incunables as an alternative plural.

issue, the issue of a book is the total number published at one time. This may be only part of the first impression (or subsequent impressions), so there can be first, second etc issues of an impression.

juveniles, a term widely used in the antiquarian book trade for children's books, especially those of the Victorian era and earlier.

large-paper, a descriptive term applied to books printed on leaves bigger than those of the normal edition. Large-paper copies were made either for presentation or for selling at a higher price to those willing to pay. Sometimes the page proportions are horribly wrong so that the text appears like a postage stamp stuck on the middle of a large envelope. Booksellers will always try to charge more for large-paper copies, but they should be paid for only according to their merits.

limited edition, an edition of a book limited to a given number of copies. Where the limitation goes above a thousand it ceases to have much significance and where it is unstated it raises a big question mark.

miniature books, very small books, collected because of their dwarfishness. John Carter suggests that any volume measuring less than 2in × 1½in should qualify for the title.

modern face, printing types where the difference between the thick and the thin strokes is strongly marked are modern face types. They were truly modern in 1815, but went out of vogue later last century, when old-face types again took over. Some fine modern faces have been designed in recent years so the style is again popular.

monograph, a book which deals exclusively with one subject or one part of a subject.

morocco, an attractive grained leather derived from goatskin, often dyed red, but also common in other colours. Levant and Niger are types of morocco; crushed morocco is a variety with the grain pressed flat but still discernible and a favourite with the best binders of the arts and crafts movement.

nice, for various reasons, some books wear badly in their original bindings—the first edition of Ouida's *Moths*, three volumes, 1880, is a notorious example—so when a dealer comes across such a book in unusually good condition he justifiably calls it 'nice'. Unfortunately, the word is seriously overworked by undiscriminating booksellers and is sometimes applied to books in a state less than good.

old face, printing types of the styles popular up to the end of the eighteenth century showed no marked contrast between thick and thin strokes. When they were revived in the nineteenth century they were referred to as old-face types.

parchment, a material much like vellum (qv), but got from sheepskin. Inferior parchment is sometimes called forel.

part-issue, the issue of a book in serial parts. Until the appearance of *The Pickwick Papers*, only inferior fiction, illustrated books and occasional works of reference were issued in parts. The term is used of the regular numbers of Addison's and Steele's *The Spectator* and similar magazines, but these were not conceived of as building up to a single unified book.

pigskin, leather from the pig, when properly processed, provides an extremely hardwearing but unattractive covering for books.

pirated edition, an edition of a book produced without the consent of the author or owner of the copyright.

points, the features such as misprints, corrections, advertisements etc used as guides for distinguishing one issue or edition of a book from another.

presentation copy, a copy of a book clearly presented by the author, or possibly the illustrator, and not merely signed by him. A copy of *The Origin of Species*, presented by T. H. Huxley to Herbert Spencer, would be a valuable association copy but not strictly a presentation copy.

private press, a privately owned press usually devoted to the production of fine books or those which would be unlikely to succeed in the ordinary way of trade.

provenance, the history of a book's ownership. This can be determined by bookplates, by the owners' names written in the book, or by information obtained from old sale catalogues or booksellers' lists.

publisher's cloth, where an entire issue, impression or edition has been bound by or for a publisher in uniform cloth, the books are said to be in publisher's cloth.

quarter binding, a binding where the leather or other material covers the spine, with some overlap on either side, but with no protective corners.

raised bands, the binding cords of a book when they are allowed to show through the leather of the spine as decorative ridges. A book may have false bands.

rebacked, when only the spine of a book has been renewed it is said to be rebacked. Where possible, portions of the old spine are retained and overlaid on the new to preserve as much as possible of the original binding.

russia, russia leather is prepared from cowhide and somewhat resembles calf, though it is blander to the touch. It has been used but little for books during the past 150 years.

section, an alternative word for a gathering, but booksellers' rather than bookbinders' jargon.

shaved, a book whose edges have been severely trimmed but not actually cropped.

sheep, sheepskin leather, termed 'sheep', is not ideal for bookbinding as it tends to peel in strips. When new it looks very like calf.

signature, the letter or other sign printed on the lower margins of the first and (sometimes) subsequent pages of a gathering. A whole gathering is often referred to as a signature.

signed copy, this is taken to mean a copy of a book signed by the author and/or the illustrator and not by anybody else, however notable.

state, the different states of an issue are the variations arising from changes made before any portion of an edition was published. It is sometimes hard to distinguish between state and issue.

sugar paper, is a soft, rather coarse paper, often grey-blue, but also found in other drab colours. It is so named from its being the material traditionally used in Britain for making small sugar bags. In the eighteenth and early nineteenth centuries, when it was also used for covering the plain boards in which books were originally issued, it was normally a laid paper, which is one made upon a wire mesh where the wires are set parallel and leave their marks on the finished paper. These marks can be seen when the paper is held to the light. Nowadays, the marks can be imitated on paper which is not truly laid so that the sugar paper sometimes used on modern books may really be *wove* paper, which is the usual paper of our times.

sunned, when the covers of a book have been more or less bleached by sunlight, they are sometimes euphemistically described by booksellers as sunned.

three-decker, a book in three volumes, but the term is used almost exclusively of Victorian novels in this form.

ties, ribbons or strips of leather attached to the front edges of the covers of some books and intended to be tied together when the books are not in use. On modern books they have no more than nuisance value as they serve no discernible purpose except to reduce the price of the book when they inevitably become worn and fall off.

titling piece, the thin leather label on the spine, bearing the title of a book. Titling pieces, or lettering pieces, were generally lettered *in situ* as the gold would have rubbed off in the course of sticking the label to the spine. Some books bound in materials other than leather have paper titling-pieces.

top edge gilt, describes a book with the top edge cut and gilded. Books may have top and fore-edges gilt, or all edges gilt.

trimmed, all books which have their edges smooth are in fact trimmed, but some people apply this term to books which have had the work rather roughly done.

unbound, not in a binding and applied to a book or pamphlet which has never been bound.

uncut, a book that is uncut has all the edges of its leaves in the rough state. An uncut copy is *not* one in which the leaves have not been separated by a paperknife or binder's plough.

unopened, an unopened book is one where the pages have not been slit apart. Some books which have survived in this condition for 200 years and more seem condemned to eternal spinsterhood as few collectors have the courage to open them after so long.

vellum, the inner side of calfskin, cured, but not tanned, to produce a very durable material, nearly white and smooth enough to be written upon. If not subjected to extremes of dampness or dryness it will outlast leather as a covering for books.

vignette, a small illustration or decoration used on a title-page or at the beginning (headpiece) or ending (tailpiece) of a chapter. Any small illustration not contained within a border is also known as a vignette.

woodcut, an illustration printed from a block of wood on which a design has been cut. The best authorities say that a woodcut is cut along the grain of the wood and a wood engraving is graved on a cross-section. Bewick woodcuts are undoubted wood engravings and the mid-nineteenth-century pictures in the *Illustrated London News* are indisputably woodcuts proper. But in many cases—eg the later work of some of Bewick's pupils—it is almost impossible to tell without an examination of the original blocks.

wrappers, are paper covers, but the term is reserved for descriptions of books and pamphlets originally issued in such covers.

yellowbacks, cheap books published for sale at railway bookstalls during the nineteenth century, bound in boards, usually yellow in colour.

xylography, the art of wood-engraving.

Note that **first printing** has two meanings. The term is used as an alternative for 'first impression', but it is also applied to the first appearance in print of a work later issued in another form. The first printing of Rudyard Kipling's poem, 'Recessional', was in *The Times*, 17 July 1897. Its first separate issue was in 1898, when it appeared as an eight-page booklet bound in grey-green wrappers, and it was first collected in *Recessional and Other Poems*, 1899, limited to twenty-five copies in white buckram.

Abbreviations used in booksellers' catalogues

(not completely standardised)

ads., adverts., advertisements
a.e.g., all edges gilt
A.L.S., A.L.s., autograph letter, signed. The second form is better
app., appendix
bd., bound
bg., binding
bds., boards
bkd., backed, as in 'mor.-bkd. bds.' for 'morocco-backed boards'
buck., buckram
b. & w., b.w., black and white, used of uncoloured illustrations
cf., calf
cl., cloth
col(d)., colour(ed)
cond., condition
cont., contemp., contemporary
contr., contributor, contribution
dec., decor., decorated, decoration
d.w., dustwrapper
ed., editor, edited
ed., edn., edition
eng., engr., engraved, engraving
endp., e.p., endpaper
ex-lib., ex-library
facs., facsimile

fp., front., frontis., frontispiece
g., gt., gilt
hf., half, as 'hf. bd.' for 'half bound'
h.t., half-title
imp., imperial (size of paper)
imp., impr., impression
impft., imperfect
inscr., inscribed, inscription
jt., joint
intro., introd., introduction
leath., leather
lge., large
L.P., large paper
ld., ltd., limited (of an edition)
marg., margin, marginal
mco., mor., morocco
n.d., no date
n.p., no place, no publisher, or no printer
o.p., out of print
or., orig., original
p., pp., page, pages
p.d., paste-down, as 'p.d. e.p.', 'paste-down endpaper'
pict., pictorial
pl., plt., plate
pol., pold., polished
port., portrait
P.P., privately printed
pres., presentation
pt., part
ptd., printed
pub(d)., published
qtr., quarter
remd., removed, as 'e.p. remd.' for 'endpaper removed'
repd., repaired

rev(d)., revised
sig., signature
sm., small
sp., spine
t.-label, title-label
T.L.s., typewritten letter, signed
trans., translated, translation
unb(d)., unbound
vell., vellum
vig., vignette
w.a.f., with all faults
wraps., wrappers

In the higher reaches of bibliography, **'r'** denotes the recto (front side of a leaf) and **'v'** the verso (back side).

A short bibliographical guide for collectors

A comprehensive bibliography suitable to the needs of collectors of every taste would fill many large volumes. This list is intended mainly as a bare foundation on which collectors can build their own personal bibliographies of the books they most desire to possess.

The budding bibliophile intent on collecting a particular author is often frustrated because he does not immediately know how or where to obtain the essential details about his author's works. Hitherto, most of the books written on collecting in general have been surprisingly unhelpful in this, so it is hoped that the list of bibliographies of individual subjects and authors which follows will go some way towards filling a want, though, regrettably, for reasons of space, more authors have had to be left out than have been put in. Many of these special bibliographies are exceedingly hard to find, but a really determined collector should be able to track down copies for consultation, if not for purchase.

It can generally be assumed that where no place of publication is given, the books were published in London.

GENERAL WORKS

Aldis, H. G. *List of Books Printed in Scotland,* 1904

Bateson, F. W. (ed) *The Cambridge Bibliography of English Literature,* 5 vols, 1957 (see also under Watson, below)

Besterman, Theodore. *World Bibliography of Bibliographies*, 4th edn, 5 vols, Geneva, 1965-6

Binns, Norman. *An Introduction to Historical Bibliography*, 1953

Block, Andrew. *The English Novel 1740-1850*, 1939

Brussel, I. R. *Anglo-American First Editions*, 2 vols, 1935-6

Carter, John. *Binding Variants in English Publishing*, 1932

——. *Publishers' Cloth, 1820-1900*, New York and London, 1935

——. *Taste and Technique in Book-Collecting*, Cambridge, 1948

——. *ABC for Book-Collectors*, 3rd edn, 1961

Chapman, R. W. *Cancels*, 1930

Collier, J. Payne. *Bibliographical Account of the Rarest Books in the English Language*, 1865

Collinson, R. L. *Bibliographies Subject and National: A Guide to Their Contents, Arrangements and Use*, 1951

Duff, E. Gordon. *Fifteenth Century English Books*, 1917

Esdaile, Arundell. *A List of English Tales and Prose Romances Printed before 1740*, Bibliographical Society, 1912

Ghosh, Jyotish C. and others. *Annals of English Literature 1475-1950*, 1961

Halkett, S. and Laing, J. *Dictionary of Anonymous and Pseudonymous Literature of Great Britain*, ed by J. Kennedy and others, 8 vols, 1926-56

Keynes, Geoffrey. *Bibliotheca Bibliographici*, 1964

Kunitz, S. J. and Haycraft, E. *British Authors of the Nineteenth Century*, New York, 1936

—-——-. *British Authors of the Twentieth Century*, with supplement, 2 vols, New York, 1956-9

Lowndes, W. T. *The Bibliographer's Manual of English Literature*, 4 vols, new edn by Henry G. Bohn, 1857

McKerrow, Ronald B. *An Introduction to Bibliography*, Oxford, 1927 (3rd imp, 1948)

Muir, Percy H. *Points, 1874-1930; 1866-1934*, 2 vols, 1931-4

Northup, C. S. *A Register of Bibliographies of the English Language and Literature*, New Haven, Yale University Press, 1925

Pollard, A. W. and Redgrave, G. R. *Short-title Catalogue 1475-1640*, 1926

Riches, Phyllis M. *Analytical Bibliography of Universal Collected Bibliography: Comprising Books Published in the English Tongue in Great Britain and Ireland, and the British Dominions*, 1934

Rosner, Charles. *The Growth of the Book Jacket*, London and Cambridge, Mass, 1954

Sadleir, Michael. *Excursions in Victorian Bibliography*, 1922

——. *The Evolution of Publishers' Binding Styles*, 1930

——. *XIX Century Fiction*, 2 vols, 1951

Smith, F. Seymour. *An English Library*, revised and enlarged edition, 1963

Taylor, A. and Moser, F. J. *The Bibliographical History of Anonyma and Pseudonyma*, University of Chicago Press, 1951

Wing, Donald. *Short-Title Catalogue 1641-1700*, 3 vols, New York, 1945-51, index vol, Charlottesville, Va, 1955

Watson, George. *The Concise Cambridge Bibliography of English Literature 1600-1950*, 1958

AERONAUTICS

Brockett, Paul. *Bibliography of Aeronautics*, Washington, DC, 1910

AGRICULTURE

Aslin, Mary S. Rothamsted Experimental Station, Harpenden —*Library Catalogue of Printed Books and Pamphlets on*

Agriculture 1471-1840, 2nd edn, 1940, supplement, 1949, *Catalogue of Serial Publications*, 1953

Fussell, G. E. *The Old English Farming Books*, 1947

—--. *More Old English Farming Books*, 1950

Loudon, J. C. *An Encyclopaedia of Agriculture*, 1825

Perkins, W. F. *British and Irish Writers on Agriculture*, 3rd edn, 1939

AMERICA

Blanck, Jacob. *Bibliography of American Literature*, 4 vols, New Haven, 1965

Bradford, T. L. *Bibliographer's Manual of American History*, ed S. V. Henkels, 5 vols, Philadelphia, 1906-10

Brown, J. C. *Bibliotheca Americana*, 3 parts in 5, New York, 1961-3

Cowan, R. E. and R. G. *Bibliography of the History of California 1510-1930*, 3 vols, San Francisco, 1933

Evans, Charles. *American Bibliography*, 14 vols, Chicago and Worcester, Mass, 1903-34-55

Hargrett, Lester. *Bibliography of Constitutions of the American Indians*, Cambridge, Mass, 1947

Hill, F. P. and Collins, V. I. *Books Printed at Newark NJ*, privately printed, 1902

Peterson, C. Stewart. *Bibliography of County Histories of the 3,111 Counties in the Forty-Eight States*, revised edition, Baltimore, 1946-50

Raines, C. W. *Bibliography of Texas*, 1896, facsimile reprint, Houston, 1955

Sabin, Joseph. *A Dictionary of Books relating to America*, 29 vols in 15, Amsterdam, 1961 (also available is a Readex Microprint with magnifying glass, published at New York, no date given)

Smith, Charles W. *Pacific Northwest Americana*, 3rd edn, ed by Isabel Mayhew, Portland, Oregon, 1950

Streeter, Thomas W. *Bibliography of Texas*, 3 vols, Cambridge, Mass, 1955-56

Wickersham, James. *Bibliography of Alaskan Literature*, Cordova, Alaska, 1927

AUSTRALIA

Miller, E. M. *Australian Literature, A Bibliography*, revised edn extended to 1950, ed by F. T. Macartney, Sydney, 1956

Spence, S. A. *Bibliography of Selected Early Books and Pamphlets relating to Australia 1610-1880*, 1952

BEES

Scottish Beekeepers' Association. *Catalogue of the Moir Library*, Edinburgh, 1951

BIRDS

Anker, Jean. *Bird Books & Bird Art*, Copenhagen, 1938

Harting, J. E. *Bibliotheca Accipitraria*, 1891 (falconry)

Irwin, Raymond. *British Bird Books: A Guide to Modern British Ornithology*, 1952

Mullens, W. M. and Swann, H. K. *A Bibliography of British Ornithology from the Earliest Times to the End of 1912*, 1917, supplement, 1923

——— and others. *A Geographical Bibliography of British Ornithology to the End of 1918*, 1920

BOTANY

Arber, Agnes. *Herbals, Their Origin and Evolution*, 2nd edn, enlarged, 1938

Blunt, Wilfrid. *The Art of Botanical Illustration*, New Naturalist series, No 14, 1950

Jackson, B. D. *Guide to the Literature of Botany, Including Nearly 6,000 Titles not in Pritzel*, Index Society, 1887

---. *Vegetable Technology: A Contribution towards a Bibliography of Economic Botany*, Index Society, 1882

Pritzel, Georg A. *Thesaurus Literaturae Botanicae Omnium Gentium*, new edn, ed by Dr C. Jesson, Milan, 1950

Render, Alfred. *The Bradley Bibliography. A Guide to the Literature of the Woody Plants of the World Published before the Beginning of the Twentieth Century*, 5 vols, Arnold Arboretum, Harvard University, 1911-18

CANADA

Peel, Bruce B. *Bibliography of the Prairie Provinces*, Toronto, 1956

Staton, F. M. and Tremaine, Marie. *Bibliography of Canadiana*, 2 vols, Toronto, 1959-65

CHILDREN'S BOOKS

Darton, F. J. H. *Children's Books in England*, 1932

Muir, Percy H. *English Children's Books, 1600-1900*, 1954

Rosenbach, A. S. W. *Early American Children's Books*, ed A. E. Newton, Portland, Maine, 1933

CRICKET

Gaston, A. J. *A Bibliography of Cricket*, 1895

Taylor, Alfred D. *Catalogue of Cricket Literature*, 1906

DRAMA & THEATRE

Arnold, J. F. and Robinson, J. W. *English Theatrical Litera-*

ture 1599-1900, 1970 (based on *A Bibliographical Account of English Theatrical Literature*, by Robert W. Lowe, 1888)

Baker, Blanch M. *Dramatic Bibliography*, New York, 1933

Brown, T. Allston. *History of the American Stage*, New York, 1870

Genest, Rev J. *Some Account of the English Stage 1660-1830*, 10 vols, 1832

Greg, Sir W. *A Bibliography of the English Printed Drama to the Restoration*, Bibliographical Society, 1939-52

Harsage, Alfred. *Annals of English Drama, 975-1700*, Philadelphia, University of Pennsylvania Press, 1940

Haskell, Daniel C. *List of American Dramas in the New York Public Library*, New York, 1916

Hill, Frank P. *American Plays Printed 1714-1830, A Bibliographical Record*, Palo Alto, California, 1934

Loewenberg, Alfred. *The Theatre of the British Isles, Excluding London; A Bibliography*, 1950

McGuire, Paul. *The Australian Theatre*, Sydney, 1949

Nicoll, Allardyce. *A History of Early Eighteenth Century Drama*, 1925

——. *A History of Late Eighteenth Century Drama*, 1927

Ward, Sir A. W. *A History of English Dramatic Literature*, 3 vols, 1899

FISH & FISHING

Dean, Bashford. *A Bibliography of Fishes*, 3 vols, New York, American Museum of Natural History, 1916-23

Westwood, Thomas, and Satchell, T. *Bibliotheca Piscatoria*, 1883

GENEALOGY

Harrison, H. G. *A Select Bibliography of English Genealogy*,

A short bibliographical guide for collectors with Brief Lists for Wales, Scotland and Ireland, 1937

GEOLOGY

Challinor, John. *The History of British Geology: A Bibliographical Study*, 1971

GYPSIES

Black, G. F. *A Gypsy Bibliography*, Gypsy Lore Society, 1914

HISTORY

Dutcher, George M. and others. *A Guide to Historical Literature*, New York, 1931

Scott, John. *Bibliography of Works relating to Mary Queen of Scots*, Edinburgh, 1896

ILLUSTRATION

Abbey, J. R. *Life in England in Aquatint and Lithography 1700-1860, from the Library of J. R. Abbey*. A Bibliographical Catalogue, 1953

Bennett, Whitman. *Practical Guide to American 19th Century Color Plate Books*, New York, 1949

Bland, David. *A History of Book Illustration*, 1969

Darton, F. J. H. *Modern Book-Illustration in Great Britain*, 1951

Hamilton, Sinclair. *Early American Book Illustrators and Wood Engravers*, New York, 1958

Levis, Howard C. *A Descriptive Bibliography of the Most Important Books in the English Language relating to the Art and History of Engraving*, 1912

Weber, Carl J. *A Thousand and One Fore-Edge Paintings,* Waterville, Maine, 1949

INSECTS

Lisney, A. A. *A Bibliography of British Lepidoptera 1608-1799,* 1960

LAW & CRIME

Beale, Joseph H. *A Bibliography of Early English Law Books,* Cambridge, Mass, Harvard, 1926

Cumming, Sir J. *A Contribution towards a Bibliography dealing with Crime and Cognate Subjects,* no date

MEDICAL & SCIENTIFIC

Garrison, F. H. and Morton, L. T. *Medical Bibliography,* 2nd edn, 1965

Osler, Sir William. *Incunabula Medica,* 1923

Zeitlinger, H. and Sotheran, H. C. *Bibliotheca Chemico-Mathematica: A Catalogue of Works in Many Tongues on Exact and Applied Science,* 2 vols and 3 supplements, 1921-41

MUSIC

Day, C. L. and Murrie, Eleanore B. *English Song Books, 1651-1702,* Bibliographical Society, 1940

Dean-Smith, Margaret. *A Guide to English Folk Song Collections 1822-1952,* Liverpool University Press and English Folk Dance and Song Society, 1954

Scholes, P. A. *A List of Books about Music in the English Language,* no date

NAVAL & MILITARY

Cockle, M. J. D. *Bibliography of English Military Books,* 1900

Manwaring, G. E. *A Bibliography of British Naval History,* reprint, 1970

POLITICAL ECONOMY

McCulloch, J. R. *Literature of Political Economy: A Classified Catalogue,* 1845, reprinted by London School of Economics, 1938

PRINTING, BINDING & PRIVATE PRESSES

Bigmore, E. C. and Wyman, C. W. H. *Bibliography of Printing,* 2nd edn, 2 vols, New York, 1945

Craig, Maurice. *Irish Bookbindings, 1600-1800,* 1954

Duff, E. Gordon. *Early English Printing,* 1896

— - —. *William Caxton,* Chicago, 1905

Fletcher, W. Y. *English and Foreign Bookbindings,* 2 vols, 1895-6

Franklin, Colin. *The Private Presses,* 1969

Isaac, Frank. *English and Scottish Printing Types,* 2 vols, Bibliographical Society, 1930-2

Matthews, Brander. *Bookbindings, Old and New,* London and New York, 1896

Mitchell, William S. *A History of Scottish Bookbinding, 1432-1650,* Edinburgh, 1955

Roberts, W. *Printers' Marks,* London and New York, 1893

Tomkinson, G. S. *Select Bibliography of Principal Modern Presses,* First Edition Club, 1928

Weale, W. H. J. and Taylor, L. *Early Stamped Bookbindings in the British Museum,* 1922

See also under Cobden-Sanderson, Morris and Whittinghams in the individual author section.

RELIGION, PHILOSOPHY ETC

Darlow, T. H. and Moule, H. F. *Historical Catalogue of Printed Editions of the Holy Scripture in the Library of the British and Foreign Bible Society*, 2 vols in 4, 1903-11, reprinted New York, 1963

Gillett, Charles R. *Catalogue of the McAlpin Collection of British History and Theology 1500-1700*, New York, Union Theological Seminary, 1927-30

Louttit, C. M. *Handbook of Psychological Literature*, Bloomington, Indiana, 1932

Rand, Benjamin. *Bibliography of Philosophy, Psychology and Cognate Subjects*, New York, 1905

TRANSPORT

Ballen, Dorothy. *Bibliography of Roadmaking and Roads in the United Kingdom*, 1914

National Liberal Club. *Early Railway Pamphlets 1825-1900*, Gladstone Library, 1938

Peddie, R. A. *Railway Literature 1556-1830*, A Hand-list, 1931

TRAVEL & TOPOGRAPHY

Anderson, John P. *The Book of British Topography: A Classified Catalogue of the Topographical Works in the Library of the British Museum*, 1881

Bradshaw Collection. *Catalogue of Irish Books in the University Library, Cambridge*, 3 vols, 1916

Chubb, Thomas. *Printed Maps in Atlases of Great Britain and Ireland*, 1927

Cox, E. G. *A Reference Guide to the Literature of Travel, Including Voyages, Geographical Descriptions, Adventures, Shipwrecks and Expeditions*, 4 vols, Seattle, University of Washington, 1935-49

Gross, Charles. *Bibliography of British Municipal History*, New York, 1897, reprint, Leicester University Press, 1966

Hancock, P. D. *Bibliography of Works Relating to Scotland, 1916-50*, 2 vols, Edinburgh University Press

Humphreys, A. L. *A Handbook to County Bibliography*, 1917

Mendelssohn, Sidney. *South African Bibliography*, 2 vols, 1910

Mill, H. R. *Catalogue of the Library of the Royal Geographical Society*, 1895

Staton, F. M. and Tremaine, Marie. *Bibliography of Canadiana*, 2 vols, Toronto, 1934-59

Taylor, C. R. H. *Pacific Bibliography*, Wellington, NZ, 1951

BIBLIOGRAPHIES OF INDIVIDUAL AUTHORS

AINSWORTH: Harold Locke—*Bibliographical Catalogue of the Published Novels of William Harrison Ainsworth*, 1925

ARNOLD: Thomas B. Smart—*The Bibliography of Matthew Arnold*, 1892

AUSTEN: Geoffrey Keynes—*Jane Austen: A Bibliography*, Nonesuch Press, 1929

BACON: R. W. Gibson—*Francis Bacon, A Bibliography*, 2 volumes, 1950-59

BARRIE: B. D. Cutler—*Sir James M. Barrie: A Bibliography*, New York, 1931

BEAUMONT & FLETCHER: S. A. Tannenbaum—*Beaumont and Fletcher: A Concise Bibliography,* New York, 1938

BECKFORD: G. Chapman and J. Hodgkin—*A Bibliography of William Beckford of Fonthill,* 1930

BEERBOHM: A. E. Gallantin and L. M. Oliver—*Max Beerbohm: A Bibliography,* Soho Bibliographies, 1953

BELLOC: Patrick Cahill—*The English First Editions of Hilaire Belloc,* 1953

BEWICK: S. Roscoe—*Thomas Bewick: A Bibliography Raisonne,* 1953

BLAKE: Geoffrey Keynes—*A Bibliography of William Blake,* New York, Grolier Club, 1931

BORROW: T. J. Wise—*A Bibliography of the Writings in Prose and Verse of George Henry Borrow,* 1914

BOSWELL: F. A. Pottle—*The Literary Career of James Boswell, Esq., Being the Bibliographical Materials for a Life of Boswell,* 1929

BRIDGES: G. L. McKay—*A Bibliography of Robert Bridges,* 1933

BRONTES: T. J. Wise—*Bibliography of the Brontë Family,* 1917

BROOKE: Geoffrey Keynes—*A Bibliography of Rupert Brooke,* Soho Bibliographies, 1954

BROWNE: Geoffrey Keynes—*A Bibliography of Sir Thomas Browne,* 1924

BROWNING, E. B.: H. B. Forman—*Elizabeth Barrett Browning and Her Scarcer Books,* 1896

BROWNING, R.: L. N. Broughton, C. S. Northup, R. Pearsall —*Robert Browning: A Bibliography, 1830-1950,* Ithaca, NY, Cornell University Press, and London, 1954

BUNYAN: F. M. Harrison—*A Bibliography of the Works of John Bunyan,* Bibliographical Society, 1932

BURNS: James Gibson—*The Bibliography of Robert Burns,* 1881

BURTON: N. M. Penzer—*Annotated Bibliography of Sir Richard Francis Burton*, 1923

BYRON: T. J. Wise—*A Bibliography of the Writings in Verse and Prose of George Gordon Noel, Baron Byron*, 2 vols, 1932-3

CARLYLE: I. W. Dyer—*A Bibliography of Thomas Carlyle's Writings and Ana*, Portland, Maine, 1928

CHAUCER: E. P. Hammond—*Chaucer: A Bibliographical Manual*, New York, 1933

CHURCHILL: F. Woods—*A Bibliography of the Works of Sir Winston Churchill*, 1963

COBDEN-SANDERSON: A. W. Pollard and Edward Johnston—*Cobden-Sanderson and the Doves Press*, San Francisco, 1929

COLERIDGE: T. J. Wise—*A Bibliography of the Writings in Prose and Verse of Samuel Taylor Coleridge*, 1913 and supplement, 1919

CONRAD: T. J. Wise—*A Bibliography of Conrad*, 2nd edn, 1921

COOK: Sir M. Holmes—*Captain James Cook: A Biblographical Excursion*, 1952

COPPARD: G. H. Fabes—*The First Editions of A. E. Coppard, A. P. Herbert and Charles Morgan*, 1933

CRANE: Gertrude C. E. Masse—*A Bibliography of First Editions of Books Illustrated by Walter Crane*, 1933

DIBDIN: William A. Jackson—*An Annotated List of the Publications of the Rev. Thomas Frognall Dibdin*, Cambridge, Mass, 1965

DICKENS: Thomas Hatton and A. H. Cleaver—*A Bibliography of the Periodical Works of Charles Dickens*, 1933

J. C. Eckel—*The First Editions of the Writings of Charles Dickens*, revised edition, 1932

DODGSON: S. H. Williams and F. Maden—*The Lewis Carroll*

Handbook, revised and brought up to 1970 by Roger Lancelyn Green, 1970

DONNE: Geoffrey Keynes—*A Bibliography of Dr John Donne,* 1932

DOUGLAS: Cecil Woolf—*A Bibliography of Norman Douglas,* Soho Bibliographies, 1953

DOYLE: H. Locke—*A Bibliographical Catalogue of the Writings of Sir Arthur Conan Doyle 1879-1928,* 1929

DRYDEN: Hugh Macdonald—*John Dryden: A Bibliography,* 1939

EDGEWORTH: Bertha C. Slade—*Maria Edgeworth 1767-1849,* 1937

ELIOT: Donald Gallup—*T. S. Eliot: A Bibliography,* new edn, 1969

EVELYN: Geoffrey Keynes—*Bibliography of John Evelyn,* 1927

FITZGERALD: W. F. Prideaux—*Notes for a Bibliography of Edward Fitzgerald,* 1901

FROST: W. B. S. Clymer and C. R. Green—*Robert Frost: A Bibliography,* Amherst, 1937

GALSWORTHY: H. V. Marrot—*A Bibliography of the Works of John Galsworthy,* 1928

GIBBON: J. E. Norton—*A Bibliography of the Works of Edward Gibbon,* 1940, reprint 1970

GILL: E. R. Gill—*Bibliography of Eric Gill,* 1954

GOLDSMITH: T. Scott—*Oliver Goldsmith Bibliographically and Biographically Considered,* New York, 1928

GRAY: C. S. Northup—*A Bibliography of Thomas Gray,* New Haven, Yale University Press, 1917

HAGGARD: J. E. Scott—*Bibliography of the Works of Sir Henry Rider Haggard,* 1947

HARDY: A. P. Webb—*A Bibliography of the Works of Thomas Hardy*, 1916

HAZLITT: Geoffrey Keynes—*A Bibliography of William Hazlitt*, 1931

HOBBES: H. Macdonald and Mary Hargreaves—*Thomas Hobbes: A Bibliography*, 1952

HOUSMAN: John Carter and John Sparrow—*A Bibliography of A. E. Housman*, Soho Bibliographies, 1952

HUDSON: G. F. Wilson—*A Bibliography of the Writings of W. H. Hudson*, 1922

JAMES: Le Roy Phillips—*A Bibliography of the Writings of Henry James*, New York, 1930

JOHNSON: W. P. Courtney and D. N. Smith—*A Bibliography of Samuel Johnson*, reissue, Oxford, 1925; supplement by R. W. Chapman, 1939

JONSON: S. A. Tannenbaum—*Ben Jonson: A Concise Bibliography*, New York, 1938, supplement, 1947

JOYCE: John H. Slocum and H. Cohoon—*James Joyce: A Bibliography*, 1953

KEATS: J. R. Macgillivray—*Keats: A Bibliography*, University of Toronto Press, 1949

KIPLING: Flora V. Livingstone—*A Bibliography of the Works of Rudyard Kipling*, New York, 1927, supplement, Cambridge, Mass, Harvard University Press, 1938

LAMB: J. C. Thomson—*A Bibliography of the Writings of Charles and Mary Lamb*, Hull, 1908

LAWRENCE, D. H.: E. D. McDonald—*A Bibliography of the Writings of D. H. Lawrence*, Philadelphia, 1925, supplement, 1931

LAWRENCE: F. A. Clements—*T. E. Lawrence: A Reader's Guide*, Newton Abbot, (in preparation)

MANSFIELD: Ruth E. Mantz—*The Critical Bibliography of Katherine Mansfield,* 1931

MARLOWE: S. A. Tannenbaum—*Christopher Marlowe: A Concise Bibliography,* New York, 1937, supplement, 1947

MASEFIELD: C. N. Simmons—*A Bibliography of John Masefield,* 1930

MAUGHAM: R. Toole Stott—*A Bibliography of the Writings of W. Somerset Maugham,* 1956

MEREDITH: M. B. Forman—*A Bibliography of the Writings in Prose and Verse of Meredith,* Bibliographical Society, 1922, supplement, 1924

MILLAY: Karl Yost—*A Bibliography of the Works of Edna St Vincent Millay,* New York, 1937

MORRIS: H. B. Forman—*The Books of William Morris Described, with Some Account of His Doings in Literature and in the Allied Crafts,* 1897

MUIR: E. W. Mellown—*A Bibliography of the Writings of Edwin Muir,* 1966

NEWTON: G. J. Gray—*A Bibliography of the Works of Sir Issac Newton,* no date

O'NEILL: Barrett H. Clark—*A Bibliography of the Works of Eugene O'Neill,* New York, 1931

POPE: T. J. Wise—*A Pope Library,* 1931

POTTER: Jane Quinby—*Beatrix Potter: A Bibliographical Check List,* New York, 1954

POWIS: L. E. Siberell—*A Bibliography of First Editions of John Cooper Powis,* Cincinnati, 1934

RAY: Geoffrey Keynes—*A Bibliography of John Ray,* 1951

RICHARDSON: W. M. Sale—*Samuel Richardson: A Bibliographical Record of His Literary Career,* New Haven, Yale

University Press, 1936

RUSKIN: T. J. Wise and J. P. Smart—*Complete Bibliography of the Writings in Prose and Verse of John Ruskin*, 2 vols, 1889-93

SCOTT: J. C. Corson—*A Bibliography of Sir Walter Scott 1797-1940*, Edinburgh, 1943

SHAKESPEARE: W. Ebisch and L. L. Schuecking—*A Shakespeare Bibliography*, 1931, supplement, 1937. William Jaggard—*A Shakespeare Bibliography*, Stratford-on-Avon, 1911, reprint, 1913

SHAW: Geoffrey H. Wells—*A Bibliography of the Books and Pamphlets of George Bernard Shaw*, 1928

SHELLEY: T. J. Wise—*A Shelley Library*, 1924

SPENCER: F. R. Johnson—*A Critical Bibliography of the Works of Edmund Spenser, Printed before 1700*, Johns Hopkins Press, 1933, supplement by Dorothy F. Atkinson, 1937

STEVENSON: W. F. Prideaux—*A Bibliography of the Works of Robert Louis Stevenson*, new edn, 1917

SWIFT: H. Teerink—*Bibliography of the Writings of Jonathan Swift*, 2nd edn, ed by A. H. Scouten, Philadelphia, 1963

SWINBURNE: T. J. Wise—*Bibliography of the Writings in Prose and Verse of Algernon Charles Swinburne*, 2 vols, 1919-20

TENNYSON: T. J. Wise—*Bibliography of the Writings of Alfred Lord Tennyson*, 2 vols, 1908

THACKERAY: H. S. Van Duzer—*A Thackeray Library*, New York, 1919

THOMAS, D.: J. A. Rolph—*Dylan Thomas: A Bibliography*, 1956

TROLLOPE: Michael Sadleir—*Trollope, A Bibliography*, 1928

VAUGHAN: E. L. Marilla—*A Comprehensive Bibliography of Henry Vaughan,* University of Alabama Press, 1948

WALPOLE: A. T. Hazen—*A Bibliography of Horace Walpole,* New Haven, Yale University Press, 1942

A. T. Hazen and J. P. Kirby—*A Bibliography of the Strawberry Hill Press,* New Haven, Yale University Press, 1942

WALTON (Izaak): P. Oliver—*A New Chronicle of the Compleat Angler 1655-1936,* New York, 1936

WELLS: Geoffrey H. Wells—*The Works of H. G. Wells 1887-1925,* 1926

WHITE: E. A. Martin—*A Bibliography of Gilbert White, the Naturalist and Antiquarian of Selborne,* revised edn, 1934

WHITTINGHAMS: Arthur Warren—*The Charles Whittinghams, Printers,* New York, 1896

WILDE: C. S. Millard ('Stuart Mason')—*Bibliography of Oscar Wilde,* 1914

WILLIAMSON: I. W. Girvan—*A Bibliographical and Critical Survey of the Works of Henry Williamson,* 1932

WISE, T. J.: G. E. Haslam—*Wise after the Event: A Catalogue of Books, Pamphlets, Manuscripts and Letters relating to Thomas James Wise,* Manchester Central Library, 1946

William B. Todd—*Thomas J. Wise: Centenary Studies,* Austin Texas,, University of Texas Press, and Edinburgh, 1960

WOOLF: B. J. Kirkpatrick—*Bibliography of Virginia Woolf,* 1957

WORDSWORTH: T. J. Wise—*Bibliography of William Wordsworth,* 1916

YEATS: Allan Wade—*A Bibliography of the Writings of W. B. Yeats,* Soho Bibliographies, 1951

Index

Illustrations are indicated by italic figures

Index

Index

Index